1969

This book may be kept

FOURTEEN DAYS

A SHORT HISTORY OF ETHICS

A SHORT
HISTORY OF ETHICS

GREEK AND MODERN

BY

REGINALD A. P. ROGERS

FELLOW AND TUTOR OF TRINITY COLLEGE, DUBLIN

LONDON
MACMILLAN & CO LTD
NEW YORK · ST MARTIN'S PRESS
1965

First Edition 1911
Reprinted 1913, 1921, 1926, 1930, 1937, 1945, 1948
1952, 1960, 1964, 1965

MACMILLAN AND COMPANY LIMITED
Little Essex Street London WC 2
also Bombay Calcutta Madras Melbourne

THE MACMILLAN COMPANY OF CANADA LIMITED
70 Bond Street Toronto 2

ST MARTIN'S PRESS INC
175 Fifth Avenue New York NY 10010

PRINTED IN GREAT BRITAIN

PREFACE

THIS book is mainly descriptive but also critical.
My primary object has been to provide a brief and
accurate *description* of the leading Greek ethical
systems, and of those systems which appear to represent
the best types of modern philosophic Ethics, from
Hobbes to the end of the nineteenth century; systems
which may be regarded as contemporary are excluded. My secondary object has been to show
by *criticism* and *comparison*, the connecting links
between systems and the movements of thought by
which new systems arise—movements which express
both reaction and expansion. Scholastic doctrines
receive little attention, because, as the title indicates,
they do not come within the scope of the work;
the omission is not intended to suggest that the
philosophy of Thomas Aquinas is antiquated or wanting
in depth—from what I know of it I conclude that
it is remarkably profound and subtle,—but as his
system, in its non-theological features, is largely a

v

commentary on, and expansion of, Aristotelianism, its omission in an elementary history is, I think, justified. Some other familiar names are omitted, because I have sought to give types of thought rather than names of thinkers. Reid's ethical doctrines, for example, are, in my opinion, represented by Butler's, and those of the French empiricists by Hume. J. J. Rousseau, though his influence was wide, is not mentioned, because his teaching was an appeal to the feelings rather than a systematic philosophy. More recent systems like those of Wundt, Paulsen, Nietzsche, and the Pragmatists are also omitted.

This book is, as I have said, mainly descriptive, but I wish to emphasise the importance of recognising that a critical history of philosophy may be used as a method of positive philosophical construction, and that its results need not be negative or sceptical. The history of thought shows that the idea of objective human good contains, in some of its forms, a contradiction, or an irrational element, which it is the business of Pure Ethics to expose and, if possible, to remove. The method of historical criticism examines the different attempts that have been made to remove this irrational element, and selects provisionally that system which appears, on the whole, the most satisfactory from a logical and practical point of view.

The history of Ethics shows that the irrational element is due to a conflict between two opposite tendencies. The first is to lay undue stress on the emotional constituents of the Good; I believe the only *logical* issue of this is Exclusive Egoism (Cyrenaics, Epicurus, Hobbes), which solves the difficulty only at the cost of admitting that objective social good is a self-contradictory conception. The second tendency is represented by Moral Purism (Cynics, Stoics, Kant), which uses the principle that the satisfaction of particular feelings or of the feelings of particular individuals cannot be the right guides to conduct; by a strained use of this true principle it is inferred that pleasure has no ethical worth. The eighteenth-century intuitionists recognised the difficulty, but they took the wrong way of escape; they endeavoured by various artifices to prove that conscience and the desire for happiness lead, or ultimately will lead, to the same result, namely, a general harmony between the pleasures of all persons. But assuming that such a social harmony could result, it would be merely external, not inward and spiritual; the irrational element cannot be abolished in this artificial way.

Evolutional Naturalism has shown that different forms of life are not independent, and that the idea of an organism is not that of a single isolated body, but a form connecting the individual with the past of living Nature. But the Rational Idealists have effected what is more important for Pure Ethics in leading us to the notion of the *inward* unity between the individual manifestations of the higher forms of consciousness ; this is the *unity of self-conscious Reason*. Without this notion the irrational element in Ethics cannot be removed. It is through this unity that individuality is transcended without being abolished. The reality of " common good " depends on this transcendence, the recognition of which alone makes it possible for a person to identify social good with his own.

As this book is of an elementary character, I have avoided metaphysical arguments as far as possible. But the preceding remarks illustrate the truth, which should never be forgotten, that a complete philosophy of Ethics involves some very profound metaphysical problems. For some writers the practical and speculative views are almost inseparable, *e.g.* Plato and Hegel : in others, *e.g.* Kant and Aristotle, the two can be separated for a time, but not when the final problems are faced ; Aristotle's ideal life, *theoria*, is the union of speculative and practical wisdom, and connects his Ethics with his Metaphysics; Kant, though teaching that the practical and speculative spheres are distinct for human experience, often implies that the distinction is not final, being due to the present limitation of our faculties. The two apparently opposite schools of Rational Idealism and Pragmatism agree at least on this point that our practical and speculative Reason have a common root. The Ethics of the " moral sense " school is the least dependent on metaphysics, but this is not in its favour, being merely the result of superficiality.

I have written a comparatively long " Introduction," in the hope that it will be useful to those who are beginning the subject ; it is intended chiefly to define the scope of Ethics, and to give an idea of the nature of the problems that arise. Fixed meanings are given to some words for the sake of definiteness, but it will be found that few systems have a precise terminology, and that the terminologies of those which are precise differ *inter se.* This inexactness is partly due to the fact that writers on Ethics often treat the subject as a branch of popular literature rather than as an exact science, partly to the fact that the ideas of Ethics are so complex and so liable to change and development, even in the individual mind, that it becomes exceedingly difficult, if not impossible, to combine philosophic breadth with precision in the use of terms. Spinoza, in his *Ethica,* was able to overcome this difficulty, but it is a curious fact that no one else uses his terminology and definitions, and that his admirers have found it necessary to explain his thoughts in language less precise than his own.

Besides the works of the writers themselves—where this was possible—I have used various histories of philosophy, especially Ritter and Preller's *Historia Philosophiae Graecae*, the histories of Ueberweg and Windelband, and Höffding's *History of Modern Philosophy*. In dealing with Hegel, I have made use of the language of Wallace's translations.

I desire to express my gratitude to Dr. Mahaffy for reading the proof-sheets and giving me the benefit of his wide experience, and to Professor J. I. Beare and Mr. G. W. Mooney for many useful criticisms and suggestions.

January 1911.

CONTENTS

INTRODUCTION

	PAGE
Subject-matter of Ethics	1
Ultimate Ends	3
Good and Moral Good	6
Ethical Judgments, Virtue and Vice, Right and Wrong, Good and Bad	9
Moral Obligation, Duty, Free-will	11
Motive and Effect	12
The Ethical Scale. Idealism and Realism . . .	14
Good and Knowledge	15
Moral Virtues and Special Virtues	17
Will, Character, Person, and Self	21
Goodness and Utility	22
Happiness, Pleasure, and Well-being	23
Subjective and Objective Good	24
General Problems	26

xi

PART I

GREEK ETHICAL SYSTEMS

CHAPTER I

PAGE

THE SOPHISTS, SOCRATES, AND THE SOCRATIC
    SCHOOLS 31
    A. THE SOPHISTS 31
    B. SOCRATES 34
    C. THE CYNICS 37
    D. THE CYRENAICS 39

CHAPTER II

PLATO 41
    A. THE IDEA OF JUSTICE 43
    Method 43
    The Cardinal Virtues 44
    Justice in the Individual 46
    Its Worth for the Individual. . . . 47
    Social and Private Good 47
    The Ideal State 47
    The Ideal Ruler 48
    Education of the Rulers. . . . 50

    B. THE THEORY OF IDEAS 52
    The Absolute Good 55
    The Ideal and the Actual . . . 57

    C. PLEASURE, GOOD, AND RATIONAL ORDER. . 59
    Is Pleasure the Good ? 60

CONTENTS

PAGE

C. PLEASURE, GOOD, AND RATIONAL ORDER (*contd.*)—

The Harmonious Life 61

Reason in the Universe 62

CHAPTER III

ARISTOTLE 64

The Separation of the Sciences 64

The Highest Science 65

Method 65

Criticism of some Ethical Theories 66

General Conception of Well-being 67

Division of Virtue 68

Characteristics of Moral Virtue 69

The Doctrine of the Mean 70

Voluntary Actions and Responsibility . . . 72

Temperance 73

Courage 74

Justice 75

Friendship 76

Self-Love and the Love of Others 76

Pleasure, Pain, and the Good 77

Knowledge and Virtue 78

The Ideal Life 79

GENERAL VIEW OF THE ETHICS OF PLATO AND
ARISTOTLE 82

CHAPTER IV

EPICURUS 85

Theory of Knowledge 86

Physics 86

PAGE

ETHICS 87

    Virtue 88

    Social Virtues 89

CRITICISM OF EGOISTIC HEDONISM . . 90

CHAPTER V

THE STOICS 93

    Knowledge and Well-being 93

    Theory of Knowledge 94

    Physics 94

ETHICS 95

    Virtue and the Good 96

    Virtue and Knowledge 98

    Resignation 98

    Pleasure and Emotion 98

    Modifications 100

    The Ideal Man 100

    Social Ethics 101

    Summary 102

CRITICISM 103

CHAPTER VI

GENERAL SURVEY OF GREEK ETHICS . . 105

PART II

MODERN ETHICAL SYSTEMS

INTRODUCTION

PAGE
Intervening Systems 113
Influence of Greek on Modern Ethics 115
Moral Obligation 118
Naturalism and Intuitionism 119
Other Types of Ethical Thought 123

CHAPTER I

EARLIER NATURALISM 125
　A. EGOISTIC NATURALISM—HOBBES . . . 126
　　Philosophy and its Worth 126
　　Division of Philosophy 127
　　Materialism 127
　　Psychology 128
　　Action, Pleasure, Pain, Good, Evil . . . 129
　　Will 130
　　The Desire for Power—Egoism . . . 130
　　Exclusive Egoism 132
　　The Warfare of Man with Man . . . 132
　　Articles of Peace ; the Laws of Nature . . 133
　　Civil Government the Guardian of the Laws
　　　of Nature 135
　　Summary of Hobbes' Ethics 136

PAGE

A. EGOISTIC NATURALISM—HOBBES (*contd.*)—

CRITICISM 137

    Criticism of Hobbes' Ethics . . . 137

    Inconsistencies in Hobbes' General Philo-

      sophy 140

B. RATIONALISTIC NATURALISM—SPINOZA . . 143

CHAPTER II

ENGLISH INTUITIONISM 147

A. RATIONAL INTUITIONISM

    Cudworth—Immutable Morality, Reason . 148

    Clarke—The Rules of Righteousness . . 149

    Criticism 151

B. AESTHETIC INTUITIONISM 152

    Shaftesbury—Virtue and Happiness . . 153

    Criticism 156

    Hutcheson—The three " Calm Determinations" 156

    Criticism of " Moral Sense " 158

C. SYMPATHETIC INTUITIONISM

    Adam Smith—The " Impartial Spectator " . 160

CHAPTER III

ENGLISH INTUITIONISM (*continued*) 163

D. AUTONOMIC INTUITIONISM—BUTLER . . . 163

    Method 163

    The Social Nature of Man 164

    The Moral Nature of Man 166

    Man is a Law to Himself 167

    Human Nature a System 167

    The System of Active Principles . . . 168

PAGE

Applications 170

Conscience and Reasonable Self-Love . . 172

CRITICISM 172

     Relation of Butler to the Greeks . . 174

     Individualism and Responsibility . . 175

CHAPTER IV

SYMPATHETIC NATURALISM—HUME. . . . 177

Impressionism 178

Morals a Science 178

Reason and Passion 178

Moral Sense and Virtue 180

Motive and Moral Approbation 181

Natural and Artificial Virtues 182

Obligation 183

Motive to Justice 183

Origin of Justice 184

Pleasure, Sympathy, Utility 185

CRITICISM 185

     Impressionism 185

     Psychological Hedonism 188

     Defect in Naturalistic Methods . . . 188

     Influence of Hume 189

CHAPTER V

MORAL PURISM—KANT 191

Relation to Preceding Systems . . . 191

The Goodwill; Motive and Effect; Duty and

     Inclination 193

PAGE

The Categorical Imperative 194

Illustrations 195

Humanity an End in Itself 196

Autonomy and the Kingdom of Ends . . . 197

Autonomy 198

Connection between the Three Forms of the
Categorical Imperative 199

Free-will and the Laws of Nature 199

Happiness and Virtue; the Three Postulates of
Morality 200

Good and Moral Law 202

Particular Duties 202

CRITICISM 202

    Formalism 202

    Virtue and Happiness 203

    Motive and Effect 204

    Nature and Freedom 206

PERMANENT INFLUENCE OF KANT . . . 207

    Links between Kant and Subsequent Systems . 209

CHAPTER VI

GERMAN RATIONAL IDEALISM 211

A. FICHTE 211

B. SCHELLING 213

C. HEGEL

    Introductory 215

        1. Logic 216

        2. The Philosophy of Nature . . . 217

        3. The Philosophy of Mind . . . 217

                                                          PAGE
The Philosophy of Mind 217

  I. *Subjective Mind* (The Soul, Conscious-
      ness, Reason) 218

  II. *Objective Mind* 221

      (*a*) Legal Right 222

      (*b*) Morality 223

      (*c*) Social Ethics 224

  III. *Absolute Mind* 227

D. REMARKS ON THE ETHICS OF GERMAN RATIONAL
    IDEALISM 227

  Relation to Naturalism and Intuitionism . 229

  Relation to Positivism and Subsequent Systems 230

CHAPTER VII

UTILITARIANISM 234

  A. EGOISTIC UTILITARIANISM—JEREMY BENTHAM . 235

    Virtue, Motive, Punishment 236

  B. SYMPATHETIC UTILITARIANISM—J. S. MILL . 237

    Proof of Utilitarianism 237

    Sanctions 237

    Quality of Pleasures 238

    Self-Sacrifice and Conventional Morality . . 239

    Virtue as an End 240

    Criticism of Bentham and Mill . . . 240

  C. INTUITIONAL UTILITARIANISM—HENRY SIDGWICK 242

    Problem and Methods of Ethics . . . 242

    Criticism of Common-Sense and Dogmatic
      Intuitionism 244

    And of other Methods 244

                                                              PAGE
Philosophic Intuitionism 245
    The Rational Axioms   245
    Proof of Utilitarianism 246
    Utilitarianism and Common-sense .   . 247
    Applications, Positive Morality   .   . 248
    Egoism and Altruism   248

D. GENERAL CRITICISM OF UTILITARIANISM .   . 249
    Ethical Hedonism 250
    Quantification of Happiness .   .   . 253
    Logical Defect in Utilitarian Idea of Good .   254
    The Unity of Good   256

CHAPTER VIII

EVOLUTIONAL NATURALISM   257
    Historical Position   257
    Evolution 258

A. CHARLES DARWIN 259

B. HERBERT SPENCER 261
    The End imposed by Nature—Life   . 261
    The Subject of Ethics 261
    Good and Bad   262
    The Ethical End—Pleasure .   .   . 262

    Spencer on the Evolution of Conduct
      The Four " Views "   .   .   . 263
      Feeling and Function   .   .   . 263
      The Sense of Duty   .   .   . 264
      The Individual and the Type   . 265

PAGE

Limit of Social Evolution . . . 266

Egoism and Altruism 266

Compromise 269

Spencer's Theory of Justice

" Sub-Human " Justice 269

Human Justice. The Formula . . 271

The Sentiment and the Idea of Justice . 271

Error of Communism 272

Authority of the Formula of Justice . 273

Applications 273

Criticism of Spencerian Ethics

Are the Fittest to Survive the Ethically

Best ? 274

Ethical Judgment Free, not Mechanical . 274

Confusion between Naturalism and In-

tuitionism 275

Hedonism and the Limit of Evolution . 278

C. THE DIFFERENT TYPES OF EVOLUTION . . 279

CHAPTER IX

ENGLISH RATIONAL IDEALISM. 282

T. H. GREEN 282

Relation to Predecessors. 282

Metaphysic 282

Will, Reason, and Freedom of Will . 283

The Good Will—Criticism of Hedonists and

Kant 284

Moral Good 285

PAGE

Character of the Moral Ideal 285

Origin of the Ideal 286

Development of the Ideal 287

CONCLUDING REMARKS 288

Applied Ethics 290

INDEX 293

INTRODUCTION

THE following questions will serve to give the reader a general idea of the nature of the problems which Ethics [1] attempts to solve:—Is happiness the ultimate end of action? Is virtue preferable to pleasure? How do pleasure and happiness differ? What is meant by saying that I *ought* to perform some particular action, or to respect some general precept such as the keeping of promises? Am I under any obligation to seek the welfare of other persons, as well as my own? If so, what is the right proportion between the two welfares? What is meant by "freedom of the will"? Is feeling or reason the right guide to conduct? What do the terms "good," "right," "obligation," "duty," "conscience" signify, practically and theoretically?

These problems and others associated with them form the subject-matter of Ethics, which may be described as the science which investigates the general principles for determining the true worth of the ultimate ends of human conduct. These principles, if they could be discovered and exactly formulated, so

[1] The word "ethics" was originally a plural (τὰ ἠθικά, the science of morals), but it is now generally used as a singular. The same applies to "mathematics," "physics," "metaphysics," and other words of like termination.

that the rules of conduct could be deduced from them, would constitute Ideal Morality. Positive Morality is the body of laws (the ethical code) accepted by an age or community as correct principles for determining the true worth of actions, and expressed in the form of judgments of approval and disapproval. For example, the Positive Morality of our age approves of industry, temperance, honesty, and a regard for human life, while it condemns their opposites.

It must not be taken for granted that Positive Morality and Ideal Morality coincide, since the former is partly based on unreflecting traditions, conventions, and customs; it is often inconsistent with itself, and varies in different times and countries. The burning of so - called witches and the torture of persons suspected of crime or heresy were once regarded as justifiable. At the present time vivisection is con-demned by some, whereas others, equally humane and intelligent, hold that, if properly restricted, it is a justifiable method of seeking for the cures of diseases. The divergence between the moral customs of civilised and of savage nations is well known; cannibalism, polygamy, the destruction of infants and of old persons,—these and other extraordinary customs have been justified by the Positive Morality of certain savage tribes.

But since Ethics cannot detach itself completely from the accepted morality of the community, and since it must start from some kind of data, ethical writers—as the sequel will show—usually assume provisionally that the Positive Morality to which they are accustomed contains valuable truth. They endeavour to exhibit the general principles underlying this Positive Morality, to criticise or justify them, and possibly to extend them beyond their commonly recognised limits. The origin, in the individual and the race, of common moral judgments is also much discussed in modern Ethics, in the belief that light will thereby be thrown on the validity of those judgments.

Ultimate Ends.—The end of a deliberate action is that for the sake of which it is performed; it is something which the agent wishes to realise. Some ends are pursued chiefly, or altogether, as means to the realisation of other ends; wealth, for example, though an end of many actions, is sought—except perhaps by misers—as a means of acquiring power or happiness. An *ultimate* end, however, is one that is desired for its own sake, quite apart from its utility in helping towards the attainment of other ends.

Ethics deals with the ultimate ends of human conduct. This characteristic distinguishes it from every other science and brings it into close connection with Metaphysics, which, as understood by Aristotle, investigates the ultimate principles underlying all reality.

That the ethical problem arises quite naturally may be seen by inquiring into the *reasons* for undertaking any inquiry, or for performing any deliberate action. If we ask, for instance, why Geometry is studied, three answers may be given. First, because there exists in some minds a free spontaneous interest [1]

---

[1] An interest may be described as anything that attracts or tends to attract attention, so that a person is led to think, act, or feel in a particular way, and finds some degree of satisfaction in such thoughts, actions, or feelings. Desire is a movement of the mind towards an object or end that interests. Thus desire and interest are inseparable. But they are not

in geometrical knowledge, and the pursuit and capture of such knowledge gives direct satisfaction. This is an ethical answer, for it means that Geometry is good for those whom it interests; and as we shall see, that which interests and satisfies desire is good, when considered by itself alone. But no human occupation is quite isolated; we must therefore pursue the question further, and inquire whether the external effects of a study of Geometry are also good. Secondly, then, we find that Geometry is studied because it is useful for other sciences, such as Astronomy, Statics, Engineering, and Architecture. This, however, is not an ethical answer; we must next inquire what are the reasons for studying Astronomy and the other sciences. Besides the answer that they gratify a spontaneous interest, and are so far good, we may reply that Astronomy (say) is useful for navigation, and navigation is useful for commerce, war, and travelling. If we followed such trains of reasoning to their conclusions we should find that the ultimate justification—over and above the constantly operating spontaneous interest—for engaging in these pursuits, is that they help men to achieve objects which are desired, at least partly, for their own sakes. It is the function of Ethics to provide general principles for estimating the real worth of these ultimate ends, or to criticise the general principles that are used for this

synonymous ; a desire is a particular conscious state, but an interest may be permanent—*e.g.* a man may take a permanent interest in football, but he has not a permanent desire to watch or play the game. Again, a desire when it is satisfied ceases to occupy consciousness, but the satisfaction of an interest consists partly in the fact that it occupies consciousness and receives more attention than other things. We do not desire to go to the theatre when we are watching a play, but interest may be present in full vigour.

purpose. Thirdly, Geometry is studied because of its educational value. It is the business of Ethics to estimate the *real worth* of the spontaneous interests which education helps to foster and to gratify

All of these answers converge to one point, and if we ask the question more generally we shall be led to the same conclusion; pursuits and studies are undertaken, and deliberate actions performed because they tend either directly or indirectly, or in both ways, to satisfy one or more human interests. They are valued either as means or as ends, or as both means and ends.

We are now confronted with the main problem of Ethics. Are the satisfactions of these interests, the attainment of these desired objects, *good in themselves*, or is there some ultimate criterion, some principle or set of mutually consistent principles by which we may determine the intrinsic excellence of the satisfaction of these interests? One might be disposed to think that the mere existence of such interests in human nature would be a sufficient justification for trying to satisfy them. If this were so the science of Ethics might stop at this point. But the answer is not so simple ; the difficulties in Ethics are due to the following causes, which compel further inquiry. (1) It is not possible for an individual to satisfy all his interests, and he must therefore use some principle of ethical selection, according to which some interests are to be preferred to others. (2) Some interests, if they are allowed to absorb the attention beyond a certain limit, are destructive of their own satisfactions, and interfere with the satisfaction of other interests. This is true, for example, of the interests arising from

bodily appetites; these, if indulged too far, lead to
sensual cravings, and to bodily and mental ill-health,
thereby diminishing the force and vigour of other
interests.   (3) The interests of one person often conflict with those of others, and Ethics has to try to
find a practical harmony between the interests of the
different members of society.

The first two causes give rise to Individual Ethics,
the third to Social Ethics.

Good and Moral Good.—Ethics seeks for a principle
that will determine the true worth of the ends of conduct.   That which is apprehended as having true
worth is said to be good.   Accordingly, Ethics has
sometimes been called the Science of the Good, so far
as this is attainable by human conduct, *i.e.* by human
actions deliberately aiming at ends.

Strictly speaking "good" is a conception that
cannot be accurately defined.   In a sense the main
problem of systems of Pure Ethics is to determine
this conception with greater accuracy, and Applied
Ethics aims at giving a practical meaning to the
conception in concrete life.   The following remarks
are intended, not to give an exact definition of "good,"
but to render more intelligible the nature of the
problems "What is good?" and "What is moral
good?" and to show how these problems naturally
arise.

"Good," "desire," and "interest" are closely connected with each other.   Though we cannot follow
Hobbes in identifying "good" with that which any
one desires,—for a person's desires may be misleading
or they may conflict with each other, or with those
of other persons,—yet it is true that the satisfaction

of a desire is good, when considered by itself alone, apart from its possible interference with other desires. More generally, that which, whether preceded by desire or not, is consciously approved by a person *for its own sake* is good, when considered by itself alone. In this limited sense a pleasurable feeling is good ; or the attainment of any desired end, such as the passing of an examination, or the acquisition of wealth ; or any occupation that interests. In the same limited sense the satisfaction of any interest is good.

But this view of good is clearly narrow and incomplete. Some pleasurable feelings, for example, may be followed by injurious consequences ; wealth may yield less satisfaction to the possessor than a moderate competence ; and when we say that wealth is wrongly acquired, we generally mean that it was acquired in a way that interfered with the interests of other persons. Here we reach the difficulty which is the original stimulus to ethical inquiry. When different " goods " or " interests " are practically incompatible, we require an ethical scale to determine which is to be preferred. In comparing one limited good with another, we may have to consider (as Bentham did in reference to pleasures) the quality, duration, and intensity of the satisfaction yielded by each, as well as the tendency which each may have to help or hinder the attainment of other goods by the agent or by other persons. In this way there arises a natural distinction between immediate and remote good. Immediate good gives a simple momentary satisfaction experienced by a single person. Remote good, in general, is distinguished from immediate good by the fact that the satisfaction it yields is not confined to the present moment or to the experience of one individual. The ends sought by Temperance and Justice, for example, have the characteristics of remote good; a temperate man refrains from sacrificing his future interests to the pleasure of the moment; a just man does not prefer his own interests to those of other persons.

Remote good, however, for beings whose consciousness is in Time, is dependent on immediate goods, since its fruition is in moments of Time, and cannot be postponed for ever; and since society consists of persons with distinct experiences, a social remote good must be realised in the experiences of individuals. Thus Temperance is not a purely negative abstinence from the satisfaction of particular desires, nor is Justice a merely negative impartiality in the distribution of benefits; the former virtue requires that healthy desires and interests should be positively satisfied in due degree, the latter that benefits should be actually received by individuals.

Immediate good, then, is relatively simple, being either momentary or confined to a single person; but remote good is a complex whole consisting of interrelated parts, which are either immediate goods, or useful in the production of immediate goods. The fundamental difficulty which we have described as the original stimulus to ethical inquiry, may now be expressed as follows: Immediate goods often have to be surrendered in order to secure remote good, which seems, therefore, in such cases, to contain an injurious element; why should we sacrifice the interests of the present to those of the future, or our own interests for those of other persons? It will be seen that various attempts have been made to overcome this difficulty. The results are often one-sided; the Cynics, for example, tend to underrate the worth of immediate good, and the Cyrenaics overrate its worth, identifying the highest good with the pleasure of the moment. The problem presents itself inevitably to every thinking person; and the answer to it means formulating, more or less definitely, some kind of ethical scale, by reference to which the relative worths of different forms of satisfaction are to be estimated.

Moral good is defined by the ethical scale which is used to compare immediate and remote goods with each other. A morally good end is the best that it is in the power of the agent to attain by deliberate action, under the circumstances in which he is placed; it is in every case at the highest point of the scale. "Moral rectitude" and "moral virtue" are similarly defined.[1]

The systems hereafter described are to some extent attempts to formulate the structure of the ethical scale—true or accepted—and to determine the source of our knowledge or beliefs concerning it.

Ethical Judgments, Virtue and Vice, Right and Wrong, Good and Bad.—Ethical Judgments may be regarded as being judgments about deliberate actions, about the persons performing those actions, or about the ends at which the actions aim. In such judgments, as made in ordinary life, the adjectives "good," "virtuous," and "right," and their opposites, are applied indiscriminately to persons, actions, and ends; but it would be better to apply "good" and "bad" to

[1] See p. 18.

B

ends, "virtuous" and "vicious" to persons or types of personal character, and "right" and "wrong" to deliberate actions. The ethical principle which determines the worth of ends determines also the judgments about actions and personal characters. To give an example we must anticipate. According to the Utilitarians the greatest happiness of the greatest possible number is the best of all ends, and the statement of this provides a principle of ethical judgment by which actions, ends, and characters are to be judged. It may be taken as proved that the health of the community tends towards the attainment of this end. If, therefore, a person who is recovering from a contagious disease deliberately enters a crowded assembly, his action is wrong, his end (perhaps amusement) is bad in so far as it conflicts with the higher end, and his character, if such actions are habitual with him, is so far vicious.

"Right" as applied to actions is, however, more definite than "good" as applied to ends. One attainable end may be better than another, and yet both may be relatively good; in such cases only the action that tends to realise the best attainable end is right; we do not say that one action is "more right" than another, but that one action is right and another is wrong.

Practically we must distinguish between actions objectively and actions subjectively right. An objectively right action, under given circumstances, is the one that truly realises the best end; a subjectively right action is one that the agent believes will realise the best end. These two actions do not *prima facie* coincide.

Moral Obligation, Duty, Free Will.—Moral obligation expresses the conscious relation of an agent to a law which he believes is the best to obey under the given circumstances, and which it is possible for him to obey. We say that the agent "ought" to obey such a law, and this is equivalent to saying that it is his "duty" to obey it. "Duty" and "moral obligation" commonly (though not necessarily) imply the existence of temptations to go wrong. To do one's duty is to prefer the higher good to the lower, as determined by the ethical scale; it means action in accordance with what is best, in so far as this is possible and can be ascertained by the agent. If we agree to define elementary freedom of the will as the power normally possessed in some degree by human beings of subordinating impulses and lower goods to higher goods, then every system of Ethics presupposes freedom in this elementary sense, since conduct or deliberate action would be impossible without it.

It was remarked that actions subjectively right and actions objectively right do not *prima facie* coincide. There are indeed many cases which seem to prove that the moral judgments of individuals are mistaken. Religious and political fanatics—to take extreme instances—are often prepared to sacrifice their own lives and those of others in order to attain ends of which the morality is doubtful. The *ultimate* ends pursued by sincere fanatics are no doubt usually good; as the salvation of souls or the improvement of social conditions. But in such cases common sense condemns the means either as bad in themselves or as being unlikely to secure the good ends. The question therefore arises, whether moral obligation remains even if the moral judgment is erroneous. Those who hold that moral obligation is merely a subjective feeling, as distinct from an intuition of objective truth, have no difficulty in answering this question. But the sceptical solution should not be accepted if we can find another. According to Kant the consciousness of moral obligation *is* moral obligation, and the consequent action is objectively right. And this view is the most satisfactory if we take it to mean only that each agent should sincerely *endeavour* to realise his own convictions as to what is right; if this be not admitted moral obligation is meaningless, since the individual can have no inward guide except his own convictions. It does not follow, however, that it is objectively good that each agent should *realise* his own convictions, for these may be mistaken. Anarchists and other fanatics *ought* bravely to follow their own moral convictions, but the rest of society *ought* to prevent these from being realised. Here the moral judgment of society corrects the isolated judgment of individuals. There is therefore no absurdity in assuming that an action which an agent believes he ought to do coincides with the action which he objectively ought to do. On the other hand, if we deny this, " ought " and " obligation " cease to have any meaning.

Motive and Effect.—Conduct is equivalent to deliberate action or action done " on purpose," and is distinguished from instinctive action by the fact that one of its co-operating causes is the pre-conception of an end desired by the agent. This pre-conception (in so far as the end is desired) we may agree to call the motive of the action. The action, in so far as it contains an effect agreeing with the motive, may be said to be "free" in the elementary sense just mentioned ; the agent secures the end he has willed. But all the effects cannot possibly be contained in the motive, for every single action starts a causal series far too complicated to be pre-conceived by men. For instance, the motive for introducing gas into a house is to give light, not to suffocate its inmates, though this may be one of the effects. While motives are often very complex, it is a common mistake to fix upon one prominent feature and call it *the* motive. Thus the motive for playing football may be described as a liking for the game, though a great many other motives may co-operate—a liking for the society of other players, personal ambition, or ambition for the success of a club.

The intention is sometimes distinguished [1] from the motive, and then signifies the agent's pre-conception of *all* the ethical effects which he believes will follow. Thus the motive for committing murder may be to obtain money or to gratify some passion ; but the intention includes also the conception of various other effects which the agent knows are likely to follow,— destruction of human happiness, the violation of the right to live, etc.

Since motives undoubtedly co-operate in the realisation of ends at which they aim, the motive must be indirectly a partial test of the rectitude of an action; a good motive is good because of its tendency, if for no other reason. This is one reason why much ethical philosophy is concerned with the

---

[1] *E.g.* by Bentham.

motives of actions. Another reason (connected with the former) is that popular ethical judgments refer chiefly to the motives and intentions of acts. An act, however, cannot be said to be objectively right unless its effects are good, and its badness partly depends on the badness of its effects.[1] But since every one's power and leisure for tracing consequences is practically limited, the judgment, in so far as it is passed on a person regarded as a cause of good or bad effects, is properly passed on the intention ; the person is rightly condemned or approved for those ethical effects which he believes will follow his deliberate action.

The Ethical Scale. Idealism and Realism.— Ethics presupposes that there is a real distinction between good and bad ends, and strives to express it theoretically. Idealists, like Plato and Green, assume further that there is some perfectly satisfying end, the Absolute Good, which each individual can appropriate by right action. But even if it cannot be proved that there is an Absolute Good, an end complete in itself, and superior in worth to anything else actual or conceivable, it will still be quite logical to seek for a standard by which the *relative* worth of actions is determinable. We may not be able to find a supreme end, but we may be able to say why one end, action, or character is better than another. There may even be a best possible, and yet this best be ideally imperfect. This truth is important to remember, and gives Ethics a practical value which

[1] To reconcile this with what was said on p. 12, we must assume as a postulate that *conscientiousness* always leads to the best results in the long run. But this is one of the difficulties which ethical systems have to consider.

it could not have if it refused to admit that anything but perfection is good. We may allow, for example, that the life of a prize-fighter is better than that of an idle tramp or a burglar, but it does not follow that it is the best life conceivable. It is a mistake to suppose that the possibility of having a scale of ethical worth implies an ideal limit at each end of the scale (the Perfect and the Absolutely Bad). Every system of Ethics seeks for the *best possible* under the conditions of human life.

An ethical system which asserts that the Perfect is attainable may be called "idealistic." One which denies that we have sufficient evidence on this point, while recognising that a relative good is attainable, may be termed "realistic." Not all systems can be thus classified; it would be hard, for example, to classify Aristotle, the Stoics, or Spencer. Examples of Idealists are Plato, Kant, Cudworth, Butler, Green, and the Æsthetic Intuitionists; and of Realists, Epicurus, Hobbes, Hume, and the Utilitarians.[1]

Good and Knowledge.—Socrates held that Moral Virtue was a form of knowledge; the intemperate man, for instance, exceeds through ignorance of the true good, the sensualist is just as stupid as an ox. In one sense Socrates was right; for virtue, so far as it is expressed in deliberate action, is impossible without some degree of knowledge of the goodness of the ends to be attained; we must know at least dimly what the good is and how to acquire it, before we can deliberately seek it. Hence the ethical worth of all forms of knowledge, and of a general education,

[1] Some writers are idealists owing to their religious convictions (*e.g.* Butler).

which assists the formation of correct judgments about the ends of action.   But Socrates was evidently mistaken if he intended to assert that the knowledge of the good is not only essential but also the sufficient condition for right action.   Knowledge and reflection undoubtedly provide motives for action in varying degrees of strength, but, as Aristotle pointed out, they cannot take the place of will and habit.[1]   Moral insight (a form of knowledge) may pronounce a conceived end to be good or bad, and a knowledge of the laws of nature may prescribe the means required for the attainment of the end ; but neither of these forms of knowledge *per se* can provide the mental and physical energy required for the successful performance of the actions indicated.   Knowledge in relation to action may be compared with the regulator of a steam engine, which produces the intended effect only if all the machinery is in working order, and if there is a proper supply of fuel.[2]   Knowledge, analogously, leads usually to appropriate action, provided that the character has been rendered sensitive to true thoughts by previously cultivated habits of self-control.

The preceding discussion considers knowledge chiefly as supplying a motive to action.   But we saw that the goodness or badness of an act is partly determined by the goodness or badness of its effects.   For this

[1] See Aristotle's discussion on this. Socrates may have meant that the knowledge that an end is good contains in itself the desire to realise it, and that without this element of desire the knowledge is imperfect ; but our criticisms are based on the ordinary use of the term knowledge as mainly theoretical.

[2] This analogy should not be pressed too far ; I do not wish to suggest that vice is merely a form of inertia, since it is a matter of common experience that evil desires are active forces.

reason knowledge of the probable effects of an action on the agent and on other persons is indispensable for right action; and we may see from this that organised science is ethically useful apart from the immediate worth which it possesses through the fact that it satisfies the interests of those who love knowledge for its own sake. Chemistry is useful for medicine and surgery, and these for health, which is clearly a good. Geology is useful, because a knowledge of minerals and rocks is applicable in various ways to other sciences (*e.g.* engineering) which help men in various ways to achieve satisfying ends. Mathematics, again, is applied to such diverse purposes as the construction of machinery and bridges, to navigation, architecture, land-surveying, and life-insurance; it has thus ethical utility, because those practical arts which it helps may be directly applied to the production of goods that can be experienced by many individuals. Of course, scientific knowledge may be wrongly applied, but its good effects seem far to outweigh its bad.

Knowledge of every kind, again, is good, in so far as its pursuit and attainment give direct and permanent satisfaction. The same is true of Art, as well as of Philosophy and Science.

Moral Virtues and Special Virtues.—Virtue, we have seen, is a property of character, though indirectly applied to actions and motives. It seems desirable to make a distinction between *moral* virtues and *special* virtues. A morally virtuous man, as commonly understood, is one who consistently respects the conventional moral code, which enjoins Industry, Temperance, Honour, Justice, Charity, and so forth.

It would be hard to tabulate all the different reasons
for calling a man morally virtuous or good, but we
may say that he does not deserve the name unless he
tries consistently to attain for himself and others
those ends that have truer worth than any other
ends within his reach.   Moral virtue may, therefore,
be defined generally as the habitual tendency to
pursue, always and with consciousness, the best
attainable ends.   The nature of these ends depends
partly on the natural talents of the individual, and
partly on his desires and tastes ; but in every case
an objective ethical standard is required to regulate
the exercise of talents and the gratification of desires.
A complete ethical standard will be both individual
and social.   A standard as aiming at individual good
might forbid a man to persist in any occupation
which was more injurious to his health and happiness
than some other occupation possible for him ; and
the standard as aiming at social good will forbid
actions — such as coining money illegally — which
injure the community.   The moral virtues are the
general forms which the tendency to seek the best
(individual and social) takes in the different relations
of life.

Virtue, however, may be regarded as having a
wider meaning than *moral* virtue.[1]   A *special* virtue
may be taken to mean an aptitude for attaining by
deliberate action some special class of good ends, for
doing any good thing well ; the aptitude must include
also the *will* to do these good things.   Thus we may
speak of a good mechanic, a good scholar, a good oars-
man, — and so forth — as possessing virtues in their

---

[1] Just as ἀρετή had for Aristotle a wider meaning than ἠθικὴ ἀρετή.

respective spheres; and their social aptitudes if exercised may be called special virtues. But why are these not called *moral* virtues, and why do Honesty, Charity, Temperance, etc., receive this title? There are two reasons for this. In the first place, moral virtue is an aptitude of the whole character, and is one that must constantly be exercised; it is the *habitual* tendency to seek the best possible.[1] Now isolated virtues, like skill in music, mechanics, or oratory, though good in themselves, may interfere with the exercise of higher virtues; and, to take another example, a good golfer possesses a " special " virtue, which may nevertheless interfere with some more important duties, since excellence in a profession—and perhaps excellence in other games —is a superior end to excellence in golf, except for a professional golfer. On the other hand, the moral virtues can never be superseded — this at least is commonly assumed and may be provisionally granted. Temperance, Charity, Honour, Justice, Mercy, cannot conflict with each other if each seeks the very best in its own relations.[2] This expresses what is true in the Stoic doctrine that all moral virtues are on the same level — the highest. Secondly, public moral opinion (common-sense morality) holds that every one can and should possess all moral virtues, but does not

[1] The relation between moral virtue and special virtues corresponds to the relation between moral good and good in the general sense (see p. 6 *sq.*).

[2] That Justice is consistent with Mercy and Charity may be disputed; but the popular view, that there is an opposition, seems to be due to the belief that Justice ignores the particular circumstances and the natural disposition of the agent. In a wider sense, however, Mercy seems to be a *just* appreciation of the natural weakness of individuals in overcoming temptation ; and Justice, far from being inconsistent with Charity, seems rather to demand that Charity should be consistent with itself, that it should not benefit one section of the community by injuring another.

make the same demand for special virtues. This is partly because special virtues depend on natural gifts and are not all attainable by every one; and partly because few men can attain excellence in more than a few directions, even if they possess several natural aptitudes. But that public moral opinion does expect every one to cultivate *some* natural excellence, some special virtue, is shown by the fact that Industry and Perseverance are regarded as *moral* virtues. The moral virtues are therefore the general forms in which all special virtues ought to manifest themselves, or by which their exercise should be regulated.

The division of virtues into moral and special is contrary to ordinary usage, but appropriate in Ethics, which most conveniently regards virtue as a property of character which leads the possessor to seek and enables him to attain good ends, either in conduct generally (moral virtues) or in limited spheres of conduct (special virtues). In every system of Ethics such " special virtues " are regarded as good, either for their own sakes or for their results.

Moral virtues and special virtues are mutually related. Industry, for example, is a *sine quâ non* of the development of any special virtue.[1] And generally the true worth of any special virtue is lowered if its exercise conflicts with any of the moral virtues. On the other hand, the moral virtues are meaningless, apart from the special virtues through which they find practical expression. What worth or meaning would Charity have, for example, if there were no

[1] Industry, in the wide sense here intended, does not imply a lack of interest or enthusiasm ; it is an indispensable means of cultivating and satisfying permanent interests—*e.g.* Athletics, Art, or Science—even if these are only "hobbies" or amusements.

concrete ends which one could help others to attain except a charitable disposition,—ends that could only be realised by the exercise of special virtues ? For Charity is a disposition to help others to attain good ends. Now this can be best effected by giving them the means of attaining those good ends for themselves, so that Charity in the widest sense consists in helping others to exercise their special virtues ; [1] and it is clear that it would have no value, that it would be merely an empty form, if there were no good ends to be attained, no personal interests to satisfy, beyond the cultivation of a charitable disposition. Again, what worth or meaning would Honesty have, if there were no interests in the possession of external goods, interests that call forth special virtues to satisfy them ? Moral virtues, in short, are forms that ought to regulate the exercise of special virtues with reference to the highest good.

In what follows, Virtue will usually signify Moral Virtue, but precise determinations will depend on the context.

Will, Character, Person, and Self.—For ethical purposes these four may be almost identified. In deliberate action it is the Will that is said to act, and this action involves a cognitive element, expressing itself in a judgment as to good or bad, and influenced by the complex of feelings, desires, and other motives that bear on the action. Thus understood, the Will embraces, in one whole, cognition, feelings, and desires, as well as an undefinable element of mental force or energy which conditions the resulting appropriate physical movements. In other words, the Will is the

---

[1] According to the definition of special virtues just given.

Self, the indivisible subject of feeling and knowing as well as acting, and we shall not err in identifying it with the whole Character or Person.[1] These four terms, however, differ in *emphasis*. The word "Will" usually suggests more particularly the element of mental force or energy; "Character" emphasises the *habitual* motives from which a personal Will acts, and the nature of the ends sought and attained; "Self" appears to lay stress on *continuity of consciousness* in the same person; and the word "Person" draws special attention to the *unity* and permanence of the subject. Hence each word is useful because of its special suggestions.

Goodness and Utility.—A thing or action is said to be useful *for some purpose*, and its utility is thus determined with reference to a good which is sought for its own sake. Goodness is an attribute of an end, utility of the means to an end. A good is some kind of satisfaction of desire or interest, or a complex of such satisfactions; the useful is what enables us to attain a good. "Useful" may be applied to things, persons, or actions; for example, crutches are useful to a lame man, not good in themselves; a secretary is employed because he is useful, not because his presence is good in itself. The endurance of hardship may be useful though not necessarily good. Many things, fortunately for mankind, are both good and useful; this is often true of knowledge, which directly gratifies curiosity, is also a means of attaining other practical results, and, moreover, expands and deepens the powers of the intellect by removing error and disclosing

---

[1] Nevertheless, many writers (such as Kant) distinguish sharply between Will and Feeling, as two different faculties of the soul.

truth. Some forms of physical exercise are pleasant in themselves and also conducive to the happiness which health brings. The ideally happy life would be one in which every action was both good in itself (satisfying) and useful with reference to some future good.

These remarks explain why we often speak of a thing as being " good " for some purpose, when we really mean " useful." The useful shines by a borrowed light; it may in a sense be regarded as a part of the good to which it tends. In fact good, as an absolute end, is an inward conscious state or activity that is desirable for its own sake, though the term is very seldom used in this exact sense. Health, worldly prosperity, friendship, sympathy, honesty, and so forth are good only so far as they express themselves as some intrinsically desirable conscious state or activity in a person or persons. Externally viewed they are simply useful.

The term " utility " since Bentham's time has received a technical sense in Ethics, and signifies tendency to general happiness. This is only a part of the meaning I have attached to it.

Happiness, Pleasure, and Well-being.—In comparing Greek and modern systems of Ethics, a good deal of confusion often arises from identifying εὐδαιμονία with " Happiness " in the sense in which the latter word is used in modern English Ethics. To avoid this confusion, εὐδαιμονία is hereafter translated " Well-being." [1] It signified the permanent realisation of good by an individual. The ethical problem,

---

[1] The capital is used when the word is intended as a translation of εὐδαιμονία.

"What is the highest attainable human good?" was, for the Greeks, equivalent to "What is Well-being?" According to Aristotle Well-being consists in an activity of the soul; according to the Greek hedonists [1] (the Cyrenaics and Epicurus) it consists in the passive enjoyment of pleasures; according to the Stoics and Cynics, passive pleasures are not essential constituents of Well-being. None of the Greek moralists, then, started with verbally identifying pleasure and Well-being; some asserted that the two are really different, and even the hedonists regarded this identification as something to be proved, not to be assumed from the start. And there is nothing essentially egoistic—in the exclusive sense—in thus identifying the pursuit of the highest good by a person with the pursuit of his own "Well-being." Aristotle fully recognised that the individual cannot regard his own Well-being as something distinct from that of others; a soldier, for example, may find his own highest good in sacrificing or risking his life for the good of his country.

The word "Happiness" has, in modern English Ethics, a narrower and a more "selfish" meaning than Well-being; [2] it signifies generally the constant enjoyment of pleasure by the individual. It was therefore a *real* problem, and not merely one about the meaning of words, to determine whether the highest good attainable by each individual is his own Happiness, general Happiness, or something different from both.

Subjective and Objective Good.—These terms which

---

[1] Hedonism identifies good with pleasure (from Greek ἡδονή, pleasure).

[2] The same is true on the whole of *Glückseligkeit*, as used by Kant, which is translated "Happiness." It meant for him the constant gratification of desires whose fruition gives pleasure.

are used frequently in the following pages require some explanation. Subjective literally means existing for the experience of a conscious subject. One person's feelings of pain and pleasure, his perceptions of external objects, his sensations of colour, warmth, and light, his susceptibility to beauty and ugliness, his views on politics, and so on—all these have a subjective side, because they have features whose existence is their existence in consciousness. Now *good* must have a subjective side, because as far as we can see, it must ultimately express itself as a desirable state or activity of consciousness in one or many persons. "Objective" means existing as an object, *i.e.* having a mode of existence which either extends beyond any immediate momentary experience of any single conscious subject, or is independent of the experience of any such subject. The State, or any organised group of men, is objective in the first sense but not in the second; it is usually supposed—and here we need not dispute the question—that tables and chairs, houses and mountains—all "objects" of external nature—are objective in both senses. In Ethics the first meaning is preferable, since good cannot be independent of consciousness, though it may extend beyond any immediate momentary experience of any single person. Thus improved sanitation, because it affects a number of persons, is objectively good, and a man's health is an objective good from one point of view, since its value is not apprehended in a momentary experience, but extends through the whole life.

In general, as the examples just given show, the good of an individual is subjective in relation to the good of society, which is objective; and the good of a momentary experience of one person is likewise subjective in relation to the good of his whole life, which is objective. But usually the contrast is between the individual and society. When we say that good is *merely* subjective, we mean that the good of one individual is generically distinct from that of another, and that there is no common measure between them—I can never judge your good to be mine. The issue of this doctrine is Exclusive Egoism, which reached its high-water mark in Hobbes.

Common moral judgments presuppose that good is objective, so far as they are disinterested; the average man disapproves of a murder and approves of an act of justice, even if his own life is not directly affected by either. Such judgments further imply that the person making them, if he is consistent, submits his private feelings to a law—the moral law. In condemning or approving another's action he implicitly condemns or approves himself if ever he should perform the same action.

If good is merely subjective, how are apparently disinterested moral judgments possible? This is the question which Exclusive Egoism has to face. If good is objective how can it also be subjective? This is really the weightiest problem of pure Ethics. We have already noticed it in other forms; it may appear as a conflict between moral obligation and private inclinations, or between the rights of the individual and the claims of society, or between immediate and remote good.[1]

General Problems.—It appears then that there are

---

[1] See pp. 5, 6, 8.

certain leading problems; these will recur in the systems hereafter described. The more prominent are :—(1) The nature of individual good; (2) The nature of social good; (3) The relation between these; (4) The ethical sanctions *i.e.* the motives that exist for the individual to pursue social good, or to do what is morally right; (5) The relation between pleasure and the good; (6) (In ancient Ethics especially) the nature of Virtue; (7) (In modern Ethics especially) the ground of Duty and Moral obligation; (8) The Freedom of the Will; (9) The ethical worth of Positive Morality, *i.e.* the body of practical moral principles generally accepted in society, and recognised as binding by the average person.

PART I

GREEK ETHICAL SYSTEMS

CHAPTER I

THE SOPHISTS, SOCRATES, AND THE SOCRATIC SCHOOLS

A. THE SOPHISTS

IN the fifth century B.C. there arose in Greece a body of professional teachers of philosophy and rhetoric known as the Sophists, who may be regarded as the pioneers in ethical science, since their predecessors in philosophy devoted attention to impersonal problems dealing with the constitution of the material universe, rather than to questions of human conduct. Protagoras of Abdera [1] represents the positive and constructive, and Gorgias of Leontini [2] the negative and critical side of Sophistic teaching. To Protagoras is attributed the famous saying, " Man is the measure of all things." As applied to conduct this saying is commonly interpreted as expressing that good is entirely subjective; [3] it is relative to the individual who achieves it, and what appears to him to be good *is* good. Viewed in this light the dictum of Protagoras is one-sided, because it ignores the objective element in morality; if good exists only for the individual experiencing it there can be no objective social good. But the dictum

---

[1] Born *circa* 480 B.C.　　　　[2] Born *circa* 483 B.C.
[3] See pp. 25, 26.

31

expresses an important truth, namely, that the good
sought by practical philosophy is *personal*; it must
ultimately be experienced by one or more human
beings, for otherwise it would have no meaning.
But this principle need not be interpreted as Exclusive Egoism, since it is quite consistent with the
supposition that social good is superior to the good
of any one individual. The experience in which the
good is realised may be the collective experience of
mankind, not the isolated experience of a single
individual. The good may be objective and yet
personal.

The dictum as just interpreted may be said to
express the *principle of subjectivity* in Ethics. But
probably Protagoras intended to emphasise, not only
that each individual has a right of free judgment as
to what is good for *him*, but also that different states
or communities,—and perhaps different periods of
history—may have different moral codes which are
not universally binding; that each social group has
a right to establish the moral code that best suits its
welfare. From this point of view the doctrine expresses the ethical *principle of relativity,* which means
that the laws of social morality are subject to varia-
tion—not indeed arbitrary, but determined by the
changes in social conditions and individual circumstances. Plato's delineation of the ideal republic is
partly intended to refute this doctrine; he endeavours
to show that there is but one ideal system of political
organisation, and that all others are to be judged by
the degree in which they approach it.

Nevertheless, when applied to special cases of
conduct the principle of relativity is a truism, for it

only means that different cases may have to be
treated in different ways *if the cases really differ in
essential points*; the law, for example, distinguishes
between murder and accidental homicide, and we
should judge less severely a starving man for stealing
a loaf than a rich man for increasing his wealth by
fraud. In the ideal government the principle would
be fully exercised.[1] But it is peculiarly liable to
abuse by dishonest or illogical thinkers; with the
later Sophists its abuse led to the anarchical doctrine
that each individual may do what he likes without
reference to the good of others, that there is no
objective distinction between good and bad.

The philosophy of Protagoras was not profound
enough to explain how the good can be both personal
and objective. Gorgias accepted the principle of
subjectivity in a negative sense, as equivalent to
asserting that truth and goodness are purely subjective. The result was absolute scepticism; there
is no knowledge, in the proper sense, but only a
particular feeling in the mind of a single person;
and good has only a limited subjective nature, consisting in a single agent's momentary feeling of gratification or approval. It follows that the conception
of an objective social good is illusory from a practical
point of view, since the good of another cannot be
an end of action for me. It is not surprising to
find that the teaching of the later Sophists, following
the lines laid down by Gorgias, was purely egoistic.

[1] The principle of relativity is consistent with the uniformity of moral
law ; just as in science the law of uniformity of nature—the same causes
have the same effects—is consistent with the truth that the same event
may be followed by different events if the conditions accompanying the
antecedents differ ; fire may cook food or it may destroy property according to circumstances.

Thrasymachus,[1] for example, identified Justice with the private interests of those who have power.

The Sophistic movement is important in the history of Ethics for three reasons. First, because it arose from a desire to criticise freely conventional theories of knowledge and morality; it was essentially an appeal to nature and reason against the arbitrary forces of mere tradition.   Secondly, the Sophists were the first to mark off Ethics—as a methodical search for the highest human good—from other inquiries, a division afterwards completed by Aristotle.   Thirdly, the individualism prominent in the Sophist's teaching, expresses the important truth—which no subsequent ethical system has been able to evade—that there is no such thing as an abstract good of society apart from the good of the persons composing it.[2]   Further, each rational agent must in any case seek his own good, and therefore morality, in its historical beginning, naturally assumed an egoistic form.   The good of another person cannot be a rational end for *me*, unless I apprehend his good as mine.   Not Egoism in general but only *Exclusive Egoism*—which asserts that no person can identify the good of another with his own good—is incompatible with a regard for social good.

B. SOCRATES [3]

The later Sophists, influenced chiefly by Gorgias, moved in the direction of Exclusive Egoism, and it

---

[1] See p. 43.

[2] This may be regarded as defining the meaning of "individualism."

[3] 469-399 B.C.   Socrates was condemned to death by the Athenian Government and compelled to drink poison (399 B.C.).   The accusation was that he corrupted youth and did not acknowledge the gods which the

was mainly against this erroneous *negative* development of the conception of human good that Socrates'
criticisms were directed.   Socrates recognised the truth
contained in the principle of Protagoras; the good we
seek is human Well-being, and it can only be realised
in persons.   But it is not for that reason merely subjective; it is proved to be objective by the fact that
it can be understood by means of general conceptions,
and its realisation is determined by definite uniform
laws, which do not depend on the feelings of this or
that individual.

The doctrines ascribed to Socrates, that virtue is
knowledge and that it is one, are partly criticisms of
the moral scepticism of Gorgias, and partly an advance
towards a constructive science of Ethics.   The doctrine
of the unity of virtue is a protest against the ethical
anarchy which would reduce all morality to a matter
of private caprice.   Socrates wished to show that
virtue and human Well-being are subject to unvarying
laws independent of the fluctuating choice of individuals.   He held, further, that these laws may
be discovered and communicated to others,—virtue
is knowable and teachable.   But the saying, "Virtue
is knowledge" meant for him more than that virtue
may be known; he intended actually to identify
practical excellence of character with intellectual
insight into the true nature of actions; he who knows
what is good   must   act   accordingly   and   no   one

State recognised.   Ueberweg (*History of Philosophy*) remarks that "this
accusation was literally false ; but considered with reference to its more
profound basis, it rested on the correct assumption of an essential relation-
ship between Socrates and the Sophists, as evidenced in their common
tendency to emancipate the individual, and in their common opposition
to an immediate unreflecting submission to the customs, law, and faith of
the people and the State."

voluntarily follows evil. Vice, on the other hand, is ignorance, and the sensualist is as stupid as an ox.

Socrates wrote no treatise on the theory of Ethics; he taught by personal discussions, in which he strove not merely to teach truths directly, but to draw forth and examine the living convictions of those with whom he conversed. He taught that the starting-point of that knowledge which is virtue, is to be conscious of one's own ignorance; and that the next step is to know one's own soul, to learn what passions within the soul are opposed to wisdom, and to control them; only by such self-knowledge can freedom be acquired.

The personal influence of Socrates was the stimulus which gave rise to the subsequent Greek ethical systems. Those who came after him endeavoured to give exact systematic expression to the conviction they inherited from him, that there is a science of right living. The problem usually took the form, "What is human Well-being,[1] and how is it to be attained?" Among those who received direct instruction from Socrates, Plato was by far the greatest thinker. But two of the so-called Socratic Schools—the Cynic and the Cyrenaic, whose founders were disciples of Socrates— deserve special mention, because they represent very distinctly the two opposite poles towards which ethical theories tend to converge; the one laying stress on action and endurance, the other on pleasurable feelings, as the chief constituents of a life of Well-being.

[1] See pp. 23, 24.

C. THE CYNICS

The founder of the Cynic [1] School was Antisthenes [2] who held that the highest end was life according to Virtue, that pain might be good as contributing to Virtue, and that pleasure sought as an end was an evil. He who has Virtue needs nothing else, he is independent of the society around him and of the laws of his own State. He is a citizen of the world, and is everywhere at home, because his Well-being depends on himself alone. Antisthenes agreed with Socrates that knowledge is essential to Virtue, but held that logic, physics, and all theoretical studies are only indirectly valuable as means to Well-being. The Cynics generally identified wisdom with practical Virtue ; they held that a merely theoretical knowledge is not a source of Well-being.

The earlier Cynics appear to have accepted un-critically the Positive Morality of the age ; they held that the accepted practical virtues, Justice, Temperance, etc., are intrinsically good. Their doctrines give but little information about the true nature of Well-being, because they did not analyse the virtues, to discover their common ground. It is useless to define Well-being as living virtuously, when the only intelligible meaning of Virtue is a state of character leading to Well-being. Negatively, the Cynic system enjoins endurance of pain and a cultivation of contempt for pleasure ; it thus emphasises the truths that the

---

[1] Called " Cynic " perhaps because Antisthenes taught at Athens in the gymnasium called Cynosarges. The name is sometimes said to be derived from κύων (a dog), because of the open disregard of the school for the ordinary decencies of society.

[2] Born *circa* 436 B.C.

direct pursuit of pleasures is apt to defeat its own end, and that self-control is essential to Well-being. Thus interpreted it is a protest against sensualism. But these doctrines are only superficially opposed to Hedonism.[1]   It would be quite consistent for a pessimistic hedonist—one who believes that, though pleasure is the highest good, but little of it is attainable—to recommend the direct pursuit of Virtue and self-control as the best method of getting what we can out of a world which at the best is painful. The Cynic Ethics was still on the plane of pure Egoism, for they sought individual self-dependence, rather than social good. Their cosmopolitanism[2] seems to have been rather a contempt (real or affected) for their fellow-countrymen than a regard for humanity. In this connection, however, it may be noticed that the English word "cynic" seems expressive only of the worst negative aspect of the genuine earlier Cynicism, —namely, contempt for the excellences of others,—and does not fairly express the essence of their philosophy. The Cynic doctrine is nevertheless chiefly *negative* and *formal*,[3] whether in relation to individual or to social good; and herein lies its chief defect.

The inadequacy of the Cynic philosophy is shown by the fact that it moved afterwards in two opposite directions, the one towards Exclusive Egoism, the other towards the truer doctrine of Stoicism. This double movement was due to the ambiguity in the

---

[1] The theory that pleasure is the highest good. This is quite different from sensualism.

[2] A cosmopolitan is one who regards himself as a citizen of the world, not of any particular State.

[3] The meaning of this will be understood by contrasting the Cynic with the Cyrenaic doctrine described in the next section.

notion of the " Self." Corrupt later Cynicism regarded
the Self as an isolated unit, and taught that Well-
being lay in a contempt for society. But Stoicism
in its higher forms regarded the Self as essentially
social, and took self-dependence to mean an unflinching
performance of the duties arising naturally from the
position of the Self in society and in the universe.

D. THE CYRENAICS

The Cynics, we have seen, identified the good with
abstinence from pleasure and indifference to pain,
and Well-being for them was mainly negative. The
Cyrenaics, on the other hand, rightly held that good
must be something positive and concrete. The only
concrete good they could find was immediate pleasure.
The founder of the School, Aristippus of Cyrene [1]
identified the End of Life with the pleasure of the
moment. Knowledge and culture (they held) are
valuable so far as they lead to pleasure, and the wise
man cultivates self-control in order to get the most
out of life; he rules and is not ruled by his pleasures.
Pleasures are to be estimated altogether by their
intensity. The virtues are not ends in themselves,
but only means. Justice is conventional and not
natural, since it arises from the artificial needs of
social life; wisdom and friendship are estimated by
the pleasure they bring to the possessor.

The Cyrenaics were the first Greek representatives
of Hedonism, the doctrine that only pleasure is good.
The system of Epicurus was a more refined expression
of the same doctrine; it arose from the difficulty of

[1] Born *circa* 435 B.C.

reconciling the two Cyrenaic positions, in one of which the good is identified with the pleasure of the moment, while in the other, self-control and mastery over pleasures are recommended.[1]

[1] A general criticism of Cyrenaic and Epicurean Hedonism will be given later (pp. 90-92).

CHAPTER II

THE Cyrenaics and Cynics tried to answer the first and inevitable problem of Ethics in the form in which it was presented by Protagoras,—the determination, namely, of the good of the *individual*. That this is the primary ethical problem is clear from the fact that every conscious rational being, acting deliberately, must seek what he believes to be his own good, except in so far as his judgment is distorted by passion, or is not strong enough to influence his will; if he voluntarily seeks the good of others it is because he in some way identifies *social* good with his own. The devoted life and death of Socrates seem to prove, more clearly than his teaching, that he was convinced that social good was an end really worth pursuing for its own sake. The Cyrenaic and Cynic doctrines, however, tend towards Exclusive Egoism, whether as a pursuit of self-dependence or of pleasurable feeling. Aristotle and Plato must therefore be regarded as more sincere followers of Socrates, for with them the question of social good and its relation to individual good came to the front. Hereafter moral questions became more difficult and complex, since there is

41   c

always in human nature an apparent conflict between personal well-being and social good regarded as ultimate motives, and this conflict takes the form of a seeming contradiction in the idea of objective good.[1]

Plato and Aristotle differ, moreover, from most other Greek thinkers—not excepting Socrates—in treating knowledge of reality as an end desirable for its own sake, an integral part of well-being, not merely an external means of acquiring it. They have even a tendency to regard speculative wisdom as the highest good; but this must not be interpreted as a narrow intellectualism;[2] speculative wisdom was for them not the same thing as an abstract and merely theoretical knowledge, but included also the mental apprehension of man's true nature and his relations to the universe. Owing to this genuine love of knowledge both refused to subordinate the search for truth to a search for Well-being; accordingly Metaphysics, Logic, and Physical Science secured their disinterested attention quite as much as Ethics.

The Ethics of Plato[3] deals partly with individual good, partly with social good, and partly with the relations between the two. The *Republic*, for example, takes the wider threefold view, while the *Philebus* treats chiefly of the nature of individual good. From these two works can be derived a consistent system of Ethics, not formulated scientifically, but expressed with great literary skill in the form of imaginary dialogues between Socrates and other persons.

[1] See pp. 25, 26.   [2] See p. 82, note.
[3] 427-347 B.C., a pupil of Socrates, and founder of the School at Athens known as the Academy.

A. The Idea of Justice

The purpose of the *Republic*, which is the most important of Plato's ethical works, was to determine the nature and worth of Justice,[1] and the means of realising it in society as represented by the State. In the first book the Sophist Thrasymachus puts forth the theory that Justice is "the interest of the stronger"; [2] that for the rulers it consists in compelling obedience from selfish motives, while for the subjects, who have no political power, it means prudent obedience through fear of punishment. This doctrine, afterwards taught in a more complex form by Hobbes, is an extreme type of Exclusive Egoism. It assumes that Justice, regarded as a personal virtue aiming at the good of the whole community, is a fiction, and that no one considers it to be worthy of cultivation for its own sake. Plato wishes to show that Justice in this pure sense is essentially good, not only for Society as a whole, but also for the individual who practises it, and with this end in view he proceeds first to analyse the conception of Justice.

Method.——While recognising that Justice is fundamentally a virtue of personal character, Plato (or rather Socrates, who, as the principal character in the dialogue, may be taken as expressing Plato's views) thinks that the easiest way of determining its nature will be to consider it first in the forms in which it is manifested on a large scale, in a State or organised group of individuals rather than in single persons, and afterwards as it presents itself in the character and conduct

---

[1] δικαιοσύνη   [2] τὸ τοῦ κρείττονος συμφέρον.

of the units of the group. A State arises from the
common need for adjusting the relations between a
number of persons, who, living together, find it to the
general advantage to make a *division of labour*, each
person doing the work most suitable to his tastes or
powers, and receiving from others a share of the
surplus products of their work in exchange for the
surplus products of his own. The growth in well-
being of a society as an organic whole depends on
the degree in which this *specialisation of function*
operates, and it is here that Plato finds the germ of
the conception of Justice, regarded as an attribute of
the State.

The Cardinal Virtues.——As a State develops in
well-being the specialisation of function takes certain
well-defined forms, producing internal vitality, internal
harmony and power to resist invasion from without.
The general expressions for these forms in their
highest perfection are the four " Cardinal Virtues,"
regarded as belonging to the State as a whole. These
are Wisdom, Fortitude or Courage, Temperance, and
Justice.[1] Wisdom is directive, deliberative, the source
of wise government, and is therefore the special virtue
of the small or ruling class, who should constitute the
intellectual aristocracy. Fortitude is the characteristic
virtue of the fighting class which was ranked by Plato
next to the intellectual. It is almost identical with
strength of purpose rightly directed; it is the quality
which enables a man to resist the promptings of fear
and pain and the temptations of pleasure, and to act
in accordance with the convictions previously formed

[1] σοφία (sometimes φρόνησις), ἀνδρεία, σωφροσύνη, δικαιοσύνη. The
translations are only approximate ; even the Greek words are used by
Plato in an unusually general sense.

by right education.[1] Such convictions in a brave
man are comparable to a good dye, they cannot
be washed out by the lye of pleasure, pain, or
fear. Temperance,[2] as a quality of the State, is not
characteristic of one class more than another; it is
the virtue of order, a harmony between all classes of
the community, to be ensured by obedience on the
part of the subjects, and by wise moderation and
disinterestedness in the rulers. This harmony is
compared by Plato to the proper tuning of the strings
of a lyre.

Justice is the highest of the cardinal virtues,
because it includes all of them. It is realised in the
State when the rulers govern wisely, the soldiers fight
bravely, and the industrial classes work with energy
and thrift, all being obedient to the Reason that
governs. From an external point of view Justice is
the perfect consummation of the "division of labour,"
and is defined by Plato as "doing your own business
and not interfering with that of other people."[3] It
is the full realisation, the crown of other virtues,
which, without it, miss their end. Wisdom alone
may be ineffectual, Courage may be ill-directed, even
Temperance (including loyalty and obedience), if
separated from Wisdom and Courage, may be purely
negative and repressive, and may end in an insipid
formal harmony, whose parts possess no individuality
or strength. Justice, on the other hand, demands the
development of *individuality*, which is ensured by

---

[1] Thus ἀνδρεία includes our "moral" and "physical" courage, as well
as the active power of resisting temptations of any kind.

[2] The word σωφροσύνη as used by Plato has a much wider meaning
than our "Temperance," which is more akin to Aristotle's use of the
same word.

[3] τὸ τὰ αὑτοῦ πράττειν καὶ μὴ πολυπραγμονεῖν.

Courage, and is directed by Wisdom through the harmonising influence of Temperance. Justice, in short, is intelligence, strength, and unity combined; it is not one virtue among many, but the due combination of all.

Justice in the Individual.—Justice, however, is something more than an external adjustment of social functions; though it has hitherto been treated as such with a view to determine its complete nature by a provisional definition. Its true essence is inward and spiritual, and for this reason it must reside in the personal characters of individuals. Every member of the State is to *be* just, not by compulsion, but because he sees that it is good; only then will the State as a whole possess Justice. Hence Plato is naturally led to consider Justice as a personal virtue. Following out his method he traces an analogy between the State and the individual. To the three classes in the State—the rulers, the soldiers, and the industrial classes—there correspond in the individual the three different faculties of the soul,—Reason, Spirited Emotion[1] and Desire (including appetite). Each of these should have freedom to perform its special function, and each is an essential element in human nature. When their functions are properly fulfilled they possess virtue.[2] Wisdom is the special virtue of the rational part, Courage or Fortitude of the emotional, while Temperance consists in the obedience of the

[1] λόγος, θυμός, ἐπιθυμία. We have no word corresponding exactly to θυμός. It included "not merely anger, but all the passions and sentiments which prompt to energetic action, and which, when subordinated to Reason, are thus the natural counterpoise to the appetites of which either sensual pleasure or bodily repletion is the object." —Thompson's *Phaedrus*, p. 166.

[2] See p. 68, for the general meaning of " virtue " (ἀρετή).

emotions and desires to Reason. Justice, finally, is
the presence of all these virtues in the soul, and consists
in the free harmonious exercise of Intellect, Emotion,
and Desire under the guidance of Reason.

Its Worth for the Individual.—Justice, then, Plato
infers, is *the* virtue of the soul; it is spiritual beauty
and health, as vice is ugliness and disease; and it is
as absurd to deny that it is profitable for its possessor
as it is to deny that health is profitable to the body.
It is the indispensable and sufficient condition of
personal happiness.

Social and Private Good.—Justice in the State (as
a harmonious co-operation between different persons)
and Justice in the individual (as a harmonious co-
operation between the different faculties of the soul)
seem to be two different conceptions connected only
by analogy. But Plato, whether rightly or wrongly,
identifies them, and finds in this identification the
principle of unity between individual and social good.
The just man is he who, led by Wisdom, aims at
practically realising the conception of harmonious
and vigorous development of parts within a whole;
as he seeks to realise this ideal within his own soul,
so he seeks also to realise it in the State of which he
is a member; in both cases for the same reason—that
he loves the conception of Justice. His own Well-
being (it is implied) is reached only when perfect
Justice reigns in every soul; and with this consummation comes the Well-being of all his fellow-citizens,
which he does not separate from his own.

The Ideal State.—It follows that the first work of
social philosophy is to delineate the form of a perfect
State in which universal Justice may find expression.

Here the leading idea is that traditional forms of
government, whether democracy oligarchy or tyranny,
should be replaced by a genuine *aristocracy*, or government by those best fit to govern.[1] A knowledge and
love of Justice, with courage to enforce it, are the
essential characteristics of the rulers of the Ideal State.
Primarily among the rulers, ultimately among all
the citizens, a community of interests is to be
established as a bond of national unity. The State
is to become like an organism, in which if one member
suffers or rejoices, all the members in some degree
suffer or rejoice; the end which Justice seeks to
realise being general Well-being, not the Well-being
of any select body.

The Ideal Ruler.— If Justice existed in every soul
rulers would be superfluous; but only a few are
naturally capable of apprehending it in its perfect
beauty, and even for them this is possible only after
a prolonged mental training. Hence the vital importance of educating the rulers properly. Justice,
as we have seen, includes all the virtues, Wisdom,
Courage, Temperance, and their specialised forms, and
one might therefore suppose that all the cardinal
virtues are equally essential to a good ruler. In one
sense this is true; the rulers must possess self-control
and the courage of their opinions. But since they
have to realise Justice in the State, their crowning
virtue—the note of true aristocracy—is Wisdom,
because they must apprehend intellectually the essence
of Justice before it is fully realised, and learn what
are the practical means for realising it. The ideal
ruler is therefore a philosopher, a lover of Wisdom,

---

[1] The original meaning of the word "aristocracy."

combining intellectual insight and practical intelligence. Justice, in fact, is Wisdom *realised* in society.

Truth is usually conceived as the object of purely theoretical knowledge. But Plato, generalising the Socratic doctrine,[1] holds that the ultimate object of knowledge is the Highest Good, in the realisation of which all opposition between theory and practice disappears. Now Wisdom is the faculty by which we apprehend the truth in this broad sense. The Idea of Justice is, on the one hand, an object of theoretical knowledge, and on the other hand, its realisation is essentially good. To know the nature of Justice is to desire above all things to realise it. The ideal ruler must therefore be a "lover of Wisdom" (a philosopher), in order that he may learn the nature of Justice. Now the lover of Wisdom does not pursue Justice alone, he seeks the truth everywhere, wherever it may be found.[2] He looks, not at the isolated appearances but at the inner essence of reality. He is never satisfied with mere opinion, which pursues only the shadow of things; he seeks and obtains knowledge, which apprehends the substance of things as they really are. It is characteristic of Plato that he regards this intellectual love of truth as the spring of moral virtue, as popularly understood. The philosopher is sincere in his conduct, because he loves the truth, whether found in his own soul or in another's. He is temperate, for his joys are spiritual,

---

[1] p. 35.

[2] The mental attitude which seeks to take into account all relevant facts, in order to determine their due positions and correlations, is really an intellectual form of Justice, which was described as the co-ordination of parts within a whole, each part fulfilling its due function. Thus the Idea of Justice animates the truth-seeker from the very start of his inquiries.

not carnal. He is not covetous, for he values only the things that are beyond price. He is great-minded and courageous, for falsehood and deception are all that he fears. He sees and loves beauty, for this is the effulgence of truth. That he possesses Justice as a personal virtue follows naturally from the fact that he desires to realise the Idea of Justice wherever this is possible, whether in himself or in other persons, or in the State as a whole.

Education of the Rulers.—The education of the Rulers is to be directed towards teaching them the nature of Justice; and it must therefore aim at the cultivation of Temperance, Fortitude, and Wisdom, which are the three constituents of Justice. Without entering fully into the various schemes proposed by Plato for selecting and training the Rulers, we may say that he laid special stress on the following points.

(*a*) An education in literature.[1] A very careful selection of the best types is necessary. Literature —whether narrative or dramatic—in which gods and heroes are described as committing ignoble or indecent actions, is to be excluded, because the good influence of literature is in proportion to the goodness of the characters whom the writer regards as worthy of admiration. Example is thus accepted by Plato as a means of moral education.

(*b*) In music, luxurious and mournful styles must be abolished, because they weaken the moral fibre. Only those are to be admitted which express the tranquillity of a temperate man in prosperity, or

---

[1] Literature and Music and all forms of Art are classed by Plato under the title μουσική.

the endurance of a brave man in adversity; hereby *Temperance* and *Fortitude* are cultivated. The result of a proper education in all forms of Art (poetry, painting, sculpture, architecture, and music) is that the soul learns to love beauty, harmony, and proportion, and thus is ready, when Reason develops, to understand the nature of the good, which, in the form of *Temperance*, is the expression of harmony in society and in the individual.

(c) Gymnastic is to be included, not for the sake of the body but for the sake of the soul. The value of Gymnastic lies chiefly in its power of counteracting effeminacy and the love of luxury, and thereby making possible the development of true spiritual Fortitude.

(d) *Fortitude*, again, is to be developed and tested, not only by physical hardships, but also by passing through moral trials and temptations.

The following preparatory training is also necessary in order to develop the reasoning powers:

(e) An education in mathematics, viz. arithmetic, geometry, mathematical astronomy, and the mathematical principles of musical harmony.[1] The use of these subjects is to evoke reflection, to stimulate the mind to pass beyond the disconnected particulars given to Sense towards the general laws of the Universe, which are apprehended by Reason. Plato held also that the precision of mathematics foreshadows the perfect knowledge of real existence attainable only by Dialectic; but the mathematician does not really *know*, because he takes his first principles for granted,

---

[1] Here the influence of Pythagoras is noticeable, who taught that number and harmony were the universal properties of real existence.

without examining their evidence. The two educational ends here emphasised are the development of the powers of correct *generalisation* and of *accuracy in details.*

(*f*) We shall see [1] that Plato regarded the universe as a rationally connected system, containing no isolated parts, and that the just State is likewise an organic whole, whose proper form can be determined only by Reason. In order to prepare the mind for this view of things, those who are destined to be rulers must study the co-ordination of the sciences and their mutual dependence.[2] This may be called the *synoptic* principle in education. We learn more about things by determining their causes and their connections with other things.

(*g*) Only the mind prepared by these studies is fit for the pursuit of Dialectic, the highest of all the sciences, which deals directly with the fundamental principles of real existence. This science is also described as the study of the " Idea of the Good " which [3] is the source of all truth, goodness, and beauty. The chief rulers are to be chosen from those who are best qualified in Dialectic, since it is their function to realise the social form of the Idea of the Good, namely Justice. The corresponding virtue is *Wisdom.*

B. THE THEORY OF IDEAS

One of the chief characteristics of Plato's philosophy is that he regards perfect types as being in a sense more real than the particular objects or processes of the physical world, or than any particular mental

[1] See pp. 62, 63.   [2] See p. 49, note.   [3] See pp. 55-57.

states of feeling or sensation. The real objects of knowledge are " Ideas," [1] and the particular objects of sensible experience are true only so far as the mind conceives them as manifestations of Ideas. The Ideas are described as eternal archetypes or models of perfection, which the Creator uses to construct the physical and sensible world in space and time. By man the Ideas can only be apprehended by general conceptions which *are*, or *ought* to be, realised in the concrete world of Nature and Man. Thus the Ideas are of two kinds: [2] first, those which are actualised and made use of in Science and ordinary life,—these (in their exact forms) we may call *scientific conceptions*; and secondly, *ethical* and *artistic ideals*, which are only inadequately realised in human experience. Examples of scientific conceptions are the Ideas of number, of equality, and of perfect geometrical figures; while Temperance and Justice, etc., as described in the *Republic*, are examples of *ethical ideals*. As regards artistic ideals, Plato appears to have included them all without analysis under the one Idea of Beauty; the same Idea is manifested in everything that is truly beautiful, whether it be a melody, a human form, a moral character, or a political constitution. But beauty [3] for Plato had a wider meaning than for us; for him it was almost equivalent to the ethically good or perfect, and its highest expression is to be found in the ordering of societies by Temperance and Justice; in general, anything properly fitted for its place or function in the scheme of things is beautiful. Only

---

[1] εἶδος or ἰδέα.

[2] Plato does not draw special attention to this distinction, but only confusion can result from ignoring it.

[3] τὸ καλόν.

the soul, however, and a society composed of souls, is beautiful in the strict sense, since beauty of physical form is merely a reflection or outward show of inward spiritual beauty.

Though these ethical ideals are eternal types of perfection that yield to no man's convenience, yet Plato recognises that lower degrees of excellence are both possible and desirable. We may approach towards the perfect State, or towards perfection of character, though both may be unattainable in this life. There are, indeed (as the Stoics afterwards insisted) no degrees of perfection, but there are lower and higher stages that may have to be passed through on the road to perfection. In this admission —which is implied at least indirectly in Plato's works—he shows that practical moderation, that dislike of extravagance, which is a characteristic of all great thinkers.

Scientific conceptions—the Ideas actualised in Nature and used by men—are not apprehended by Sense, but only by intuitive Reason. Sense gives us only the detached particulars, but Reason apprehends the universal Idea in the particulars; it recognises that the objects of sensible experience are actually related and combined by Ideas. The Ideas of equality, of straight lines and circles, are too exact for Sense to apprehend. Number, again, is one of the simplest illustrations of the co-ordination of particulars by Ideas; by it the "many" and the "one" are united, whereas for Sense, everything is detached and appears to exist by itself alone.

In like manner (Plato meant) the ethical ideals are not known by particular feelings of pleasure, but

only by Reason. Pleasure, indeed, has its proper
position, and is an essential part of the good, but it
is not the criterion, nor is it to be allowed to judge
of what is good or bad. An ethical ideal, like a
scientific conception, is a co-ordination of parts
within a whole, but cannot be directly presented to
Feeling.

The Absolute Good.—From the preceding it may
be gathered that the Ideas are, in some sense, to be
conceived as principles of connection between diverse
elements, or forms of the " one in many." Now, if
we follow out this thought consistently, we are compelled—as Plato was—to conclude that there is one
fundamental or highest Idea, by which all different
Ideas are connected ; for otherwise these Ideas would
be isolated, and would suffer from the same defect as
the particulars of Sense. Different Ideas are to be
conceived as manifestations of the highest Idea,
which Plato calls the " Absolute Good," or " the
Idea of the Good." [1] The Idea of the Good is not
a merely abstract conception, nor is it identical with
any particular existing object ; rather, it reveals itself
in everything that truly exists. It is the source of
all truth, of knowledge, beauty, and moral goodness.
Its apprehension by the soul is knowledge, its in-
dwelling in the soul is virtue, its shining forth to
the soul (it may be through the medium of sense) is
beauty. Its manifestation in the State is Justice. In
the *Republic* Plato expresses the belief that a knowledge
of the Absolute Good can only be achieved through
a long course of education by a few specially gifted
minds. It may, therefore, be apprehended by Reason,

[1] ἡ τοῦ ἀγαθοῦ ἰδέα. *Rep.* Bk. VI.

but its nature can only be described by an analogy :
As the sun illumines the sensible world and is the
source of the eye's power of vision, and of nourishment and growth in all living things, so the Good
illuminates the intelligible world and gives the soul
power to know and to grow in knowledge and virtue.
The Absolute Good is the source of all knowledge
and also the highest object of knowledge.

The " Idea of the Good " was, for Plato, an object
of mystical faith rather than of rational intuition,
and he does not claim to know very much about it.
It has been interpreted in various ways by commentators. By some it is identified with God, by
some with the system of archetypal Ideas which the
Creator uses to construct the real Universe, by some
with the ultimate Laws of Nature, and by some with
the Final Cause of the Universe. All these interpre-
tations are probably correct in some degree, but they
are scarcely more definite than Plato's own description, which, as he recognises, is unavoidably mystical.
Clearly we cannot describe the Absolute Good until
we have apprehended it.[1]   Plato probably meant to
express, what he afterwards stated more explicitly in
the *Laws*, that the Universe is a rational system, and
that the true nature of anything depends on its
position in the system.[2]

The Idea of the Good, however, is not to be
pursued merely in order to satisfy the speculative
intellect that everything really existing is good, or
a means thereto. The Rulers are to study Dialectic,
the Science of the Idea of the Good, for a practical
purpose, in order that they may be able to realise

[1] Cf. Green (Chapter IX.).   [2] pp. 62, 63.

Justice in Society,—Justice being in fact the social manifestation of the Idea of the Good.

The Idea of the Good is, therefore, on the one hand, an eternally existing object of the *speculative* intellect, and, on the other hand, it is, or contains, a practical or ethical ideal (*e.g.* Justice) which ought to be realised, but is not yet realised. Here we have a serious opposition between the ideal and the actual, an opposition already seen in the division of the Ideas into two classes.

The Ideal and the Actual.—Plato asserts that only the Ideas truly exist. Now we have seen that Ideas are either ethical ideals (*e.g.* Justice) or scientific conceptions (*e.g.* number). It is comparatively easy to admit that the latter are truly existent, so far as they are actualised in nature and used successfully in experience; but great difficulties arise when we inquire how ethical ideals, not yet realised, can be regarded as truly existing. The following alternative explanations naturally suggest themselves.—

1. That ethical ideals are imaginary types of perfection, which are nevertheless useful for urging men towards improvement. This is the common-sense, realistic view,[1] that there is a cleavage between the existent and the non-existent good, whose realisation is desirable, but perhaps impossible, and certainly not inevitable so far as we know. This interpretation is, however, inconsistent with most of Plato's writings.

2. That ethical ideals are, and always were, realised in a supersensible world with which the soul may have communion in the present life. He who has such communion is the true philosopher, who sees

[1] See p. 14.

things in their spiritual perfection and guides weaker
souls into the light of truth.   In a like spirit Keats
addresses the great poets :—

> Bards of Passion and of mirth
> Ye have left your souls on earth !
> Ye have souls in heaven too,
> Double-lived in regions new !

According to this view the supersensible world alone
truly exists; the physical world is more than half
illusion; it exists only in so far as it is good—that
is, manifests Ideas—but on the whole it is a mere
shadow of existence.   Evil, therefore, is a negation;
in the soul it is mere illusion, and for that reason
it is not a real object.[1]   Knowledge of what exists is
identical with Well-being and virtue.

3. That ethical ideals, though not yet realised in
the world, in Nature, and in human experience, will be
realised in the future; then and not till then will the
world truly exist.   According to this theory, ethical
progress is inevitable, and it is in a sense a creation
of the world, a transition from non-existence to
existence.

4. Lastly, there is the view (a development of the
preceding) that ethical ideals truly exist, provided
the whole universe is taken into account.   The part
as a part is imperfect, but as co-ordinated with other
parts it shares the absolute perfection of the whole.
Things now *seem* imperfect, because we must think
them in isolation; but if we could trace their lines
of development, and take a complete view of space
and time and whatever is beyond them, we should see

---

[1] This view of evil is open to the objection that the mental state of
illusion is itself the evil thing, and is not a mere negation.

that everything is perfect because the whole is perfect.[1]
Evil, by this interpretation, consists in taking a merely
partial view of things and is the same as error.

We should, I think, accept the second, third, and
fourth of the explanations just given as being, on the
whole, most in accordance with Plato's doctrines.   The
theory of the Absolute Good is intended to express
his conviction that the ideals of morality and art,
and true scientific conceptions, come from the same
source.   The Idea, the Ideal, the truly existent, and
the Highest Good, are coincident.   External Nature
truly exists in proportion to its perfection, its conformity to Ideas.   A State truly exists in proportion
to its Justice, its conformity to the Idea of a co-
ordinated system of persons, each performing his
proper function.   The individual soul, in like manner,
truly exists—that is, realises its own proper nature—
only in so far as it conforms to the Idea of Justice,
which in this connection means the harmonious
exercise of its different parts—knowledge, emotion,
and appetite—under the control of Reason.

C. PLEASURE, GOOD, AND RATIONAL ORDER

The *Philebus* contains an inquiry into the nature
of individual good, under the form :—Is the good,
as personal Well-being, identical with pleasure, or
with the exercise of intelligence, or is it something
superior to both ?   The two possible constituents
of the good were in some degree suggested by the
Cyrenaic and Cynic theories, and the *Philebus* may
be regarded as a criticism of their one-sided views.

[1] See pp. 62, 63.

Is Pleasure the Good ?—Plato uses the following arguments to prove that pleasure is not the sole constituent of the good.

1. The good is an ultimate end, being desired for its own sake; it is perfect and sufficient, so that no addition to it can increase its worth; it is sought by every intelligent being and completely satisfies desire. But mere pleasure has not these characteristics; indeed, if unaccompanied by knowledge, perception, and memory, it can scarcely be said to rise above the threshold of consciousness, or if it does, it is like the consciousness of an oyster; it is therefore either an indifferent object of desire or unsatisfying.

2. Since the good, wherever present, is essentially desirable, its different manifestations cannot be opposed to each other—it is in harmony with itself. Therefore pleasure *per se* cannot be the good, for different pleasures often conflict with each other.

3. The good is an ultimate end, but pleasure is in many cases a restoration of some kind of bodily harmony that has previously been disturbed; as such it is a process or a " becoming," [1] a movement towards an end beyond itself, not an end in itself. Plato holds that the pleasures of appetite, especially, have this characteristic, since appetite depends on pre-existing wants. Such pleasures, again, are not positively desirable, since their nature consists only in the removal of pain, discord, or want. We conclude that as some pleasures are not essentially good, pleasure *as such* is not essentially good; its worth depends on its accompaniments.

Is Mental Activity the Good ?—It is also true that

[1] γένεσις.

no mental state devoid of the feeling of pleasure can be identified with the good. A life of mental activity consisting in the exercise of wisdom, intellect, knowledge, and memory would not satisfy desire if the person were incapable of feeling pleasure and pain. No man is satisfied with mere thinking, he must also find pleasure in his thoughts. Therefore, the good, since it is not merely what ought to satisfy, but what does, when apprehended, satisfy desire,[1] must contain pleasure as a constituent.

The Harmonious Life.—Since pleasure and mental activity are both essential to the good and neither is sufficient, it follows that Well-being must consist in a due combination of both. The proportions of feeling and mental activity that constitute the "mixed" life, are to be determined by wisdom, fulfilling its highest function of rational judgment.

From this point Plato is led to an analysis of pleasures; the general conclusion being that those accompanied by pain or precedent want are of less worth than "pure or unmixed" pleasures—those free from attendant pain.[2] For this reason aesthetic and intellectual pleasures are preferable to sensual, which are always preceded by want and accompanied by pain. "Necessary" pleasures—those accompanying the normal exercise of the appetites, must, nevertheless, be included in the life of Well-being. To these must be added the pleasures of Art and Science, of reflection and self-knowledge, the pleasures arising from health and temperance, and from all the recognised

---

[1] See pp. 6, 7.
[2] The reader will see that the standard by which Plato in this connection judges pleasures was afterwards used by Epicurus and other hedonists.

moral virtues, but above all, the pleasure of contemplating truth. The general sense of Plato's argument is that pleasurable feeling and mental activity are both essential to personal Well-being, and his doctrine is thus a correction of the one-sided theories of the Cynics and Cyrenaics. The result reached in the *Republic* is fundamentally the same, for it was there urged that the best life for the individual is one in which intellect, emotion, and appetite work together in a harmony determined by Reason.

Reason in the Universe.—This perfect blending of pleasure and mental activity which constitutes the life of Well-being, is caused by symmetry, measure, and beauty. But these are more akin to wisdom than to pleasure ; for conscious Reason, the over-ruling Mind, is the source of the order and perfection of the universe. Plato concludes that the good of the individual is more closely allied to wisdom than to pleasure ; Reason and not Feeling is to determine what is good.

In the *Laws*, the same idea of rational order, symmetry or measure, is used as an ultimate explanation. What truly exists is perfect, imperfection being due to taking a limited—and so far false—view of things. The whole universe is directed by the over-ruling Mind, Who orders all details for the welfare of the whole. Each part has its appropriate position, and, in particular, men have their proper functions, whether to do or to suffer. Plato therefore rejects the Protagorean dictum [1] and asserts that God, not man, is the measure of all things. The Ideas of divine

[1] See p. 31.

order and harmony, not the wishes and feelings of finite human beings, contain the ultimate explanation of the universe. The ideal for each lower soul is to become dear to God and to grow like Him. The greatest of all evils for man is the excessive love of self; man should rather love those who are higher in the kingdom of souls, and strive to reach their level. The soul consists of a mortal part and an immortal, and knowledge is the activity of the immortal part. In the *Phaedo* we are told that the mortal part belongs to the body, which impedes the immortal soul in its flight beyond the things of Sense. Reason or intelligence, as the faculty of apprehending truth, is the proper regulator of human actions. Ignorance is the chief source of evil, and it practically means a failure to recognise one's proper position and work in the scheme of the universe. It is clear that this is an extension, beyond the limits of the State, of the Idea of Justice described in the *Republic*; not only the perfect individual, not only the perfect State, but also the whole Universe is an ordered system in which each member has its due function.

CHAPTER III

The Separation of the Sciences.—The predecessors of
Plato had a tendency to give special weight to one
department of reality without recognising that their
views were one-sided. Thus the earlier Greeks identified the universe with external Nature, and Philosophy
for them was a kind of abstract Physics. With the
Sophists there came a humanistic movement which
culminated in Socrates; Ethics and Politics now
attracted most attention, man and the State being the
chief objects of intellectual interest. With Plato all
this one-sidedness was abolished; his system was
synthetic, his object being to discover fundamental
principles everywhere, and to find the connecting links
between them. In the same dialogue we often find
discussions on metaphysical, theological, ethical, educational, and physical problems running into each other
in a manner which shows that he regarded all truths
as parts of one great system, as so many webs in the
network of reality. Aristotle's conception of philosophy
was fundamentally the same as Plato's, but he saw
that an increased knowledge of classified details was

[1] 384-322 B.C.; born at Stagira in Thrace, a pupil of Plato, tutor to
Alexander the Great, and founder of the Peripatetic School at Athens.

essential to the growth of the Sciences, and he therefore devoted separate works to Metaphysics, Ethics, Politics, Psychology, and many of the natural sciences. In the subsequent development of science the need for a division of labour naturally led to further specialisation by different inquirers. This departure from the Platonic ideal of co-ordinated truth [1] has in more modern times been kept in check by two causes: by the occasional appearance of "synthetic" systems of Philosophy, like Hegel's, Comte's, or Spencer's; and by the recognition of the fact that co-ordination between different sciences is often a rich source of progress, as may be inferred from the titles "Physiological Chemistry," "Physical Geology," and from the dependence of many applied sciences (as Medicine) on the results of a variety of other Sciences.

The Highest Science.[2]—Aristotle in his *Ethics* defined good as "that at which all things aim," and the highest good or *the* good, as that which is desired for its own sake. The highest good of mankind forms the subject of the highest science, and this is "Political Science." [3] It deals with the good of the State, which is greater, more perfect, and more divine than the good of any single individual. Yet, since the State is composed of individuals, one part of "Political Science" takes the form of an inquiry into individual good, so far as this is attainable by action; and this is the subject of the *Ethics*.

Method.—Aristotle recognises that Ethics is not an

[1] See pp. 52, 56.
[2] See *Ethics*, I. 1.
[3] This included the Ethics of Society and of the Individual as well as what is now called Political Science. In Greece, before the growth of cosmopolitanism, society was identified with the State, not with humanity.

exact Science like Mathematics or Logic. The results are only general and not always exact. The proper person for the inquiry is one who has had wide experience of life, a general education, and control over his emotions. The sources of information are intuitive perception, personal experience, and the communicated experience of others. The data thus acquired are to be collected and reduced critically to general principles; thus the method, so far as popular social morality is concerned, is mainly inductive.

Criticism of some Ethical Theories.——That the highest human good is the same as Well-being [1] is universally admitted, but there are different views as to the precise nature of Well-being. The vulgar often identify it with pleasure, wealth, or honour; but these cannot be final ends, for some pleasures are not desirable, wealth is only a *means* to Well-being, and honour is sought rather to increase our confidence in our own virtue than as an end desirable for its own sake. Plato's doctrine that there is an absolute good, which is the *a priori* source of the excellence of all good things,[2] must also be rejected as contrary to experience, since there are many things rightly called "good," though having nothing in common except that they are actually desired;[3] this applies, for example, to wisdom and pleasure, which are both desirable. Again, the Cynic theory, that Well-being is identical with the possession of Virtue, cannot be accepted as final, since the worth of Virtue has to be estimated by the nature of the mental activities to which it leads; regarded

[1] εὐδαιμονία, see p. 23.   [2] See p. 55.
[3] Nevertheless, as we shall see, Aristotle recognises that there is a true general conception underlying Well-being and virtue, and this was partly Plato's meaning.

as a merely inactive possession, it is useless and almost meaningless.

General Conception of Well-being.—Aristotle is led to a provisional and formal definition of Well-being by the following considerations. In the first place, Well-being must be complete in itself,[1] since it is not a subordinate end, but an unconditional good desirable for its own sake and preferable to any other. Secondly, man's Well-being must consist in the fulfilment of the work or function for which he exists, and in which his true being finds expression. The nature of this function can only be determined by considering the nature of the human soul. Now the human soul consists of two parts, the rational and the irrational which may be considered apart, though they are actually inseparable. The irrational part consists of an unconscious element,—which is the source of generation, nutrition, and growth, and is common to all forms of life—and of the conscious element of emotion and desire which is shared by man with the lower animals.[2] Only the rational element is peculiar to man. His emotions and desires are naturally under the authority of Reason which is the proper regulator of his conscious actions. In the exercise of Reason, therefore, and in the regulation of emotion and desire by Reason, man fulfils his true function, the end for which he exists. Thirdly, since the life of Well-being is complete and all-satisfying, the function of the man who lives this life has reached its highest excellence, and this is equivalent to saying that he possesses virtue. Finally, Well-being is not attainable in a

[1] αὐτάρκης.

[2] ψυχή (soul) meant for Aristotle the principle of life, whether in the animal or the plant.

single moment, but requires for its realisation the
whole life of a man in its normal length from maturity
to death. " For as one swallow or one day does not
make a spring, so one day or a short time does not
make a fortunate or happy [1] man." From this discussion there emerges the definition of Well-being or
human good as " an activity of the soul in accordance
with virtue in a complete life." [2] This activity must
be conscious, and either purely rational or in obedience
to Reason. It is to be understood that the unconscious nutritive process is only a one-sided and partial
aspect of the human soul ; the same applies to emotion
and desire, which, however, being forms of consciousness, are to be accepted as constituents of Well-being,
so long as they submit to the authority of Reason.

The definition just given is formal, because it does
not determine the content of Well-being. The problem
now to be considered is, what is the nature of that
virtue, which, when it expresses itself as activity, leads
to Well-being ?

Division of Virtue.—The Greek word for " virtue " [3]
signified literally *excellence,* and so the fitness of an
organised structure or of an artificial product for the
end for which it exists and by which its true nature
is defined. The eye, for example, has virtue when
it sees well, the body when it is in health, a knife
has virtue when it cuts properly. A virtue of the
conscious human soul is thus any permanent mental
state which helps towards the realisation of the end
for which man exists,[4] this end being rational activity.

---

[1] εὐδαίμων, possessing Well-being.
[2] ψυχῆς ἐνέργεια κατ' ἀρετὴν . . ἐν βίῳ τελείῳ.   [3] ἀρετή.
[4] It is important to observe that, for Aristotle, the end for which man
exists is not something external to his soul, but an inward conscious activity.

For practical purposes, therefore, a human virtue may be described as any praiseworthy mental state that is permanent.[1] There are two kinds of virtue corresponding to the two conscious parts of the soul : (1) Intellectual Virtue,[2] including knowledge, practical and theoretical, belongs to the rational soul when it performs well its function of knowing and discovering the truth ; (2) Moral Virtue[3] is attributed to the irrational but conscious part of the soul in its relation to Reason, when emotions and desires are subordinated to Reason, and thereby fulfil their proper function, the facilitation of rational activity. Thus temperance and courage are instances of moral virtues, for the one expresses the permanent control, by Reason, of the desire for pleasure, the other of the emotion of fear.

Characteristics of Moral Virtue.—Moral virtues spring from habit.[4] They are not innate in the sense of being naturally implanted qualities in us, for habit cannot alter any natural quality ; *e.g.* a stone naturally falls, and you cannot habituate it to rise by repeatedly throwing it up. There are, however, in man natural capacities for acquiring virtues, while the actual acquisition is due to habit. The moral are thus contrasted with the intellectual virtues, which are generally imparted by teaching.[5] Again, morally virtuous

---

[1] Both intellectual and moral virtues are termed ἕξεις (permanent states).

[2] διανοητικὴ ἀρετή.   [3] ἠθικὴ ἀρετή.

[4] ἔθος, connected with ἦθος, whence the title ἠθική, from which the word "Ethics" is derived.

[5] Aristotle's psychology is here open to criticism. Intellectual virtues, just as much as moral, are habits, since they are acquired by the gradual assimilation of ideas, not, as a rule, by the sudden reception of truth from others. This gradual assimilation is the formation of a mental habit by mental action. The real distinction is that moral virtues are acquired habits of regulating irrational impulses, whereas intellectual virtues are forms of knowledge.

actions are *deliberate,* because Reason acts consciously
towards the realisation of a pre-conceived end.   It
follows that such actions must be done *for the sake
of what is good,* since Reason aims at good ends.
Knowing, though essential, is not by itself strong
enough to enforce right conduct; Reason must avail
itself of the force of habits acquired by frequent
repetition of good acting.   Aristotle appears to assume
that the natural aptitudes for acquiring moral virtues
are implanted in all, and that these aptitudes have
originally enough strength to make *possible* the gradual
formation of good habits; or perhaps he meant that
Reason has originally enough directive force to select
the best aptitudes for cultivation.

The Doctrine of the Mean.—According to Plato
the good man is he in whom knowledge, emotion,
and desire work in perfect harmony, no part of the
soul tyrannising over the rest, and each part exercising its due activity.[1]   This is one of the many
connecting-links between Plato and Aristotle, whose
doctrine of the Mean is a special way of expressing
the same truth.   Aristotle, we have seen, assumes
that man, *qua* man, has a special function, some work
or activity in the exercise of which he manifests his
true essence and finds his Well-being.   But what is
true of the race is also true of the individual soul
and its different parts.   Every person has a special
function, and so have all the parts of his soul;
these functions, when duly exercised, issuing in the
appropriate work or activity.   Now we find that every
perfect work, whether of Science, Art, or Nature,
possesses the characteristics of being *a mean between*

---

[1] pp. 46, 47.

two extremes, the one of excess and the other of defect.
Every kind of excellence is such a mean, and this
is true of Moral Virtue,[1] which is the excellence of
man in the sphere of action and emotion. Temperance,
for example, is a mean between intemperance and
asceticism, courage between cowardice and rashness.
Accordingly, Aristotle defines Virtue as " a permanent
mental state, expressing itself in deliberate actions,
and lying in a relative mean fixed by Reason, that is,
as the man of practical wisdom would fix it." [2] It
is implied that the permanent mental state is created
by habitual actions of the same type as those to which
it leads ; thus a man becomes temperate by constantly
acting temperately ; hence Virtue is a kind of habit.

In this definition certain points are further
developed by Aristotle. First, morally good actions
are deliberate, not impulsive ; this is because the
virtuous man, *qua* rational, aims at a rationally
conceived end, and he is not satisfied with blindly
following the promptings of irrational impulses without weighing their merits. The end, therefore, must
be judged to be good, and this is expressed by saying
that the action must be done " for the sake of what
is noble." [3] Secondly, the path of Virtue is but one,
whereas the paths of vice are many, being characterised
by every degree of excess or defect.[4] Thirdly, the
middle path is not given by mechanical *a priori* rule,
as in arithmetic ; it is known only by the man who is

---

[1] In the rest of this Chapter, "virtue" will signify "moral virtue"
unless otherwise stated.

[2] ἕξις προαιρετικὴ ἐν μεσότητι οὖσα τῇ πρὸς ἡμᾶς, ὡρισμένῃ λόγῳ καὶ
ὡς ἂν ὁ φρόνιμος ὁρίσειε.

[3] τοῦ καλοῦ ἕνεκα.

[4] Plato expressed the same idea in saying that the good is determined
by "measure." See p. 61.

a practical expert in right conduct. Certain practical rules may indeed be given for finding the mean, but, in the long run, instinctive moral intuition is the final court of appeal. Such intuition is partly innate, and partly the result of the experience of those who constantly seek the right path.

The following are illustrations of the doctrine that virtue is a mean between two extremes in action or in emotion [1] :—

Excess.	Mean.	Defect.
Rashness	Courage	Cowardice
Licentiousness	Temperance	Apathy
Extravagance	Generosity	Miserliness
Bad Temper	Good Temper	Servility
Flattery	Courtesy	Rudeness

Justice is a mean in the peculiar sense that it lies between the vice of taking more than one's share, and the opposite defect of taking less.

Aristotle remarks that his theory is not to be strained too far; it is (we might say) a sign-post pointing towards Virtue rather than an exact definition. Again, to some vices there corresponds no mean; thus there is no mean in adultery or murder or theft. Still it might be argued that those vices are the products of *excessive* passions such as licentiousness, fury, malice, or covetousness.[2]

Voluntary Actions and Responsibility.—An action

---

[1] The names of the virtues are printed so as to represent the idea that the mean is often nearer one extreme than another.

[2] Practically, the Doctrine of the Mean is equivalent to identifying moral excellence with rational moderation in all things, and is thus closely akin to the Platonic doctrine of the personal virtues of Temperance and Justice as expounded in the *Republic*, and to the Harmony Theory of the *Philebus* (see pp. 46, 61). In philosophic form, however, it is inferior to Plato's view, because it lays no stress on the idea of the co-ordination of parts within a complete whole. As a guide to conduct it has a show of

is voluntary when the agent is the original cause of the action, there being no external compulsion. Into a deeper discussion of this Aristotle does not enter; he evidently assumes that the Ego or Self can be an original source of actions—a doctrine which naturally leads to the Kantian theory of the Autonomy (self-determination) of the will.[1] A man is held responsible and is praised or blamed for voluntary actions only. He is justly blamed for not cultivating virtuous habits, for though the violence of his passions may now deprive him of the power of voluntary action, there was a time when he had a sufficient natural capacity for virtue to develop self-control. Ethically virtuous and ethically vicious actions and emotions are subjects of praise and blame, because they express the character which the agent himself has created by a series of voluntary actions.

Some Special Virtues, Temperance, Courage, Justice, Friendship.—The four "cardinal virtues" have with Aristotle a much narrower meaning than with Plato (in the *Republic*); he is content to take the commonly accepted detached meanings, whereas Plato generalised with a view to securing philosophic co-ordination and unity.

By *Temperance*[2] Aristotle means moderation in bodily pleasures, particularly those shared with the lower animals. Continence[3] is closely allied to Temperance, but is distinguished from it by the fact that the continent man has violent desires, whereas the temperate man either has none or

clearness and precision which disappears when we find that, as Aristotle admits, the mean cannot be fixed by a general rule, but only by the instinctive moral perceptions of a man who is already wise and virtuous.

[1] See chapter on Kant.   [2] σωφροσύνη.   [3] ἐγκράτεια.

D

has completely mastered them.   Continence is therefore the inferior virtue; but, its excess, Incontinence,[1] is more excusable than Licentiousness,[2] the excess corresponding to Temperance; because the incontinent man is urged against his will by the superior force of passion, whereas the *will* of the licentious man is corrupted, and excessive pleasure is sought deliberately.

Courage or *Fortitude*[3] is a mean between Cowardice and Rashness.   For the exercise of true Courage the following conditions must be fulfilled.   There must be real grounds for fear, and an actual feeling of fear, which is controlled for the sake of what is noble, in such a way that right action is not hindered by fear, and the man does his duty unflinchingly.   Also there must be a refusal to undertake unnecessary risks, whereby the excess of Rashness is avoided.   War is the great occasion for the exercise of this virtue. The noble *motive* distinguishes true Courage—and indeed all moral virtues—from the spurious forms. For example, those forms of courage which are due to frequent experience of danger (the courage of the veteran), or to ignorance, or to insensibility, or to passion (as the courage of the lion), are not genuine *moral* virtues; they have a value, but they are not directed by Reason.   For Aristotle the sphere of Courage is limited to physical dangers; the corresponding virtue in Plato is much wider, and includes not only "moral" Courage (in the current sense) but also the mental force by which any kind of emotional temptation is resisted.[4]

The whole of Book V. of the *Ethics* is devoted to

---

[1] ἀκρασία.   [2] ἀκολασία.   [3] ἀνδρεία.
[4] See pp. 44, 45.   Plato's ἀνδρεία includes the σωφροσύνη and ἀνδρεία of

the discussion of *Justice* and allied virtues. Plato, we have seen, attached a comprehensive philosophical meaning to the Greek word translated "Justice"; Aristotle, on the other hand, tries to fix and analyse the meanings actually used, and finds that they are various. In the first place Justice often signifies obedience to the Law of the State. As the laws professedly aim at the good of the subjects, the word came to signify the perfection of *social* Virtue; and, finally, since he who does his duty towards his neighbour is said to be virtuous, Justice is often identified with *complete* Virtue. Aristotle, however, is chiefly concerned with Justice in a narrower sense, as the virtue expressing itself in actions dealing with personal property. This "particular Justice" is again subdivided into (1) Distributive [1] Justice and (2) Corrective [2] Justice. Distributive Justice uses two principles; one is that a man is to receive profit from an undertaking in proportion to the amount that he contributes; the second is that he is to contribute to public expenses in proportion to his possessions. We might illustrate the first by invest-ment, the second by taxation. Corrective Justice deals with infringements of the law of the land; the penalty or compensation is measured by the degree of the injury, and has not (as in the case of Distributive Justice) any reference to the special circumstances of the persons involved.

Justice assumes various other forms. When considered without any special reference to political

---

Aristotle. Plato's ἀνδρεία is inseparable from his σωφροσύνη, but the former lays more stress on the active resistance to be overcome in order to preserve the harmony expressed in the latter virtue.

[1] διανεμητική.　　　　　　　　[2] διορθωτική.

law, it is Fairness of Mind,[1] which implies a spontaneous love of Justice apart from legal sanctions.

Friendship [2] was a favourite subject of discussion with the Greek philosophers. Aristotle holds that there are three forms of Friendship; it may be based on utility, on pleasure, or on goodness of character. But the first two forms are transient; that which is based on goodness in both parties is Friendship in the true and permanent sense; it includes the advantages of both the other types, for the good are both useful and pleasant to each other. Friendship is also essential to Well-being, for man is by nature social, and the exercise of this virtue stimulates many excellent activities which would otherwise lie dormant. (This is a criticism of the Cynic theory that the wise man is independent of others.) That activity of the soul which constitutes Well-being is indeed inward, yet it is dependent on the possession of some external goods, and a friend is the " greatest of external goods." But, more than that, a friend is an inward spiritual possession, and is in truth " a second self " whose Well-being we can share. Life is essentially a good and pleasant thing for the good man, and thus to be conscious of the existence of a good friend is to increase our own Well-being, by sharing the life-activities which constitute another's Well-being.

Self-Love and the Love of Others. [3]—Traditional moral judgment, Aristotle remarks, condemns Self-love as a vice; yet, as a matter of fact, every man pursues chiefly his own interests, and it appears to be reason-

---

[1] ἐπιείκεια.   [2] φιλία.

[3] The Greek words for Friendship and Love (as here used) are the same (φιλία). This connects the present discussion with what precedes. φιλία is here contrasted with φιλαυτία.

able that a man should love himself most. The explanation of this paradox is to be found in the ambiguity of the word "self." The bad man loves only his irrational self, and therefore he grasps more than his share of money, honour, bodily pleasures and other things by which this lower self is gratified. But the "Self" as a whole contains a rational part, which is the proper director and judge of man's actions. Thus he who truly loves himself obeys Reason;[1] loving noble deeds above all things, he serves others as well as himself, and will sacrifice his wealth and even his life for another, if the attainment of true good requires it. But the bad man is an enemy to himself as well as to others, since he gratifies his lower self, which, being only a part of the whole, is really his *false* self.

Pleasure, Pain, and the Good.—That the pursuit of pleasure and the avoidance of pain form the strongest of all motives to action cannot be denied, and legislators make use of this truth in inflicting punishments. But what is the ethical value of pleasure? What is its true worth in the scale of goods? That pleasure is *a* good must be admitted, because it is naturally desired for its own sake, not merely as a means to some other satisfaction. But pleasure cannot be the sole and sufficient constituent of complete Well-being, because it is a matter of general experience that some pleasures are evil, owing to their unhealthy concomitants. All excess, too, is bad, and this is true of pleasures.[2] It follows that pleasure

---

[1] See p. 67.

[2] Aristotle is appealing to general experience; otherwise this argument would be a *petitio principii*. An excess of the highest good could not be bad!

is not *the* good, not the *supreme* good. Aristotle's general conclusion (if we allow that he is consistent, which has been questioned) is that pleasure is an essential element of Well-being, but it is not the only constituent thereof.[1] In the seventh book (commonly attributed to Eudemus) pleasure is defined as an "unimpeded activity" of the soul, and is there regarded as almost identical with Well-being, which was defined as a perfect activity.[2] It is clear, however, that Aristotle valued the *nature* of the activity quite as much as the feelings accompanying it; and if pleasure is to be identified with Well-being this will be not merely because it is an unimpeded activity, but rather because of the intrinsic excellence of the activity which makes it "unimpeded." On the whole, Aristotle thinks that the worth of pleasure is to be determined by something outside the mere feeling, by some objective criterion. He evidently wishes to strike a mean between the Cynic and Cyrenaic theories. The apparent contradiction in Aristotle's view seems to arise from his not fixing the *meaning* of "pleasure," which in one place he regards as a *passive* feeling, and in another as a mental *activity*.

Knowledge and Virtue.—Socrates identified Virtue with practical insight,[3]—knowledge as applied to action. Aristotle admits that the virtues and practical insight are in fact inseparable, but he claims that they are not identical. Virtue without the intellectual element (insight) is merely natural or instinctive, not moral, since Moral Virtue is defined as the habitual sub-

[1] This agrees with Plato's doctrine as expressed in the *Philebus*. (See pp.60-62.)   [2] See p. 68.

[3] φρόνησις.   (See p. 35.)

ordination of desires and emotions to Reason. Conversely, he who possesses practical insight possesses every moral virtue, because practical insight, in its complete form, is itself created by virtuous actions, and will again lead by preformed habits to the appropriate actions.

Aristotle seems to agree with Socrates that he who *really knows* what is right cannot but do right. The incontinent man, even when free from temptation, only *opines* or *feels* that he should control his desires. His desires may rise to such a strength as to overcome these opinions or feelings, though they could never vanquish true knowledge.[1] Aristotle might have added, in conformity with his doctrine of Virtue, that habit as well as knowledge is essential to Moral Virtue. Yet his tendency in this discussion is to adopt the Socratico-Platonic view that clear knowledge takes possession of the will as well as of the intellect. If this view is accepted we shall have to admit that a dipsomaniac, who is as incapable of resisting temptation as a stone is incapable of flying, has poisoned his intellect as well as his will, and is unable to apprehend distinctly what he is doing. Aristotle, however, admits that the incontinent man may have a knowledge of the *general* principles of right action (*e.g.* that excess is bad, and that pleasure in moderation is good), but desire impels him to make a wrong application of the general principle in the particular case.

The Ideal Life.—Well-being has been defined by

[1] See especially *Ethics*, Book VII. 5 (at end). In this discussion a sharp contrast is drawn between ἐπιστήμη (knowledge) and δόξα (opinion), which judges by πάθος (feeling). The contrast was a favourite one with Plato and with the Stoics (pp. 49, 98).

Aristotle as an activity of the rational soul in accordance with Virtue.[1] Now Virtue, in general, is the quality which enables its possessor to perform his proper function well; therefore, since rational activity is the highest function of the human soul, it follows that the moral virtues are the various forms taken by Reason in the individual as means to its own free activity.[2] But these forms are not created by Reason alone; they arise partly from the actual conditions in which Reason finds itself. These conditions are the particular bodily and mental structure of the individual, and the structure of the society of which he is an integral part. Reason aims at moulding these conditions to suit its own activity; thus it endeavours to regulate desires and feelings—which spring from the body and the irrational part of the soul; it seeks also to produce social harmony in order that its activity may not be hindered by the mutual conflict of individuals. The moral virtues are thus the forms by which Reason, seeking to realise itself, would regulate the individual soul, and the society or State composed of individual souls.

It follows that the moral virtues are not ends in themselves; they are only means adopted by Reason to acquire its freedom; they are the best means possible under the given conditions. Thus the ultimate question of Ethics still remains to be considered:—What is the *positive* nature of the highest good, the ideal life which consists in a perfect activity of Reason? Aristotle in reply describes it as "*theoria*," by which he means a life spent in the unimpeded apprehension and discovery of the Truth;

[1] p. 68.   [2] See pp. 67, 77.

this is the proper function of the rational soul. As a perfect activity the life of *theoria* is unimpeded and is therefore pleasant in the highest degree ; in it, therefore, any conflict between pleasure and good is for ever abolished. It is also desirable for its own sake and complete in itself, and thus fulfils all the conditions of Well-being.[1] It far transcends the activities of the moral virtues, which are only called out by the imperfections of man and of society. (Courage, for example, would be useless in an ideal society, and temperance would not be required in a soul for whom the most pleasant activities were also the best.) The activities of moral virtues are human, but the ideal life is divine ; indeed Aristotle is forced to admit that the perfect life is unattainable by man in his present condition ; for it demands not only leisure and freedom from worldly toil and trouble, but also immortality—else were it imperfect. It belongs to God alone. Yet man has something divine in him, and he should strive after the perfect life ; even though he be not immortal, he should live as if he were immortal, by giving full scope to the activity of his true Self—Reason.[2]

---

[1] See pp. 67, 68.

[2] The life of *theoria* (ἡ θεωρητικὴ ἐνέργεια) is the pursuit and capture of Truth in the widest sense, not merely the abstract truth of scientific propositions. *Theoria* is a looking into the heart of things, the absorption of the soul in reality, the fusion of subject and object. It is doubtless what Spinoza meant by the *Amor intellectualis Dei*, the pure activity of the thinking soul freed from sensual disturbances. Aristotle reminds us that it is an ideal unattainable in the present life, and it may therefore be described as mystical. But whereas the mystic trance is usually describ d as a state of passive *feeling*, *theoria* is of a much higher order, since it makes room for the activity of the intellect as well. Some of Aristotle's philosophy (*Metaphysics*, Bk. XI.) suggests that he held the view that in this divine activity *individuality* is transcended ; if this is so, Love as well as Knowledge is a constituent of the life of *theoria*.

GENERAL VIEW OF THE ETHICS OF PLATO AND ARISTOTLE

We have seen that there is a very close agreement between the ethical results reached by Plato and Aristotle—so far as the individual good is concerned; especially in the conception of the life of Well-being as a harmony between the functions of the soul, including pleasure as well as intellectual and aesthetic activities. There are also some other points of agreement. Aristotle's conception of the ideal life (*theoria*), in which he transcends popular morality, illustrates a characteristic common to the post-Socratic Greek philosophers, namely the tendency to regard the best and wisest men—whose Well-being is also the greatest —as living a spiritual life apart from and above the lives of ordinary men. This view is the offspring of the Platonic doctrine that Dialectic, the highest human activity, is possible only for a select few.[1] This did not mean that only the wise men have rights, or even that they have more rights than ordinary men; on the contrary (according to Plato) they are to rule the State for the good of the whole, and Aristotle's teaching was the same when he said that the good of the State is something nobler and more perfect than the good of any individual. Further, Plato and Aristotle have this in common, that they regard the capacity for knowing the truth as the highest attribute of man. For this reason they are sometimes called intellectualists.[2]

[1] See p. 52 (*g*).
[2] An Intellectualist is one who places knowledge above feeling in the ethical scale.

This tendency was partly due to their own tastes; both pursued knowledge for its own sake, and finding in this the highest satisfaction, they too hastily concluded that others must do the same. Yet they were not extreme intellectualists, for they accepted *pleasure* and the apprehension of beauty [1] as essential constituents of a life of Well-being. They saw, however, the defects of mere Hedonism; the search for pleasure *per se* is futile, for the very attainment of pleasure depends on our having desires for other things besides pleasure. On the whole, both taught indirectly that the acquisition of knowledge for its own sake, though not the only desirable activity, is yet the best, and yields the most pleasure.

In social Ethics both taught that the individual has a duty to Society as represented by the State. The moral virtues, as presented by Aristotle, have social as well as individual worth; they are forms of the control exercised by Reason for the general Well-being of Society. According to Plato (as we have interpreted him) what gives force to social obligation is the rational love of the idea of a symmetrical co-ordination of parts within a complete whole; this co-ordination being good in itself is deemed desirable in the State and in the individual—it is Justice realised. This explanation of the grounds of social obligation is somewhat ideal and abstract, nor would it be likely to appeal to the average citizen; in any case sympathy and other social instincts, as well as a recognition of the advantages which the individual reaps from social

---

[1] τὸ καλόν. This word is used of both physical and moral beauty. Cf. p. 53 and p. 71 (third note).

order, are required to give force to the Platonic conception of Justice.

But though the character of the ethical ideal was the same for Aristotle and Plato, their methods were very different, as the preceding pages have shown. Plato everywhere seeks unity and co-ordination ; he generalises where Aristotle divides, analyses and seeks to discover the practical meaning of ethical terms.[1] The same tendency led Aristotle to separate Ethics from the other sciences, though indeed his doctrine of *theoria* seems to imply that the unity and co-ordination of knowledge is the ideal of Ethics. Again, Plato, as we have seen, tended to identify the ethical ideal and the truly existent. Aristotle, however, was more of a realist ; he was too cautious to assert that the highest conceivable good is attainable by man.

[1] Compare their treatments of the cardinal virtues, p. 44 *sq.*, p. 73 *sq.*

CHAPTER IV

EPICURUS

THE philosophy of Epicurus[1] was a refined and modified form of the Cyrenaic Ethics combined with the Atomism of Democritus. This system, like the Stoic, found great favour with the Romans. It was fervidly advocated by the great poet Lucretius, and in a lighter vein by Horace.

Epicurus regarded Philosophy as the scientific pursuit of Well-being; for him knowledge is only a means, not an end in itself. Logic and Physics are subordinate to Ethics, and have no worth except as productive of Well-being. The use of a theory of knowledge (Canonic) is to distinguish between the true and false guides to Well-being; and Physics is to be studied in order that man, by understanding his exact position in the material universe, may be delivered from superstition—the fear of the unknown. The hedonistic value of Science as productive of mechanical devices which increase the conveniences of life, was ignored by him, for the simple reason that Science at that period was not productive, but mainly theoretical. He held that Mathematics and exact

[1] 341-270 B.C., born at Samos, taught at Athens.

definitions and divisions (Dialectic) together with almost all formal sciences, are useless because they do not contribute to Well-being.

Theory of Knowledge.—The Epicurean Canonic aims at investigating the criteria of truth and the grounds of knowledge. The source of all our experience is perception through the senses. The only criterion of truth is direct sensation, or clear memory of past sensations; similarly the only criterion of good is pleasure or the absence of pain. The real elements of experience are given immediately in perception, and the question of their external existence cannot arise, because there is no possible external standard accessible to our minds. Error only arises when we make judgments that go beyond sensation. An opinion is true when it is confirmed by sensible experience; otherwise it is false.

Physics.—Here Epicurus was a materialist; he completely abandons the doctrine that knowledge is confined to sensation, and that sensations are the objects of knowledge—an inconsistency due to his neglect of Logic. He asserts the existence of a universal extra-mental matter, consisting of innumerable atoms, moving through internal spontaneity and mutual impact, these being the only two possible sources of motion. The only form of reality is matter, for besides the atoms and empty space there exists nothing real. The soul is a subtler form of matter, consisting of the finest atoms spread through the body. Nature does not work with an end in view, but is a blind concourse of atoms " ruining along the illimitable inane." [1]   In spite of this, Epicurus (most curiously) asserts the

[1] Tennyson's *Lucretius.*

freedom of the will as a postulate indispensable to
Well-being, and explains it by the irrational spontaneity
by which the atoms move out of the straight line [1]
without external influence.[2]

ETHICS

As immediate perception is the only test of truth,
so the immediate feelings of pleasure and pain are the
only motives to action.   The latter doctrine (psychological Hedonism) is used by Epicurus to support his
ethical Hedonism, from which he does not clearly
distinguish it.   Well-being, the end of life, consists
in the enjoyment of pleasure, and there is no other
good.   In proof of this he appeals to the principles,
(a) that pleasure is the primary and natural end at
which all sentient beings aim, and that pain is a
universal and necessary object of aversion, and (b) that
it is a matter of universal experience that we always
use feeling as the standard by which to judge whether
anything is good or bad.   But although all pleasures
are intrinsically desirable, reason and memory inform
us that they should not be pursued indiscriminately,
since the enjoyment of some may be followed by pains
that outweigh the pleasurable feeling.   Thus the
highest good is not the pleasure of the moment, but
the pleasure of the whole life.   In this respect
Epicurus differed from the Cyrenaics.   Pleasures are
therefore to be measured, not by their intensity alone,

---

[1] In the same way, presumably, the soul or will, being an atom moves
out of its normal course freely, *i.e.* without external compulsion.   The
theory, it may be noticed, is inconsistent with Newton's First Law of
Motion.

[2] For criticism of Materialism see chapter on Hobbes.

but also by their duration, stability, and freedom from attendant and consequent pain.[1] It is inferred from this that the pleasures of the mind are superior to those of the body, because they include the pleasures of memory and hope, as well as those arising from present sensations. Pleasures, moreover, are to be found, not only in movement, but in rest, in freedom from disturbance.[2] This is a second point in which Epicurus differed from the Cyrenaics. He seems indeed to have held that we should be satisfied with tranquillity of mind, since the most intense pleasures are apt to be followed by pains which make the game not worth the candle.

Virtue.——Epicurus' estimate of virtue is similar to that of the Cyrenaics, but he seems to prize more highly the ordinary moral virtues. These are not ends in themselves, as the Cynics and Stoics said, but indispensable means for getting the greatest possible enjoyment out of life. Prudence [3] is the crown of the virtues, because it consists in an appropriate selection of pleasures. Temperance is a means of acquiring the maximum total of pleasures by exercising moderation in every kind of indulgence. Courage in the Aristotelian sense, as the virtue of a warrior, appears to have received no notice from Epicurus. This is partly due to the fact that Aristotle was on intimate terms with his pupil, Alexander the Great, and would therefore have reason for admiring the courage of a soldier ; whereas Epicurus, living in a narrower academic circle, had no sympathy with the joys of battle, and preferred a life of social peace.

---

[1] Cf. Bentham (chapter on Utilitarianism).   [2] ἀταραξία.
[3] φρόνησις.

The hedonistic value of Fortitude (in the Stoic sense) is, however, strongly emphasised by Epicurus as a means of banishing pain, and, according to Seneca (the Roman Stoic) the Epicurean precepts for acquiring pleasure are practically the same as the Stoic laws of virtue. The Epicurean theory is however far less inspiring; where the Stoics teach that true greatness of soul will face and triumph over every misfortune, the Epicureans urge us to run away from everything unpleasant. Examples of this are: Epicurus' artificial doctrine of free will, plainly invented to avoid the unpleasant feeling that we are not free; and his saying that death, the most terrifying of all things, is not an object of fear, for when we are, death is not, and when death is, we are not.

Social Virtues. — These have an egoistic basis. Justice is conventional, not natural.[1] It springs from the need felt by each rational member of society for an adjustment of claims, with a view to preventing the suffering which must result to *him* from social conflict. Justice is thus a compact entered into by the different members of a society, by which each individual agrees to abstain from injuring others, on the understanding that they are to abstain from injuring him. This conception was afterwards more fully developed by Hobbes. Epicurus placed a high value on Friendship, and taught that the possession of friends is the richest source of life-long Well-being; wisdom cannot find any jewel of equal worth.

[1] Cf. the Cyrenaic theory.

CRITICISM OF EGOISTIC HEDONISM

The practical conclusions drawn from the principles of Epicurus will largely depend on the taste and susceptibility of the individual using these principles. Epicurus approved of the recognised social and individual virtues because he happened to find pleasure in them; but for others, the same starting-point might lead to exclusive Egoism, to tyranny, and—according to circumstances—to acts of extreme injustice. Herein lies the social danger of Epicureanism. Whether the doctrine be true or not, it would, if generally accepted, be injurious to society; partly because of the misinterpretation to which it is particularly liable; partly because its consistent application often prevents the exercise of talents which might be of the greatest service to society. Only in a community in which social and individual interests were in perfect harmony,—in which, for example, rich men loved philanthropic activity,—would it be possible to regard it as a harmless doctrine.

The more fundamental question, Is Epicureanism a *true* doctrine? must now be briefly considered. Four questions have to be answered, of which the first two are psychological, and the second two are ethical:—

(*a*) Is all desire for immediate pleasure? If we answer in the affirmative, it follows that the pleasure of the moment is the only possible motive of action, and there is no room for a philosophy of Ethics. But it is plainly not true, *e.g.*, that I get my tooth extracted for the immediate pleasure of having it extracted; nor, unless I have an appetite, do I eat for the immediate pleasure of eating. And in general the motives of most of our actions are something more than a desire for immediate pleasure. Thus the psychological basis of the Cyrenaic Ethics is insecure.

(*b*) Is all my desire for a pleasure which is to be distributed uniformly over my whole life? The affirmative answer to this was accepted by Epicurus as the psychological basis of Hedonism, though he confounded this question with (*a*) and with (*c*) below.[1] A little reflection will show that very few isolated deliberate actions aim directly at the pleasure of the whole life. On the whole, therefore, though pleasure is an object of desire and pain is an object of aversion, it is not true that all desires, all motives, aim solely at pleasure, or the avoidance of pain. That Epicurus should have thought so was plainly due to the narrowness of his interests, his contempt for science, literature, and art, which are subjects of human activity, not merely because of the pleasures they afford, but also because of their characteristic contents, which provide motives for investigating them.

(*c*) Is it true that all men *judge* pleasure to be the highest good, the most desirable of all objects? Do they take it as the *ultimate* standard by which all their actions *ought* to be judged? According to Epicurus they do; but if this is true, they must do it unconsciously (and therefore there is no strictly ethical judgment involved), for it is a matter of experience that many people deny that they regard

[1] Cf. Mill (chapter on Utilitarianism).

pleasure as the highest good.   We are thus led to
the vital ethical question :—

(d) *Is* pleasure the Highest Good ?   Does it, when
attained, give more satisfaction than anything else
could ?   Is the true worth of any attained object
directly proportionate to the degree of pleasure it
affords, and independent of everything else ?   Aristotle
and Plato have given a general answer to this ; they
point out that pleasure is an essential constituent,
but not the sole constituent, of the Good ; pleasure
per se is not completely satisfying ; it must be associated
with and determined by objects possessing characteristics which are something more than pleasure-giving.[1]

[1] See pp. 59-62, pp. 77, 78.   Further criticisms of Hedonism are given
at the end of the chapter on Utilitarianism.

CHAPTER V

THE STOICS

The Cynic Doctrine that Virtue is the highest good, and that its possession is in itself Well-being, was further developed and modified by the Stoics.

The founder of the Stoic[1] School was Zeno of Cyprus.[2] Among his followers the best known were Cleanthes, a pupil of Zeno, and Chrysippus,[3] who in turn succeeded Zeno as heads of the School. Famous later Stoics were Seneca,[4] Epictetus[5] the slave, and the Emperor Marcus Aurelius.[6] Panaetius[7] of Rhodes and his pupil Posidonius[8] (who was heard by Cicero) taught an eclectic and less rugged form of Stoicism mingled with Platonic and Aristotelian elements, and helped to popularize the system among the Romans.

Knowledge and Well-being.—The attitude of the Stoics and Epicureans towards knowledge contrasts strongly with that of Plato and Aristotle, since they taught that knowledge is only a means of Well-being, not an end in itself. Accordingly the Stoic and Epicurean systems of philosophy are distinctly ethical, whereas those of Plato and Aristotle have a much wider scope. The Ethics of Zeno and Epicurus, should, therefore be considered in connection

---

[1] The name Stoic is derived from Στοά, the painted porch in which Zeno taught.

[2] *Circa* 340-265 B.C., taught at Athens. [3] B.C. 280-209.

[4] A.D. 4-65.   [5] A.D. first cent.   [6] 121-180 A.D.

[7] *Circa* B.C. 180-111.   [8] *Circa* B.C. 135-150.

with their Logic and Physics, which they investigated for ethical purposes. It will be seen, however, that the scientific and logical theories of these two schools are quite different. The Stoics laid more stress than Epicurus on the importance of Logic and the formal sciences, and the theories of cognition of the two schools have little in common.

Theory of Knowledge.—Truth, according to the Stoics, consists in the actual correspondence of a perception with its object; without such correspondence rational action is impossible. There is no external test of truth; knowledge or irresistible belief is its own criterion, it carries certainty with it, for it is a mental representation which "grasps" the object.[1] This contrasts with the Epicurean theory that our knowledge is only of sensations. The Stoics held that we have, besides the perceptions of sense, certain primary conceptions shared by all men alike. These are *natural*, because they are evoked by normal experience. Some of them are fundamental notions in Science and Ethics (*e.g.* right and wrong); they are apprehended by Reason.

Physics.[2]—Here the Stoics show a curious inconsistency; they assert on the one hand that everything real, including the soul, is material. On the other hand they believed in the existence of a Soul of the World, a Divine Spirit, animating matter and producing in it the motion which is not inherent in it. The ultimate grounds of things are thus God and formless matter existing at opposite ends of the scale. In their attempts to abolish this inconsistency between

---

[1] καταληπτικὴ φαντασία.

[2] Physics, here, as with Epicurus, means the science of the nature of things.

Theism and Materialism, the Stoics adopted a form
of Pantheism, asserting that the Being of God is
immanent in every particle of matter. The ethical
importance of the two sides of their doctrines (the
spiritual and the material) springs from the inferences
which they drew from them : first, that the laws of
matter are inflexible, and that man, if he wishes to
reach Well-being, must learn what they are, and adapt
his wishes to the destiny which they shape for him
by inevitable necessity ; secondly, that these laws are
not blind, but directed by a universal World-Reason,
and that consequently the search for Well-being is
not a vain one.   Thus the Stoic system is characterised
by a constant effort to transform, by the power of
Reason, submission to the blind forces of Nature into
rational faith in an over-ruling Providence.

ETHICS

Epicurus raised immediate *Feeling* to the highest
pinnacle in Ethics ; the Stoics went to the opposite
extreme and elevated *Reason* at the expense of Feeling. The cardinal doctrine of the Stoic Ethics is
said to be expressed in the dictum that Well-being
—the end of life—consists in living in conformity
with Nature. By "Nature" is meant generally the
necessary laws of the universe and, in particular,
those laws which are manifested in man and his
physical surroundings. This doctrine is regarded by
the Stoics as an application to mankind of the wider
principle that every living thing has a primitive
impulse towards self-preservation and consciousness
thereof, and that it follows its nature in giving
practical expression to this impulse. Since the Self

of Man is self-conscious active Reason,[1] the precept
"follow nature" means for him the same as "act
rationally." That Reason and Nature, properly
understood, lead to the same actions, is also an
inference from the principles that the laws of the
world are the product of the universal Reason which
puts life and activity into inert matter.

The precept "follow Nature," or "obey Reason,"
may, however, be interpreted in a variety of ways.
An Epicurean, for example, might say that it is in
the highest degree natural and reasonable to seek the
maximum of private pleasure. Hence it is not in
the general precept that the characteristic feature of
Stoicism is to be found, but in the application of
this principle, in the closer determination of the
practical meaning of the words, "life according to
Reason" or "Nature."

Virtue and the Good.—The Stoics, in applying the
doctrine "follow Nature" or "Reason," identify good
with that which is *naturally* desirable. They classified
objects of choice or aversion as follows. Good things
are those which necessarily benefit whenever they are
present, and they are on this account the objects of
rational or natural desire; they are in short desirable
in themselves. These good things are, in general,
the moral virtues, particularly Practical Wisdom,
Justice, Courage, and Temperance.[2] Evil things are
the opposite of these, viz., Folly, Injustice, Cowardice,
and Intemperance; these are the general forms of evil,
evil being characterised by the property that it is
naturally injurious, and therefore intrinsically undesirable. Between things good and evil there lies

[1] Compare Aristotle, pp. 67, 77.   [2] The *Cardinal Virtues*, see p. 44.

an intermediate class of things indifferent,[1] which in themselves are neither essentially beneficial nor essentially injurious; instances are life, health, pleasure, beauty, strength, wealth, good repute, good birth; as well as their opposites, death, disease, pain, ugliness, weakness, etc. These are neither good nor bad from the moral or absolute point of view, but they are more or less preferable, according to the conditions under which they appear. On the other hand, " good " and " absolutely good " are synonymous; the moral virtues are desirable under all circumstances and the vices are always undesirable. It follows with strict logic that all good things are equally good, and all bad things equally bad—*peccata paria*; there is no scale of excellence—for otherwise the goodness or badness of anything would be relative and variable, not absolute, since it would depend on the presence or absence of other things.

A further inference is that moral virtue is not a state capable of increase or diminution—like the temperature of a body—but a disposition possessing no degrees, like the straightness of a stick. This is a criticism of the Aristotelian doctrine that Virtue is a habit formed by repeated action, its strength or weakness depending on the frequency of repetition. Not that the Stoics ignored the value of habitual action as a means of acquiring Virtue; they meant rather that the strengthening of habits is only a progress towards Virtue, and that a man is not, strictly speaking, morally good, and therefore does not possess Well-being, until he has reached moral perfection.

---

[1] τὰ ἀδιάφορα.

Virtue and Knowledge.—The virtues are inseparable. They have common theoretical principles and a common end, and he who has one has all. This is because they are products of the one Reason expressing itself in action. Hence they are forms of knowledge of practical truth. Practical Wisdom is a knowledge of what acts are good, bad, or indifferent; Temperance is a knowledge of what objects should be sought, avoided, or regarded as indifferent; Justice is a knowledge of what is due to every one; and Courage is a knowledge of what is or is not a proper object of fear. Practical Wisdom deals with duties, Temperance with impulses, Courage with endurance, and Justice with social distribution. The vices, in like manner, are forms of ignorance; the judgments from which they spring are based on opinion, not on knowledge.[1] These views express the Stoic interpretation of the Socratic doctrine that Virtue is one and is knowledge.

Resignation.—The ethical importance of acquiring knowledge of scientific laws arises from the consideration that if we know what must happen, we are able to adapt our wishes to the inevitable, and are more likely to obtain Well-being than by vainly struggling against it. This Resignation is a form of rational control of the desires and is assisted by concrete knowledge. The Stoic Resignation was partly acquiescence in the necessary course of events, and partly a submission to the over-ruling rational Providence.

Pleasure and Emotion. Self-Control ("Apathy").— The focus of all the negative tendencies of Stoicism is an opposition to Hedonism. Virtue, and Virtue

---

[1] A Platonic distinction. See pp. 49, 79, note.

alone, is essential to Well-being, and pleasure is only
an indifferent object of choice; it is not a natural
end or motive of action, but only a *result*[1] of action.
The primary impulse of living creatures is not (as the
Cyrenaics and Epicureans say) directed towards pleasure,
but towards self-preservation. The ethical worth of
pleasure is dependent on the actions from which
it results; thus the pleasure of fools is to be distinguished from the calm joy of the wise man.[2] In
truth both pleasure and pain are emotions,[3] and all
emotions are regarded with suspicion by the Stoics,
because of their tendency to become unrestrained;
in their extreme forms they are *irrational* and *unnatural* disturbances of the mind. Intemperance,
an excessive love of pleasure, is the source of the
greatest mental confusion, and a type of the evil
common to all emotions, since it means a complete
departure of the mind from right reason, and self-control. Extreme emotion is a disease of the soul. The
four primary emotions are fear, pain, pleasure, and
desire. Just as the virtues are forms of knowledge,
so the emotions are forms of opinion, and are
therefore unworthy of regard, not being based on
truth. Among the Stoics there prevailed, however,
different estimates of the moral worth of pleasure and
other emotions, some asserting them to be absolute
evils, and others admitting that pleasure and some
calm emotions were allowable. But all were unanimous
in maintaining that emotion is not a good (*i.e.* an

---

[1] ἡδονή, they held, is not a τέλος but an ἐπιγέννημα.

[2] The contrast is between ἡδονή (identified by the Stoics with violent
pleasure) and χαρά (calm pleasure).

[3] πάθη. The Stoic criticism is chiefly directed against violent emotions:
quiet emotions they sometimes approved of.

absolute good) and that it cannot be compared with Virtue. "Apathy"[1] they prized as one of the chief qualities of the wise man, but they took it often to signify, not absence of feeling, but control of the emotions by Reason. In this control consists freedom. The wise man was even permitted to enjoy certain quiet rational emotions, which are the *results* but not the *ends* of virtuous action.

Modifications.—The harshness of the Stoic theory was somewhat modified—at the cost of consistency— by their division of actions morally "indifferent" into three classes: first, those which are befitting[2] (because Reason selects them), as the honouring of parents and brothers and actions stimulated by patriotism and friendship; secondly those which are disapproved by Reason; and thirdly, actions genuinely indifferent, as the breaking of a twig or the holding of a pencil. Morally right actions[3] or moral duties are to be carefully distinguished from these. Such modifications are attempts to escape from the *negative formalism* arising from the identification of goodness with Virtue and Virtue with practical knowledge; until the concrete objects of this knowledge are specified, the whole theory tends to move in a useless logical circle.

The Ideal Man.—We have said that the post-Socratic Greek ethical thinkers had a tendency to regard the best men—who also possess the highest Well-being—as living a spiritual life apart from and above the lives of ordinary men. This tendency finds its strongest expression in the Stoic picture of the

---

[1] ἀπάθεια, literally "absence of emotion."
[2] τὰ καθηκόντα.   [3] τὰ κατορθώματα.

ideal man or the " wise man." He possesses all the
moral virtues in the highest degree; and since the
moral virtues are forms of Reason, which, again, is the
source of all that is even relatively desirable, he alone
is able to use properly those excellent qualities that
are not denominated good absolutely, but derive their
worth from the moral goodness of the agent. The
wise man alone is the perfect prophet, poet, orator,
logician and judge, and is in every respect perfect.
He has Well-being and is free because he controls
his emotions. Various extreme statements are attributed to the Stoics in this connection. They are
reported as saying that the majority of mankind are
fools. The wise man, had he existed, would have
been a " superman," intrinsically superior by nature
to ordinary men. But the conception was partly
intended as an ideal, and it was taught that the ideal
was seldom attainable even by the members of the
Stoic School. It may have served a useful purpose
by counteracting the self-dependent spiritual pride to
which Cynicism and Stoicism were liable.[1]

Social Ethics—Justice, Cosmopolitanism, Friendship.
—The Stoics taught, in opposition to Epicurus and
the Cyrenaics, that Justice is a law of Nature, a
product of universal Reason and not a mere convention.

---

[1] The Stoic wise man is generally described (as in the text) as a being
perfect at everything. This view is clearly exaggerated. But there is
another interpretation which probably contains the thought which the
greater Stoic teachers wished to express; namely, that a man cannot be
perfect at anything unless he has the highest kind of moral wisdom
—strength of will combined with keen insight into truth, both practical
and theoretical. This is the quality of *genius*, and is not possessed by
ordinary men Cf. Plato on the Lover of Wisdom (pp. 49, 55, 56), and
Aristotle on the life of *theoria*. Whether ordinary men can by effort
attain to this height either in this life or in the next, is a question left
undecided.

By this doctrine the Stoics strengthened the foundations of the cosmopolitanism [1] which had already been laid by the Cynics. Though all men are in a sense fellow-citizens of the same State (humanity) the wise man will take a practical part in the affairs of the narrower political group to which he belongs. He will be interested in the education and life of his fellow-citizens, especially under the more perfect forms of government. Friendship is only possible between the wise and virtuous, for it is based on that likeness of character which makes sympathy possible; a friend, as Aristotle says, is a second self.

Summary.—The following are the chief features in Stoic Ethics—

1. Well-being consists in acting rationally, or in accordance with the nature of man, a nature partly self-determined, partly determined by the eternal laws of the universe, laws which are themselves expressions of Reason, and are thus in conformity with man's self-determining nature.

2. Rational action and morally virtuous actions are the same.

3. For the individual the result of rational action is self-dependence and freedom, which follow from controlling the emotions. Thus Virtue, not pleasure, is to be our guide. Hence also follows resignation, from the consciousness that the laws of Nature are both reasonable and immutable.

4. From the social point of view there results an extension of the areas of duties to all beings possessing Reason, that is, to the whole of humanity.

---

[1] The theory that man is a "citizen of the world," and that he has social duties to all humanity. The name signifies the transition from the State morality of Plato to the wider view.

CRITICISM

The greatness of the Stoic Ethics consists in its assertion of the power of the soul to resist misfortune and suffering. The means recommended, however, are chiefly negative; pain is to be resisted by cultivating indifference to every kind of feeling, whether pleasant or painful. This negative attitude towards feeling was probably not originally suggested by a belief in the supremacy of Reason. It is, at all events, quite consistent with Epicureanism for those who believe that there is more pain than pleasure in life, and that susceptibility to pleasure is always accompanied by a proportionate susceptibility to pain. Such persons might, on purely hedonistic grounds, cultivate indifference to feeling.

The Stoic theory is not, however, purely negative. The feelings are to be controlled in order that the activity of Reason may not be hindered, since this alone is intrinsically good. But whereas Plato and Aristotle regarded Reason, in the ethical sense, as manifesting itself in human life as a harmonious blending of feeling, will and intellect, the Stoics tended to identify Reason with will, using intellect as the servant of will, and ignoring the claims of feeling. This position, however, is not tenable; if the will consistently aims at a good end, the nature and worth of this end must be judged and appreciated by intelligence and feeling combined, and we have no right to say that will is on the highest level. If, on the other hand, will strives blindly to assert itself without reference to intelligence and feeling, it is irrational and can possess no intrinsic value.

The influence exerted by Stoic philosophy on popular morality and on subsequent ethical systems was very great. We owe to it the first definite expression of the idea of the authoritativeness of duty as contrasted with feeling, an idea afterwards so fully analysed by Kant, and less perfectly by Butler. Spinoza's Ethics also contains many Stoic elements, especially pantheism and the idea of resignation to necessary law.

In their theory of pleasure the Stoics emphasised, in opposition to Epicurus, the psychological truth that all desire is not for pleasure; but they made the mistake of confounding this psychological truth with the ethical theory that pleasure is not good, that it *ought* not to be an end of conduct. The doctrine common to Plato and Aristotle[1] is, however, truer and more moderate; Well-being as desired, or as attained, is not merely a feeling of pleasure, but pleasure is essential to Well-being, and a rational being desires certain ends *plus* pleasure. It might be added that the desire for pleasure or aversion from pain in the realised end is often in the background of consciousness, and for that reason escapes notice.

The negative element in the teaching of the Stoics, besides neutralising indiscriminate Hedonism, was probably the source of their cosmopolitanism. For they could see no reason why the Greek, as such, was intrinsically superior to the foreigner. But their cosmopolitanism was not merely negative, since they taught that the possession of Wisdom and Virtue is the positive ground for preferring one man to another, quite apart from differences of nationality.

[1] See pp. 60-62, 77, 78.

CHAPTER VI

GENERAL SURVEY OF GREEK ETHICS

WE shall conclude this part with a brief sketch of the development of Greek Ethics.

Protagoras states the ethical problem as a search for human good, which, he insists, must be realised in individuals. He urges that government (both moral and civil) is essential to the well-being of men living together, and that the "political virtues"[1] which are essential to government are divine gifts not further explicable. Though in this way emphasising the true worth of morality, he rests content with popular or conventional Ethics, and fails to discover any rational conception of ideal goodness that might lead to improvement in current moral doctrines.

The absence of a sound philosophic basis of morality led the more sceptical Sophists, headed by Gorgias, into a denial of the objectivity of virtue; but as this line of thought ends in ethical anarchy, we need not pursue it further.

Socrates resists the conventional tendency of Protagoras and tries to stem the scepticism and anarchy to which either public opinion or careless

[1] These would now be called social virtues.

private judgment, regarded as the basis of morality, must lead. He claims that the Good *is one*, in the sense that it is an expression of some universal principle that may be discovered by careful scientific investigation, in which public moral opinion is not to be accepted as infallible. Ethics is the science of human Well-being, the principles of which are to be discovered by the trained thinker, and taught by him to the multitude. Virtue is a form of knowledge ; to acquire Well-being we have only to discover the essential nature of the Good.

The Socratics attacked the problem at this point. Virtue is knowledge,—but of what ? What *is* the practical nature of Well-being ? The Cynics reply that moral virtue is the only good, and that the Well-being which springs from its possession is self-dependence, indifference to fortune, pleasure, or pain. But this answer is formal and negative, and the definition of Well-being as the pursuit of virtue is circular, since virtue can only be described as a mental quality leading to Well-being. What then is the content of Well-being ? To this the Cyrenaics reply that it consists in the enjoyment of pleasures *here* and *now*. Virtue and self-control are only *means* of getting the most intense pleasures. These two answers express two different sides of Socratic teaching, the Cynics laying stress on the *form*, the Cyrenaics on the *matter* of personal good. Both systems are mainly *individualistic*. The Cyrenaic represents the extreme type of egoistic Hedonism. But the Cynic cosmopolitanism, though negative—being based on a contempt for national distinctions—contains the germs of a wide humanitarian Ethics ; for it raises the question—what right has one man to a greater share of Well-being than another ?

With Plato and Aristotle Ethics became more complex, owing to their recognition of the necessity of finding a connection between social and individual good. Both, in different language, teach that ideal Well-being is a harmonious activity of the different parts of the rational soul. This comes to mean that for the ordinary citizen the life of Well-being consists in the exercise of the soul's natural capacities for action and emotion, in which no faculties of action are overstrained, and no emotion is allowed to become strong enough to violate the composite harmony. Since pleasure is the feeling of such a harmony, it is an essential constituent of the Good. Social good is conceived by Plato as the realisation in the State of the same conception of harmony (Justice). The moral virtues, as analysed by Aristotle, are certain permanent qualities of character that are required to secure this harmony both in the individual soul and in the State. Plato and Aristotle agree in distinguishing the practical goodness possible for the average man from the ideal excellence attainable only by the select few. On the whole they agree in describing the highest form of mental activity as the pursuit and attainment of the knowledge of true being; even though this ideal may never be realised. Such knowledge, according to Plato, has for its object the Good or Perfect. The manifestation of the Good in the world of sense is beauty, and thus the ideal man loves truth, beauty, and goodness, seeing that they are essentially inseparable. It is hardly possible to distinguish this view from Aristotle's teaching that *theoria* is the highest form of Well-being, since *theoria* can only mean a life of free spiritual activity having for its object all that is true, good and beautiful. Aristotle also adds that the ideal life, being a free activity, is the most *pleasant*; but in this connection he identifies pleasure with the freedom of inward spiritual activity, and he does not regard it as a merely passive feeling due to the influence of external objects on the senses. The ideal at which all may aim is further described by Plato as "likeness to God"; this agrees with the doctrine just mentioned, since the most divine attribute of man is his capacity for knowledge —knowledge not partial, but complete, and wholly corresponding to the reality of things, a reality existing in the Divine Mind as a perfect system of Ideas. In like manner Aristotle teaches that *theoria* is essentially a divine activity, but he differs from Plato—or perhaps he is only more explicit—in questioning whether the ideal is fully attainable by man. We have seen that this ideal was not the egoistic self-dependency of the Cynic, since it becomes the imperative duty of the wisest men to use their wisdom to the advantage of the State. For Aristotle, also, the good of the State is greater and more perfect than the good of the individual. To these two thinkers we owe the conception of a *social* good in which the good of each individual is only a part, yet an essential part. From this source, under the influence of the expansive yet primarily negative cosmopolitanism of the Cynics and Stoics and the missionary spirit of Christianity, there sprang the conception of a positive humanitarian ideal, unlimited by nationality.

The Stoic system is partly a reaction against the

apparent intellectualism of Aristotle and Plato.   But the reaction is *theoretically* a retrogression; for it cannot be denied that the life of highest Well-being is in some sense a *harmony* in feeling and action, whereas the Stoic Ethics destroys this harmony.   Verbally, indeed, they identify the good with a harmony of man with his own true nature, but actually they lay stress on one element in that nature, the power of control—the Will. Verbally, also, they identify self-control with Reason, but Reason signifies for them, not the co-ordination between the parts of the soul, but the suppression of emotions.   The theoretical retrogression may be described by saying, that whereas Plato attributed to each of the cardinal virtues a special and indispensable function, the Stoics endeavoured to raise Fortitude to the highest rank, thereby violating the Platonic law of Justice.

But though the Stoic system was *theoretically* a retrogression, it was *practically* an advance.   It recognises the disorders of mankind; its precepts are suggested by the practical desirability of resisting those pains and evils that cannot be altogether abolished.   At the risk of disturbing the Platonic ideal harmony, it recommends over-development of the power of control, in preference to allowing emotion the opportunity of upsetting the balance in a worse direction.   It is a prosaic ideal in ordinary life; in moments of violent temptation or suffering it becomes sublime.

Epicurus represents another form of the reaction against the apparent intellectualism of Plato and Aristotle.   In relation to the Stoics he illustrates the same antithesis of thought as the Cyrenaics in relation

to the Cynics. In his just attempt to avoid the
Cynic and Stoic *formalism*, he falls into the error of
identifying the *content* of the good with mere pleasure.
Both Stoics and Epicureans are one-sided, the one
laying undue stress on the control of feeling, the other
on the enjoyment of feeling.   The systems of Aristotle
and Plato are truer, though practically less efficient,
being dominated by scientific, aesthetic, and metaphysical interests.   For the plain man the aesthetic
ideal of order and harmony is not a strong motive :
he demands something one-sided and finds this in
pleasure or self-respect.   The harmony of self or
society directly appeals only to a few of the cultured
few.   Practically the ideal of the harmony of self
tends to degenerate into egoistic Hedonism,[1] except
in so far as this deterioration is checked by the
introduction of the Stoic element.   Subsequent
history shows that the Epicurean and Stoic principles
are effective by themselves,—the former, however,
tending towards licentiousness, the latter towards
purity of morals.[2]   The less narrow doctrines of Plato
and Aristotle have deeply influenced not only philosophy
but also popular conceptions of morality.   The
latter influence, however, was acquired by fusion
with the stronger moral and spiritual forces of
Christianity.

[1] Cf. Tennyson's poem, *The Palace of Art.*
[2] See Lecky's *History of European Morals,* chap. ii.

PART II

MODERN ETHICAL SYSTEMS

INTRODUCTION

Intervening Systems.—The purpose of this work is to give specimens of some of the more influential Greek (pre-Christian) and modern systems of Ethics beginning with Hobbes. But it seems desirable to mention some of the leading features of the Ethics of the intervening period, which was one of considerable philosophical activity, and of great interest and importance, owing to the fusion of—and conflict between—Greek and Christian ideals. Three types of philosophy are worthy of special note, the Neo-Platonic, the Patristic, and the Scholastic. Little more than their names can be here mentioned; the Patristic and Scholastic periods, in particular, cannot be adequately described without reference to dogmatic theology, and we are mainly concerned with systems which do not presuppose theological principles.

(1) The Neo-Platonists[1] tried to assimilate, without dogma, the Platonic philosophy to the mysticism suggested by Hebrew or Christian ideas. This type originated at Alexandria, and thence spread to Rome and Athens. Its principal exponents were Philo—an Alexandrian Jew—Plotinus, Porphyry, Iamblichus, and Proclus. It professed to return to the funda-

[1] From the first to the sixth century A.D.

mental conceptions of the Platonic philosophy, the conceptions of the One, the Absolute, the Good, which were identified with the Deity. The supreme realisa-tion of human reason lies in its absorption into the Absolute through a mystic ecstasy. The type is thus a blend of philosophy and theosophy.

(2) Patristic is the name applied to the writings of the earlier Fathers of the Christian Church to the end of the fifth century. Of these the most famous was Augustine.[1] Though deeply influenced by Plato, his whole philosophy is constructed on a basis of Christian theology. He taught that the highest Good is the love of God, that in this love all man's faculties reach their highest perfection, and his desires are completely satisfied.

(3) The Scholastic philosophy, which flourished from the ninth to the fifteenth century, endeavoured to accommodate Greek and Neo-Platonic philosophy to Christian theology. The earliest noteworthy Scholastic was Johannes Scotus Erigena.[2] He followed Plato and the Neo-Platonists, and affirmed the identity of true religion with true philosophy. But his pantheistic tendencies did not find favour with the Church. The philosophy of later and more influential Scholasticism was based chiefly on Aristotle; it separated philosophy from revealed religion, while claiming that the two are wholly consistent. This position found its strongest supporter in Thomas of Aquino,[3] the most distinguished of the Scholastics. Like Augustine, he adhered absolutely to Christian theology as taught by the Catholic Church. The main purpose of his teaching was to prove that Faith

[1] 354-430.   [2] Born in Ireland about 810.   [3] 1225-1274.

and Reason, though distinct sources of truth, cannot
conflict with each other, and, further, that Faith
removes contradictions which perplex unaided Reason.
He was a devoted student of Aristotle, whose system
he took as the most perfect representative of natural
Reason. According to Thomas, the highest good for
man is the knowledge of God; subjectively, this is an
activity of the speculative intellect having God for its
object. This teaching is regarded by Thomas as the
proper interpretation of Aristotle's doctrine of *theoria*.[1]

Influence of Greek on Modern Ethics.—From this
brief sketch the reader may gather that the Greek
systems, both ethical and metaphysical, have permeated
all European thought. It is therefore not surprising
to find that there is a very close affinity between
the Ethics of Hobbes—the founder of modern non-theological Ethics—and that of the Stoics and Epicureans.
The Physics, Psychology, and Ethics of Hobbes have
the free disinterested character of Greek thought,
though his political philosophy was undoubtedly
moulded, and corrupted, by the peculiar circumstances
of his age.[2] From the Greeks, and especially Aristotle,
Hobbes learned the usefulness of Psychology as a
preliminary to Ethics, since it helps to determine
what motives actually appeal to men; from the Stoics
and Epicureans he learned the desirableness of applying the results and methods of every science to the
determination of the laws of human welfare. From
this point of view his philosophy is the link between
the old Greek systems and the sociology of Comte and
Herbert Spencer. It will be seen, moreover, that
there is a particularly close connection between Hobbes

[1] See p. 81, and note 2.   [2] The *Leviathan* was published in 1651.

and Epicurus. On the other hand, the rigidity of Hobbes' method, and the arrangement of his arguments, make his egoism much more formidable than that of Epicurus, who despised Logic. The age in which Hobbes lived was one in which the new Physical Science, both inductive and deductive, was making great changes in man's view of his own position in the universe. The regard for method and precision which characterises genuine Science influenced Hobbes considerably. This precision produced a distinct subdivision of subjects and problems.[1] Ethics, Physics, and Theology, ceasing to be confounded, are afterwards studied with greater success.

An important result of Hobbes' clearness of method was that one of the most vital questions of Ethics became more clearly emphasised, viz., what motive has the individual for seeking the good of others as well as his own good? Since Plato[2] and the other Greeks partly recognised this difficulty, its formulation cannot be regarded as distinguishing Christian or modern Ethics. Nevertheless the question is particularly prominent in modern Ethics, owing to the social teaching of Christianity, that men should love one another.

On the whole any attempt to draw a sharp line of distinction between Greek and modern non-theological Ethics must fail. There is no modern theory, except Evolutional Naturalism, that has not its Greek counterpart. The technical use of various terms— like Egoism, Altruism, the Social Organism, Social Obligation, Moral Obligation, Duty, Conscience, Teleo-

---

[1] A revival of Aristotelianism. (See p. 64.)
[2] See pp. 43 sq., 47.

logical Ethics—conceals this truth. The difference is formal, not fundamental; the same problems recur, but they are now stated with greater clearness and precision, and discussed with more analytical thoroughness. The greater modern thinkers, too, being able to use critically the results already reached are often more profound, and take a broader view. It must be remembered that these remarks apply only to *pure* Ethics.[1] *Applied* morality changes with the social conditions, with the special characteristics of nations and individuals, with religious beliefs, and with the growth of sciences.[2] But these changes do not affect the grounds of pure Ethics. We have to distinguish between the principles of Ethics and the forces which enable those principles to be realised. Thus Christianity has favoured the growth of universal sympathy, and of the consequent organised philanthropy unknown in Greece ; it also strengthens or inhibits certain impulses and tendencies to action in various well-known ways, more particularly by the doctrine of future rewards and punishments. Evolutional Naturalism is indeed a growth of the nineteenth century, but it is likely to affect applied Ethics more than pure ; it expresses new views as to how human good is attainable, and gives new *answers* as to the historical source of our moral beliefs, but it has not altered the final problem of Ethics. Questions regarding the nature of ultimate motives and of the *general* character of the good remain unchanged,

[1] See p. 6.

[2] For example, we do not now usually attribute diseases and earth-quakes to moral wickedness, but to natural causes ; and insane persons are no longer supposed to be possessed by the devil. but to be suffering from brain disease produced by natural laws.

since mankind still consists of distinct conscious individuals each necessarily desiring Well-being.

Moral Obligation.—Though the ideas of moral obligation and duty are not peculiar to Christian or modern Ethics, questions about *motive*, of *moral obligation*, and *duty* are nevertheless more prominent in modern than in ancient Ethics. The Greeks seldom asked why an individual *ought* to pursue the good; they held that the knowledge or perception that an act or end is good *is* the motive, and where—as in unreasonable or immoral men—this motive is absent, private happiness is impossible. It was thus the influence of Socrates' teaching that prevented the idea of moral obligation from rising into prominence; he taught that if we know what is good we shall act rightly without compulsion or obligation; if we are ignorant we cannot act rightly. But when it became clearer that personal Well-being is not, *prima facie*, identical with the pursuit of objective social good, the inquiry naturally arose, what obligation is a man under to pursue objective good rather than his own Well-being? That social good is the *best* was recognised by Aristotle and Plato,[1] and if this be true we must be under a moral obligation[2] to follow it. This difficult question may be put otherwise: How can I reasonably pursue a good which I can never experience in its fulness? The good of another (it is natural to argue) is enjoyed by him and not by me, and as a motive for my action it can only be secondary or acquired. It is not too much to say that the forms of all modern systems of pure Ethics[3] have been

[1] See especially pp. 47, 48, 65.   [2] See p. 11.
[3] Evolutional Ethics is perhaps an exception, if indeed it can be regarded as pure Ethics.

determined by the attempt to solve this problem rationally. A fresh stimulus to the inquiry was given by Hobbes, who boldly cut the knot, asserting that one individual has no motive for pursuing the good of another. But the moral convictions of mankind could not rest satisfied with this solution, and the result has been a series of hypotheses, most of which express some degree of truth.

Naturalism and Intuitionism. — Many of the ethical systems hereafter described belong to one of two types, which may be termed Naturalism and Intuitionism. According to the naturalistic writers moral ideas are derived; they are the products of desires and feelings or instincts that originally have no moral predicates, and they arise by necessary laws of nature (whether physical or mental) which for all we know may be purely mechanical and undirected by Reason. Hobbes, for example, derives the laws of morality from the natural instincts of self-preservation and self-assertion ; Hume, deriving them from a variety of feelings, including pleasure and sympathy, explains their force by custom and tradition. Spencer regards moral ideas and the sense of moral obligation as due to hereditary instincts, for which no reason can be given beyond the fact that those races who do not possess them have no chance of surviving.

The intuitionists, on the other hand, hold that moral obligation and moral ideas and truths are fundamental and irreducible ; they cannot be explained as being products of non-moral forces like self-interest, animal instincts, or the love of pleasure. They commonly hold that either the morality of particular actions or the fundamental principles of morality are intuitively [1] discerned, though training may be necessary before such discernment is possible.

Naturalism is not to be identified with any doctrine which, like the Stoics' or Butler's, asserts that "Virtue consists in following Nature." The Stoics and Butler were, in fact, intuitionists. The naturalists hold that moral laws and judgments are the products of external natural laws which in themselves are neither moral nor immoral, so far as man can tell. Many of the earlier English intuitionists held that moral laws were natural, either in the sense that their excellence and the obligations to which they give rise are eternal—just as mathematical truths and the laws of physical Nature are eternal,—or in the sense that moral laws and obligations follow from the known nature of man.

It is unnecessary to enter into a long discussion of the question whether the English naturalists and intuitionists of the eighteenth century criticised each other fairly. The controversy was partly verbal, since it turned on the ambiguity of the word "Nature." Sometimes "natural" is identified with "*non-artificial*," *i.e.* not created by human design; in another sense it signifies *eternal*; in another it is attributed to anything that is the result of *necessary* laws; sometimes a thing is called natural because it is apprehended by *normal* or ordinary experience, and in this connection Nature is often contrasted with Divine Revelation, which is described as supernatural.

The distinction between these two opposite views of Ethics originated with the Greeks. Socrates, the Cynics, Plato, Aristotle, and the Stoics, were the

---

[1] Hence the name "Intuitionism."

predecessors of the intuitionists; the Cyrenaics and Epicurus of the naturalists. This is especially clear in their discussion of the question whether Justice exists "by nature" or "by convention."[1] Epicurus and the Cyrenaics assert that Justice is conventional, the others that it is natural or eternal; Plato, for example, claims that it is intrinsically and objectively good, and Cudworth (the Cambridge Platonist) follows him in describing it as an "eternal and immutable" Idea, which determines even the Deity in His actions. But all the Greeks were, in a sense, intuitionists, since they regarded personal Well-being, whether particular or universal, as the intrinsically good end by which the rightness or wrongness of actions is to be estimated. On the other hand, it might be urged that Plato was a naturalist, in the same sense that Spinoza was a naturalist.[2] On the whole, therefore, a classification of Greek systems into intuitional and naturalistic does not seem appropriate. Modern naturalists differ from what I have called their Greek predecessors in seeking less to determine what ends are intrinsically good and satisfying, than to explain the existence and force in society of accepted moral ideas and judgments. This difference is partly due to the increased recognition of the truth that a consciousness of duty or moral obligation is a fact of human nature which cannot be ignored, even if it can be explained as a product of non-moral forces.

There is an important practical difference between Naturalism and Intuitionism in connection with Free-will. The naturalists tend to regard man as entirely

[1] pp. 89, 101.
[2] Since Plato sometimes, and Spinoza always, identifies evil with negation (pp. 58, 144).

subject to the laws of external Nature, which are beyond his control; moral obligation means for them an impulse towards action, which ranks with other impulses according to its strength. The intuitionists hold that man, through moral ideas, has some control over Nature and over his own actions; moral obligation may have little *force*, but it has supreme *authority*; and it works not through blind mechanical laws [1] but by appealing to the rational consciousness of duty. The intuitionists usually admit freedom of the will as a power of doing what is intrinsically right because it *is* right. Freedom, in this sense, is a form of causality by which effects are produced through pre-conceptions of what is good. The naturalists, however, hold that the future course of events is determined by the past, and that a pre-conception of an ideal future good can determine our actions only in so far as it is itself determined by preceding events.

The naturalistic method is essentially descriptive; it does not set up an ethical standard, but merely tries to explain the origin of accepted ethical principles. It is content with describing human nature as it *is*, whereas Intuitionism attempts to determine what it *ought* to be. Strictly speaking, therefore, Naturalism is not Ethics,[2] since it deals with beliefs about good rather than with the good itself. But since the two subjects are closely connected, and the naturalists so often use intuitional axioms,[3] and since their method largely

---

[1] For a further discussion of the connection between moral obligation and free-will see chapters on Kant and Green.

[2] As described in the Introduction (pp. 1, 6).

[3] *E.g.* Spencer, on the "formula of Justice."

determines the course of ethical inquiry, it is necessary to include them as ethical writers. It is clear, for example, that if "custom" is the only source of morality, as some naturalists claim, then its commands are not unconditionally binding, and to obey them may be injurious; an intuitionist will therefore seek to discover some other source, or to amend traditional morality by using some objectively good standard.

Other Types of Ethical Thought.—The division into Naturalism and Intuitionism is most fittingly applied to the English writers of the seventeenth and eighteenth centuries, when the intuitionists— who regarded themselves as the champions of virtue against heterodoxy—were so eager to prove that morality is expressive of eternal truth, and to refute the doctrine—which they held inconsistent with this —that moral customs are created by social compacts. In the nineteenth and twentieth centuries this division is less appropriate, since the focus of interest has changed. The opposition is to a large extent replaced by one between Evolutional Naturalism and Rational Idealism. On both sides the horizon was widened, owing to the recognition that the past history of man must be taken into account if we are to understand what he is now. The evolutional naturalists teach that the character of the human race, including moral ideas and all social institutions and customs, is determined by the law of the survival of the fittest to survive, which has been operating mechanically since the dawn of life. The rational idealists, on the other hand, regard the higher social customs and institutions as creations of the self-unfolding Mind of society. They cannot properly be classed with either naturalists or intuitionists. In their independence and indifference to vulgar opinion or tradition they resemble the naturalists; but inasmuch as they resist the mechanical view of development and assert the supremacy and freedom of mind, they have more in common with the intuitionists, especially with Cudworth.

In addition to these types, Utilitarianism has been crystallised by modern thought into a distinct doctrine, which may ally itself either with Naturalism (Bentham, J. S. Mill, and Spencer) or with Intuitionism (Sidgwick). The cardinal principle of Utilitarianism is that the "greatest happiness of the greatest number" is the supreme end of conduct.

There are other doctrines which have received names and are worthy of notice, but in the following pages we shall concentrate attention on Earlier Naturalism, Intuitionism (including Moral Purism), Utilitarianism, Evolutional Naturalism and Rational Idealism. Most other doctrines are either attempts to effect a synthesis between two or more of these or are too loosely expressed to be described as philosophy.

CHAPTER I

EARLIER NATURALISM

THE sixteenth and seventeenth centuries in Europe were marked by a revival of the freedom of thought that characterised the ancient Greeks, a return to Nature, a revolt against the artificial products of the principle of authority. This was the age of Copernicus, Kepler, Galileo, Descartes, and Newton, immortal names in the history of science. The first book of Francis Bacon's *Novum Organum* [1] gave expression to the free critical side of this movement, so far as it effected physical science. In speculative philosophy the movement was specially furthered by René Descartes, [2] who taught that the only truths which the soul can accept are those which it clearly and distinctly apprehends, unprejudiced by tradition or the opinions of others; and the saying of Spinoza, [3] " truth is its own criterion," pointed in the same direction. Under the influence of the same spirit, Thomas Hobbes of Malmesbury, [4] attempted the construction, by the aid of Reason and experience only, of a complete system of Natural Philosophy which was intended to expound the fundamental principles of Geometry,

[1] 1620. [2] 1596-1650. [3] 1632-1677. [4] 1588-1679.

Physics, Physiology, Psychology, Ethics, and Politics. Hobbes' method was more deductive than that of Bacon, who laid much stress on the necessity of a preliminary induction based on the observation of particulars. The system of the former was in many ways influenced by Greek models. It is encyclopaedic, like Aristotle's; the doctrine that the effort after self-preservation is the ruling active principle in all living beings came from the Stoics; apart from these, his physics, psychology and ethical groundwork remind us most of Epicurus.

A. EGOISTIC NATURALISM—HOBBES [1]

Philosophy.—Hobbes defines Philosophy as the knowledge of effects by means of the concepts of their causes, and of causes by means of their known effects; thereby identifying Philosophy with Deductive Science based on reason and observation. The first preparation for its study is therefore Logic, which determines the principles of right reasoning. In Formal Logic Hobbes follows Aristotle, but he has a curious and inconsistent tendency to identify reasoning with a proper use of words (Nominalism). In his Logic of Method may be mentioned his conception of Cause, which he describes as the aggregate of conditions necessary and sufficient for the production of the Effect.[2]

The Worth of Philosophy.—Philosophy is partly descriptive, but her function is mainly creative; her true end is utility, the production of effects through

---

[1] The quotations from Hobbes are from the *Leviathan*, unless otherwise stated.

[2] Elements of Philosophy, *Concerning Body*, chap. ix. This definition of Cause is usually attributed to J. S. Mill.

a knowledge of causes—*scientia propter potentiam.*
The end of speculation is action, and the end of
action is the improvement of human life. This
doctrine was taught from the first by most English
philosophers, beginning with Bacon, and is the foundation of modern Utilitarianism. Hobbes, however, does
not say whether the end to be attained is general
happiness or power; nor is the doctrine consistent
with his Exclusive Egoism.

Division of Philosophy.—The two principal parts
of Philosophy are Natural and Civil. The first deals
with material bodies made by Nature, the second
with Commonwealths or bodies made by the wills
and agreements of men. Civil Philosophy is subdivided into Ethics, which treats of men's dispositions and manners; and Politics, which deals with
the natural laws that are at the basis of government.[1]
Hobbes' intention was to show that the laws of
Politics spring from the laws of Ethics—in the
above sense, as inclusive of psychology—and that
these again depend on the laws of material bodies.
He differs from modern materialists in his naïve
belief that this design can be accomplished.

Materialism.—According to Hobbes, the most
universal cause in Nature is motion, and thus it
becomes the ideal of Philosophy to explain all
phenomena, physical and mental, as effects of spatial
movement.[2] The laws of Civil Philosophy are to be
deduced from the laws of individual minds and

[1] Hobbes' conception of Politics afterwards (with Comte and Spencer)
developed into Sociology, which treats of the uniform laws naturally
operating in groups of men.

[2] The doctrine is from Epicurus, who derived it from Democritus.
(See p. 86.)

organisms mutually influencing each other, and these laws in turn are to be deduced from those of material movement.

Psychology.—Here again Epicurus is the model, but the scientific theories of the seventeenth century are also used. Everything real in the world is in space or time, and is therefore either matter or motion. Subjective or mental experience consists merely of *apparitions* produced in the subject by the sensory nerves. We wrongly suppose colour and light, as apprehended by us, to be external realities; their external causes are simply rapid movements of material particles. It seems that Hobbes regarded the Ego or Soul as a collection of *phantasmata* or appearances, the effects of material movement, but possessing no causal efficiency whatever. This view is, however, inconsistent with his ethical Egoism, which presupposes that the mind is a self-conscious real unity endeavouring to assert its own being.

The laws of mental states are to be explained by spatial movement as follows. All mental states are either Sensation, Imagination, Memory, or Desire. Sensation is the source of all our knowledge; it is caused by physical movements transmitted from outer bodies to the organs of sense. Imagination and Memory are nothing but "decaying sense"; they are due to the remains of movements originally started as sensation.

But besides passive sensations we have to explain the so-called active principles in man—the voluntary motions. These are originated by Imagination, which pictures beforehand the end to be sought, as walking, speaking, etc. The "small beginnings of motions," before they come to fruition in larger motions, are called Endeavour (*conatus*).[1] Appetite or Desire is Endeavour directed towards its cause, and is thus obscurely conceived by Hobbes as a kind of physical attraction in a definite direction, Aversion being a physical repulsion.

Psychology of Voluntary Action, Pleasure and Pain, Good and Evil.—Desire, with its opposite, Aversion, are the two forms of Endeavour or voluntary motion ; each is due to the physical forces of attraction or repulsion operating between the body and an external object. The " appearance " or " sense " of the motion of desire is *pleasure,* of the motion of aversion is *pain.* The desired object or the end of the motion of desire is called *good,* the object of aversion is called *evil.* Thus pleasure is the " appearance " or " sense " of good, and pain the appearance or sense of evil. Hobbes also defines pleasure as " a corroboration of vital motion and a help thereunto," and pain as a hindrance of the same. In this definition he tacitly assumes the Stoic doctrine that desire is naturally directed towards self-preservation.[2] He appears to

[1] It must be remembered that Hobbes, in speaking of Imagination as a cause of motion, was regarding it as a physiological process originally set up by the impact of external bodies on the sensory organs. Modern physiology would regard these "small beginnings of motion" as a stage in reflex action (*i.e.* the reaction of the organism to external stimuli) before the nervous energy has been transformed into movements of the muscles.

[2] In these descriptions of good, pleasure, and desire, Hobbes overlooks some important points. He defines good as the object of desire ; in defining pleasure, on the one hand, as a "corroboration of vital motion" and on the other hand as the sense of (successful) desire, he implies that all pleasure, and therefore all successful desire, tends to prolong the life of the agent. Good actions, those that prolong life, those that give pleasure, and those that satisfy desire are therefore identical. But Hobbes gave little or no reasons for this very sweeping conclusion. The relation between pleasure-giving and life-prolonging acts was afterwards considered more fully by Spencer, who comes to much the same conclusion as Hobbes (see chapter on Spencer).

differ from the Epicureans in making pleasure
dependent on desire, but the difference is of no ethical
importance, since he holds that the sense of desire is
always pleasure. Since good and evil depend on
desire, they are relative to the person; nothing is
absolutely good. There is no supreme or final good
in this life. "But for an *utmost* end in which the
ancient philosophers have placed felicity . . . there is
no such thing in this world, nor way to it, more than
to Utopia; for while we live we have desires, and
desire presupposeth a further end."[1] "*Vita ipsa
motus est*"; happiness in this life consists in the
constant movement of desire towards fulfilment, not
in the tranquil state of having no desires, which is
an impossible fiction.

Will.—Deliberation is an oscillation between
desire and aversion. Will is the "last appetite"
in deliberating, the desire which is decisive in trans-
forming deliberation into action. A voluntary act
is one that proceeds from the Will. Men and animals
possess free-will in the same sense; we not only *can*,
but we *must* do what we will; since a desire if
strong enough must be efficient, just as any physical
force produces its effect if it is not resisted by another
force.

The Desire for Power—Egoism.—Each individual
as a voluntary agent is conceived by Hobbes as a
centre of desires and aversions and his Felicity as "a
continual progress of the desire from one object to
another." But men in whom reason exists, seek, not
only to gratify the desires of the moment, but to
acquire the means of gratifying all future desires,

[1] *Human Nature*, chap vii 5.

and thus there arises "a perpetual and restless desire of power after power that ceaseth only in death." [1] This desire for power is not original or primitive; it is derived from the fundamental desires for self-preservation and self-gratification, the former being generally the stronger. When it is recognised that my desires conflict with those of other persons, there grows the secondary desire to control the actions of other persons. Since the means of gratifying a great many future desires are intrinsically more valuable than the actual gratification of any single desire, the Love of Power becomes the chief regulating principle of ethical judgments. It is at the root of all our admiration for "Virtue," which is defined as any highly esteemed quality that gives a man social eminence and sets him above his fellows. All mental qualities and possessions are estimated by the degree in which they gratify or oppose this passion. "The value or worth of a man is, as of all other things, his price; that is to say, so much as would be given for the use of his power; and therefore is not absolute." Riches, reputation, honour, dignity, even benevolence, courtesy and integrity, are valued only because they increase the possessor's social influence and make him an object of fear to his fellow-men. Fear is the negative aspect of the love of power; it compels men to obey those who have authority backed by force. Pity is a form of fear; it is defined as "imagination or fiction of future

[1] At this point Hobbes unconsciously abandons his materialism, and I shall make no further attempt to reconcile his ethics with his physical theory of desires; it is clear that the desire for power to attain *future* objects is only possible in a conscious Ego; it cannot be defined as a *physical* attraction towards a present object, since it involves the conception of a permanent conscious self.

calamity to ourselves proceeding from the sense of another man's calamity."[1] Natural affection and friendship are purely egoistic; they are efficient for the sole reason that "there can be no greater argument to a man of his own power than to find himself able not only to accomplish his own desires, but also to assist other men in theirs."[2] Benevolence—even to strangers—is always based on a half-conscious mutual compact or on an expectation of a good return for favours done. Even when men have gained power, they struggle ruthlessly to add thereto, in order to secure their future welfare.

Exclusive Egoism.—Thus Hobbes' doctrine is Exclusive Egoism. He does not inquire whether we *ought* to have a *disinterested* regard for the good of others; he asserts that this is impossible; and his ethics is therefore psychological, being based on a description of what he believed to be the facts of human nature as revealed to introspection. In the sequel we shall see that he attempts to explain the existence and efficacy of morality and government as a rational development of the instincts of self-preservation and self-gratification.

The Warfare of Man with Man.—All men, says Hobbes, are equal by nature, meaning that in the average they possess equal powers of self-defence—whether of bodily strength or prudence—and similar tastes. Owing to this natural equality men often desire the same ends, and thus endeavour to subdue one another by violence or by guile. Hence, "during the time men live without a common power to keep them all in awe, they are in that condition which

---

[1] *Human Nature*, chap. ix. 10.   [2] *Ib.* 17.

is called war; and such a war as is of every man against every man." This universal war is unpleasant for every one; it prevents the growth of industry, navigation, agriculture, science, literature, and the pleasures of society, and there is, "which is worst of all, continual fear and danger of violent death; and the life of man solitary, poor, nasty, brutish, and short." And though this state of warfare may never have existed universally, yet it exists in proportion to the weakness of government, *e.g.* amongst the savage American Indians; and it is exemplified in the conflicts of kings with each other. In this state of "mere nature" nothing can be unjust, nothing is either right or wrong. "Where there is no common power, there is no law, where no law no injustice. Force and fraud are in war the two cardinal virtues." Likewise there is no property, since every man takes what he can get.

Articles of Peace; the Laws of Nature.—That very egoism which originally set men at loggerheads with each other, when it becomes rational and foreseeing brings peace. The Right of Nature (*jus naturale*) is the liberty possessed by each man to use his power to preserve his own life, and is thus the supreme unconditional ground of all ethical action. The Laws of Nature are the precepts [1] which Reason enjoins as the best means for self-preservation. These laws are also Articles of Peace, because they ensure that social harmony without which happiness is impossible. The first and fundamental Law of Nature is "to seek peace and follow it," qualified by the condition that

---

[1] Hobbes is here dealing with those Laws of Nature which relate to *social* action.

if we cannot get peace we are to defend ourselves at all costs. The second Law enjoins that a man should be willing, for the sake of peace, "to be contented with so much liberty against other men as he would allow other men against himself." By this article a man surrenders his natural right to seize everything within his grasp. The voluntary and mutual surrender of rights gives a practical meaning to the words "obligation," "duty," "ought," "justice." One who has voluntarily given up his right is *obliged*—or *ought*—to act accordingly, it is his *duty* to do so. The mutual transference of right is called *contract*. The first performer of his side of a contract acquires *merit*. The third Law of Nature is "that men perform their covenants made," a covenant being a contract in which one party has already performed his part. This law is the "fountain and original of justice." The fourth enjoins gratitude, lest the giver repent him of his gift, the fifth complaisance (agreeableness), the sixth readiness to pardon one who repents, the seventh, that "in revenge, men look not at the greatness of the evil past, but the greatness of the good to follow." The eighth is against contumely, or the expression of hatred, the ninth against pride, "that every man acknowledge other for his equal by Nature." Nineteen Laws are given in the *Leviathan*, and the above specimens indicate their general character; they are the accepted laws of the strictest social Ethics. According to Hobbes they are summed up in the saying, "Do not that to another which thou wouldst not have done to thyself." Moreover these Laws of Nature are "immutable and eternal," for "it can never be that war shall preserve life, and peace destroy it." The science of these is "the true and only moral philosophy." It must be noticed, however, that these laws are not unconditionally binding; the immediate need for self-preservation, or even the *certain* prospect of obtaining power, would, on Hobbes' principles, compel a rational individual to break them ; but such contingencies do not generally arise.

Civil Government the Guardian of the Laws of Nature.—The Laws of Nature are the products of rational egoism, and will therefore be observed by any one who really *knows* what his interests are, provided the other members of the community observe the same laws. But what guarantee has any individual that others will surrender the rights that he has surrendered ? Reason alone is not in general a strong enough security. The Laws of Nature " of themselves, without the terror of some Power to cause them to be observed, are contrary to our natural passions, that carry us to partiality, pride, revenge, and the like. And covenants without the sword are but words." The only safeguard is the establishment by universal consent of a common power to enforce the laws of Nature. Men are " to confer all their power and strength upon one man or upon one assembly of men, that may reduce all their wills by plurality of voices unto one will." This is " as if every man should say to every man, ' I authorize and give up my right of governing myself to this man or to this assembly of men, on this condition, that thou give up thy right to him and authorise all his actions in like manner.' This done, the multitude so united in one Person, is called a Commonwealth. This is the generation of that great Leviathan, or rather (to speak more reverently) of that mortal God, to which we owe, under the immortal God, our peace and defence."

Summary of Hobbes' Ethics.—Thus the primitive Egoism, with which Hobbes starts, ends in the opposite extreme of Political Absolutism. The original motive of all voluntary action is self-interest; the good is purely for the self, and consists in the constant progress of desires towards fulfilment. Reason shows that the social harmony essential to private happiness can only be ensured by *general* obedience to certain precepts called Laws of Nature; these are the recognised laws of social morality. To prevent any particular infringements of these laws it is expedient that all should surrender the control of their behaviour to one man or assembly of men, giving them power to enforce obedience. Thus the State becomes the *external* criterion of morality, while self-interest is the only possible *internal* criterion. Hence the term "good," originally applied by each individual to different ends or for different reasons, comes to have a sort of objective or social meaning. What I call good, originally and naturally, is what satisfies my desire; but I consent to regard as "good" that which is approved by the Civil Government, because Reason informs me that such general consent on the part of all is the best available means of satisfying my desires. Strictly speaking, however, social good, as conceived by Hobbes, is only one form of the useful[1]; it is a means, not an end in itself, for each individual.

[1] See p. 22.

Criticism of Hobbes' Ethics.

The formal element in Egoism is unassailable; that every man, so far as he acts rationally, seeks what he believes to be his own good, is implied in the notion of individual voluntary action, in which the agent consciously puts before himself a certain end which he judges is good for *him* to realise. But we must distinguish between the *form* and the *content* of Egoism; it is in reference to the latter that Hobbes is open to just criticism. He assumes that the *content* of the good at which every person aims is the preservation of his own physical life and the enjoyment of pleasure. The narrowness of this view leads to the negative conclusion that men never desire the good of others; a doctrine false to human nature and one of the most serious defects in Hobbes' psychology—afterwards severely criticised by Shaftesbury and Butler. It is clear that almost every one, in different degrees, identifies his own good with the good of some circle of men. And it is questionable whether even the majority of men would regard the preservation of their own lives as the highest good under certain circumstances. In any case a single example of the surrender of life—and there are many—for honour, religion, family, or friends, would prove that self-preservation is not judged by all men to be the highest good. This is quite consistent with a rational—even with a hedonistic—Egoism, for it only means that a man may consider life to be not worth living, if the claims of honour, affection, human feeling, or loyalty are violated, or if certain realities upon which his happiness depends are lost to him for ever.

F

Hobbist Egoism, owing to its omissive character, may be called *exclusive*. It ignores the fact that the Ego is essentially social, and consequently has, in different degrees, ideals aiming at the good of other men, a good from which it may not distinguish its own.

Hobbes' theory of the *origin* of Government is more directly a question of Political Science and History than of Ethics; we are here concerned rather with his doctrine of the ethical meaning of a government when established. This doctrine may be traced partly to the political circumstances of the age (the civil war of Charles I.'s reign[1]), to his dread of civil disorder, and his love of social peace and the leisure which it brings. Firmly convinced that a stable and wise government, possessing power to enforce its laws, is essential to the happiness of men, he invented the theory of Exclusive Egoism to give more vividness to his picture—then by no means imaginary—of the disorders and miseries of a society without government. This caused him to overlook the fact that the moral, as distinct from the forcible, claims of the established government are conditional and not absolute; were this not recognised the ethical progress of society would be hopelessly fettered by a slavish conservatism. Hobbes' theory expresses in exaggerated form the truth that any kind of government —good or bad—tends to check the exclusive egoism of individuals or classes; egoism which, though not universal—as Hobbes taught—is nevertheless common enough to be dangerous to the welfare of society. And, though governments do not, historically, usually

[1] The *Leviathan* was published in 1651, two years after the execution of Charles I.

spring from mutual compacts, yet one of their strongest supports is the recognition by the average citizen that it is to his own advantage that the laws should be enforced; moreover, the working of a democratic state is to a large extent a matter of general agreement amongst groups seeking chiefly their own interests.

Hobbes' system is of great importance in the history of Ethics for the following reasons.[1] First, he insists on the *personal* nature of the good, just as Protagoras did;[2] there is no good of society apart from the good of its members. This is a plea for Individualism which is quite different from Exclusive Egoism. Secondly, this Individualism,[3] and indeed all Hobbes' principles except his Political Absolutism, are protests against the unreasoning forces of tradition and authority taken *per se*; obedience to these has to be justified by reference to personal good. Thirdly, in a very distinct sense, the issue of Hobbes' philosophy may be regarded as a *disproof* of Exclusive Egoism, for he shows that the position with which he starts cannot be maintained; the individual must give up his rights to a social authority and identify his will with the will of the community. Though indeed Hobbes held to the position that social good is merely useful for the individual, yet the development of thought renders such a position untenable. Minds are not isolated atoms; rational consciousness, as Kant and the Rational Idealists afterwards urged, is in its nature universal, and ultimate good ends must be in some way ends for the common consciousness of all rational beings.

[1] See also p. 143.   [2] See p. 32.   [3] See p. 34.

Inconsistencies in Hobbes' General Philosophy.

The ideas of Hobbes have so much determined the course of modern Philosophy, both by reaction and development, that it may be worth while to show that his principal doctrines do not form a consistent system. These doctrines are (*a*) Materialism, (*b*) Sensualistic Psychology, (*c*) Ethical Egoism, (*d*) Political Absolutism.

(*a*) *Materialism and Egoism.*——Hobbes wavers between *absolute* materialism, which asserts that everything real is "matter" (*i.e.* objects filling space) and *phenomenal* materialism, which asserts that matter is the only real object known to us.   His original design was to deduce everything from the laws of matter—starting from external nature and proceeding through man to society.   The laws of human actions were to be deduced from the principle that the mind is a collection of sensations and feelings, which are caused by physical impressions on the organs of sense, but have themselves no causal efficacy, no active power of producing changes.   Consistently with this view he should have regarded human societies as complex material systems, resulting from physical interactions between human bodies, in agreement with the laws of matter.   But in his Ethics and Politics he abandons Materialism.   He regards the Ego, not as a collection of impotent feelings and sensations, but as a substantial permanent and *conscious* unity, possessing feelings and interests that are actively opposed to the feelings and interests of other Egos.

Materialism as a Method.——Hobbes was an ardent supporter of material explanations, and from this point of view his materialism should be regarded as a valuable protest against the dogmatic errors of the Middle Ages, when sensible men had not enough exact knowledge of nature to raise physical science above the level of the commonplace; while the superstitious mob, ignoring the more obvious laws of nature, attributed to supernatural causes all extraordinary phenomena like comets, earthquakes, and pestilences. Hobbes, therefore, in spirit and intention at least, was one of the pioneers of modern physical science, which has made all its advances by seeking everywhere for physical laws.

Materialism as an Explanation.—But a physical explanation cannot be accepted as final. There is indeed some kind of relation between mind and matter, and since our souls dwell in material bodies, if we ignore the laws of matter, we suffer for it. But that mind in the form of conscious will has no causal efficacy is contrary to experience, which informs us —as Hobbes' egoism implies—that forethought and deliberation produce a multitude of effects, both in the physical and also in the mental world; houses and bridges are examples of physical effects, education and social institutions, of mental effects thus produced. Conscious will is a causal agency, [1] and to attribute all active causality to matter is pure dogmatism. Without going beyond everyday experience we are forced to conclude, that though the realisation of ends by conscious will is limited or conditioned by the laws of matter, it is not altogether determined thereby. Further, since our knowledge of matter is obtained

[1] The truth is vitally important in Ethics, which was defined as involving conduct or deliberate action (p. 1).

through consciousness, it would be more reasonable to infer, as Berkeley did, that matter only exists as an object of consciousness, than that matter is the only real object. Again, any explanation, even a physical one, must conform to the laws of Reason; the principles by which we *think* of matter are not themselves material.

(*b*) *Ethical Egoism and Sensualistic Psychology.*— Hobbes' psychological analysis of the Ego is defective, in the first place, through the omission of certain elements. He ignores many pure social feelings, such as sympathy and a genuine regard for the good of others. Secondly, he is inconsistent. His sensualistic psychology regards the Ego as a mere collection of isolated phantasms, feelings, and desires, but his ethical doctrine treats the Ego as a real *substantial* and permanent *unity* of feelings, desires, and interests that are actively opposed to the feelings, desires, and interests of other Egos.

(*c*) *Egoism and Political Absolutism.* — Hobbes' Egoism regards the State as a collection of mutually exclusive units. This view conflicts with his Political Absolutism, which conceives the State as an organic structure possessing a substantial unity.[1] The mutual surrender of private interests to the will of the rulers is a practical proof that the different Egos regard exclusiveness as impossible; or, philosophically speaking, that it contradicts the idea of personality.

(*d*) *Materialism and Political Absolutism* are clearly inconsistent, since it is not possible to regard the State as a material substance existing in space.

Hobbes' inconsistencies arose from the magnitude

---

[1] Hobbes expresses this by saying that the State is a "Civil Body," different in kind from spatial bodies.

of the task he attempted, a complete synthesis of the
laws of Nature, of men, and of society.   His courage
and hopefulness express the right spirit for approach-
ing the study of philosophy—the spirit of Aristotle
and Plato, and in later times of Descartes, Spinoza,
Kant, Hegel, Comte, Spencer, and many other bold
thinkers.   And though no perfect synthesis has yet
been attained, yet every thorough attempt in this
direction tends to increase the sum of human knowledge; the very inconsistencies in a great philosophic
system, by directing critical reflection towards the
solution of problems that did not occur before,
have this effect.   In the case of Hobbes this is well
illustrated by the subsequent history of English Ethics,
the course of which was primarily determined by direct
censure or unconscious and unacknowledged appreciation of his doctrines.

B. Rationalistic Naturalism—Spinoza

The chief work of Baruch (Benedict) Spinoza [1] was
the *Ethica*, which, though mainly metaphysical and
psychological, was written with the purpose of showing
men how Well-being (*beatitudo*) [2] is to be secured.[3]
He agrees with Hobbes in teaching that the laws of
social morality are originally determined by contracts
between opposing interests; but he holds that it is
only among men of undeveloped reason that these

[1] 1632-1677 (a Jew of Amsterdam).

[2] Used by Spinoza as the Greeks used εὐδαιμονία, not in the modern
sense of " happiness " (see pp. 23, 24).

[3] I have given only a few of the ethical results of Spinoza's theories
and I have scarcely said anything about his metaphysics.   Any attempt
to give a systematic and brief account of his wonderfully planned
philosophical system would be more misleading than instructive.

laws are to be regarded as merely external adjustments between opposing forces. Among rational beings the interests of all are truly and *inwardly* identical, since Reason is everywhere at harmony with itself. Here he differs entirely from Hobbes and agrees with the Stoics. Whereas Hobbes regarded knowledge as a means used by the agent to advance his own interests without regard to those of other persons, Spinoza holds that increased knowledge abolishes the distinction between my interests and those of other rational beings.

The systems of Spinoza and Hobbes both conform to the definition of Naturalism,[1] but for very different reasons. According to Hobbes there is no *a priori* distinction between good and bad *in rerum natura*, before it is created by human beliefs and conventions; but Spinoza teaches that there are no such *a priori* distinctions, because everything that *really* exists is necessarily perfect; evil, and therefore the distinction between good and evil, is subjective illusion, due to ignorance of that which truly *is*. Well-being is therefore to be found in knowledge. The highest knowledge is the knowledge of God, Who is the one Substance embracing all reality within His own Being. Practically this doctrine resembles Stoicism, for it means that Well-being consists in the peace of mind arising from the recognition that the laws of Nature are unalterable. A man who has fully grasped this truth will not be fretful or discontented, nor will he be angry, jealous, or vindictive, for he knows that men act as they do because they cannot act otherwise.

[1] See p. 119.

Spinoza has much in common with Plato and Aristotle. With them he teaches that knowledge of the truth is intrinsically good, and that this knowledge is not a mere intellectual apprehension of the formal truth of certain propositions, but an intercourse of the soul with reality.[1]   Like the non-hedonistic Greeks he identifies personal Well-being with the exercise of virtue; it is not an external reward of virtue, but *is* the best activity of the soul. *Beatitudo non est virtutis premium sed ipsa virtus.*[2]

As a profound, accurate, and sincere thinker, Spinoza must be placed in the foremost rank. By English moralists of the period—naturalists and intuitionists alike—he has generally been hopelessly misunderstood. Hume treats him as an obscurantist; the intuitionists, if they mention him, describe him as atheistical and immoral. The latter criticisms were due to his severe treatment of the orthodox views of moral obligation and responsibility. He was also opposed to the doctrines which regarded Well-being as an external reward of virtue, holding that virtue is happiness and that vice is misery, and that the vicious man is to be pitied, not condemned. Spinoza's rejection of moral responsibility was prompted, not, as some of his critics implied, by a vicious and atheistical spirit, but by an unusually deep sympathy with the sufferings of mankind, and by a recognition of the great influence of the emotions in clouding the judgment. Only the free man, according to Spinoza, is happy, and his freedom consists in the control of his emotions by Reason. But the

[1] See p. 81, and note; also pp. 49, 55.
[2] *Ethica*, v. 42. Cf. Aristotle's definition of εὐδαιμονία (Well-being) as a perfect activity (p. 68).

earlier intuitionists use the term "freedom" in a different sense, as a power of choosing between good and bad alternatives, and they hold that the consciousness of moral obligation implies that every man is free to act rightly.

Spinoza, like the Greeks, paid but little attention to the consciousness of moral obligation. But this consciousness is too strong and universal to be ignored. Subsequent naturalists accept the consciousness as a fact, but tend to explain it as a subjective feeling having no rational object. The intuitionists, on the other hand, regard our consciousness of moral obligation as direct evidence that moral obligation is a reality, that it is not merely a phenomenon of an individual's consciousness, but an objective fact.

CHAPTER II

ENGLISH INTUITIONISM [1]

THE English intuitional systems of the seventeenth and eighteenth centuries were chiefly prompted by the desire to disprove the ethical doctrines of Hobbes. Rational Intuitionism was specially directed against his political absolutism, which seemed to imply that right and wrong are determined by an arbitrary social compact, and against his attempt to reduce religious duty to fearful obedience to a Power Who is able to enforce His arbitrary wishes by rewards and punishments. The other forms of Intuitionism attacked the Exclusive Egoism of Hobbes by showing, with varying degrees of success, that society is an organic whole— *naturally*, and not artificially, as Hobbes said; that the individual cannot think of his own good as something entirely distinct from the good of others, since he has various motives leading him deliberately to pursue the good of others, either directly or indirectly.

[1] For definitions of "Naturalism" and "Intuitionism," see p. 119 *sq*.

A. RATIONAL INTUITIONISM—CUDWORTH and CLARKE

Immutable Morality.—Ralph Cudworth,[1] the leader of the " Cambridge Platonists," in his *Treatise concerning Eternal and Immutable Morality*,[2] claims that good and evil have fixed natures independent of opinion or compacts ; moral distinctions therefore cannot be determined *arbitrarily* by the will or power of man or even of God.   Mere Will can no more turn good into evil or evil into good, than it can turn black into white.   Justice is immutable and eternal ; it is natural and not artificial, that is, its laws are inherent in the essence of things.   Though these laws may not be realised in society, they are, as ideals, absolutely reasonable.

Reason versus Sense.—In proof of this doctrine Cudworth undertakes a long hostile criticism of the " sensual empiricism "[3] of Hobbes, after the manner of Plato's attack on the empiricists of his age.   His conclusion is that Sensation gives us no knowledge of permanent reality—not even of the physical world— since it is a merely passive apprehension of particular images or phantasms, which are purely subjective and transient, existing only for the subject, and only at the moment when they are experienced.   The true objects of knowledge are universal conceptions (the Platonic Ideas), which are apprehended only by Reason. Examples of such conceptions are perfect geometrical

---

[1] 1617-1688.

[2] 1731 ; published posthumously.

[3] Sensual Empiricism is the doctrine that all our knowledge is given by sensation, and our ideas of good by immediate feelings of pleasure and pain. See pp. 86, 128, 142.

figures; the various relations used in Science, as Cause and Effect and Force; and in general the meanings of almost every word; we may, for instance, *see* the image of a house, but we do not apprehend what a house *is*, except through a general conception not presented to sense. Now Justice, Duty, and Obligation, and all ethical ideas are likewise universal conceptions, which can neither be seen, touched, nor tasted; their nature and objective excellence is apprehended only by Reason, and they are as real and eternal as the truths and ideas of Science. God is the archetypal Mind, in whom exist all the eternal ideas, both of Science and Morality.[1]

The ideas and truths of Morality, therefore, according to Cudworth, are given by the same Reason which gives us a knowledge of scientific truths; practical and speculative Reason are identical. But Reason, whether practical or speculative, Cudworth insists, is essentially *active*; it is not a mere passive and formal reception of propositions.

Rational Intuitionism was taught with further detail by Dr. Samuel Clarke[2] in his Boyle Lectures (1705). He claims that the laws of morality express the eternal " fitness " or " unfitness " of actions;[3] that God does not arbitrarily create these laws, but necessarily determines Himself to act in agreement therewith; His purpose being to establish order in the whole universe. The principles of morality are as intuitively evident to Reason as those of Mathematics,

---

[1] Cudworth urges, as an argument for the existence of God, that these ideas are real and eternal, and cannot subsist except in an eternal Mind.

[2] 1675-1729, Rector of St. James's, Westminster.

[3] " Natural," " right," " good," " reasonable," and " fit " in this connection are used by Clarke as equivalent terms.

and it is as absurd to deny the one as the other.
The immorality of barbarous nations no more proves
that morality is a matter of variable compacts than
their ignorance of mathematics proves that mathematical truths are fixed by compacts. Clarke, not
without mental confusion, sometimes describes vice
as a practical breach of the law of contradiction,
and sometimes—under the form of self-will—as "an
attempt to destroy that order by which the universe
subsists." The "original obligation of all is the
Eternal Reason of things," which necessarily determines
the judgment, but not actions.

Particular duties, according to Clarke, may be
deduced from certain fundamental "Rules of Righteousness," known intuitively as eternally right, fit, and
natural,[1] and requiring no support outside themselves.
The three more general of these axioms relate to God,
our fellow-men, and ourselves. The first requires us
to honour and worship the Deity, and to obey His will,
not because He has power, but because He is good,
and knows the best means of realising the welfare
of the Universe. The second Rule of Righteousness
contains two parts: (a) The Rule of Equity, requires
"that we so deal with every man as in like circumstances we could reasonably expect that he should
deal with us"; (b) The Rule of Love or Universal
Benevolence, "that in general we endeavour by an
universal benevolence to promote the welfare and

---

[1] Clarke seems to have been influenced by a remark of John Locke's
(*Essay*, Bk. IV.), that "morality is capable of demonstration as well as
mathematics"; Locke probably got the idea from Spinoza, who worked
it out in his *Ethica*, following, no doubt, the suggestion of Descartes as
to the possibility of constructing a system of general philosophy on axioms
and reasonings as exact and certain as those on which mathematics was
supposed to be built.

happiness of all men." The third Rule of Righteousness requires that " every man preserve his own being
as long as he is able," and keep his mind and body
fit for the performance of his duty; hence follow
the obligations to temperance, industry, and content-
ment.

The " reason " for the Rule of Equity is " whatever
I judge reasonable or unreasonable for another to do
for me, that by the same judgment I declare reasonable
or unreasonable that I in like case should do for him."
Differences of relation, however, must be taken into
account; the magistrate, for example, is " not to
consider what fear or self love would cause the
criminal to desire, but what reason and public good
would oblige him to acknowledge was fit and just for
him to expect."

The doctrines of Cudworth and Clarke are, of
course, open to the criticism—to which many ethical
systems are liable—that they give little information
about the concrete nature of the good. To say that
right action is reasonable or natural, appears at first
sight to mean little more than that it is reasonable
and natural to do what is right. But the valuable
element in these systems is their insistence on the
impartiality or disinterestedness of right action, and
the consequent inadequacy of Exclusive Egoism. This
is clearly seen in Clarke's Rule of Equity. Their desire
to enforce this truth explains why they were constantly
asserting that moral and scientific truths have the same
rational characteristic; they wished to show that all
truths are universal and objective, and that they are
not created by arbitrary will. This idea of the
universality of moral truth connects Kant's Ethics

with the earlier English Rationalists, and, through the latter, with Plato and Aristotle.

Cudworth and Clarke rashly identified practical and speculative Reason without giving just grounds for so doing; that is to say they regarded the ideals of Ethics (*e.g.* Justice) and the Ideas or concepts of external Nature (*e.g.* Cause and Effect, Quantity, etc.) as objects of Reason in the same sense.[1] Kant, with greater caution and more insight, distinguishes between practical and speculative Reason, so far as human life is concerned.

The Rational Intuitionists' criticism of Hobbes is not altogether fair to that bold thinker; they represent him as saying that the distinction between good and bad is *invented* by human compacts, whereas he really meant that unswerving loyalty to such compacts is the best way for each individual to secure his own good, which is in no sense an arbitrary fiction. The "Laws of Nature," Hobbes insists, are "immutable and eternal."[2] As we have seen, the real defect in Hobbes' Ethics was the supposition that each individual necessarily pursues the gratification of his own desires, and that he identifies that gratification with the enjoyment of pleasure or the preservation of his own physical life. The criticisms of subsequent Intuitionists were specially directed against this aspect of Hobbes' philosophy.

B. Aesthetic Intuitionism

Aesthetic Intuitionism, as represented by Shaftesbury and Hutcheson, is characterised by the fact that

---

[1] Cf. Plato, pp. 52 *sq.*, 57.   [2] p. 134.

it attributes our knowledge of moral distinctions to a special practical faculty, the "moral sense," which is affected by the moral qualities of actions just as the sense of beauty is affected by the beauty in objects, and as our bodily senses are affected by the physical qualities of objects. This doctrine is partly a reaction against Rational Intuitionism, with which, however, it agrees in recognising that moral distinctions are objective, and that Hobbism is a pernicious theory. "Moral sense" was regarded, especially by Hutcheson, as a *via media* between Exclusive Egoism and the doctrine that abstract and formal Reason can influence our actions.

All the earlier English Intuitionists hold that there is no insuperable opposition between self-love and the actions prompted by a regard for virtue. Shaftesbury endeavoured to show that in the present life virtue and happiness are perfectly coincident ; the others held that the discords of the present life will be removed in the next world.

Shaftesbury.

The system of Shaftesbury [1] may be considered under three headings. First, influenced by the Rational Intuitionists, he endeavours to define the Idea of the Good after the manner of Plato; secondly, he describes the source of our knowledge of right and wrong ; thirdly, he endeavours to prove from experience that private and social morality are inseparable from happiness in the present life.

(1) *The Nature of Good.*—The goodness of any-

[1] Antony Ashley Cooper, 1671-1713, third Earl of Shaftesbury.

thing is not an attribute belonging to itself alone, but it is determined through its relation to a wider whole or system. A part of a system is good when it is properly fitted to its place in the system of which it is a part. The good of a species is higher than the good of any one individual of the species; it may therefore be good, for example, for a mother to sacrifice herself for her offspring, in order that the species may be preserved. As applied to man, this doctrine means that virtue consists in a disposition of the affections good for the whole species, and aiming directly at that good. Thus " public interest " becomes the final standard of right and wrong.[1]

(2) *The Source of Moral Knowledge.*—The intrinsic excellence of Virtue is apprehended by " moral sense," which leads us to love good affections, just as the sense of beauty leads us to love beauty. In fact, moral goodness is beauty in the sphere of the affections, for it implies a harmony or fitness of parts within a whole. Through moral sense we love the forms of Justice and Temperance, when we know what they mean.[2] No one is virtuous unless he loves virtue for its own sake. Fear of future punishment or hope of rewards can no more make a man virtuous than chaining a tiger can make it trustworthy.

(3) *Virtue and Happiness.*—Though Virtue is intrinsically lovable, it is expedient to prove that it agrees entirely with self-interest; Shaftesbury even appears to believe that the obligation to follow virtue

---

[1] This doctrine is in some degree a connecting link between Plato's teaching (pp. 62, 63)—that the order of the Universe is the End—and Utilitarianism.

[2] This doctrine is thus complementary to Rational Intuitionism and not opposed thereto ; we must *know* what Justice is, and when we know it we love it. Cf. Plato (p. 47)

can only arise from our conviction that there is such an agreement. "To be wicked and vicious is to be miserable and unhappy." This is proved by following out the idea that virtue is a harmony within "the system of the affections," and that sentient happiness results from this harmony. The affections are either (a) the "natural" affections (e.g. love of society, parental kindness) tending directly to public good; (b) the "self-affections" (e.g. resentment and love of life) which aim directly at private good only; and (c) unnatural affections (e.g. cruelty) which are wholly bad.

The virtuous man possesses public and private affections in due degree, and his own happiness results from this. But Shaftesbury deems it more important to prove that a lack of public affections, and an excess of private affections, lead to misery, than that the opposite extremes, which are not likely to occur, produce the same effect. To have the public affections strong is to have the chief means of self-enjoyment; social converse, the exercise of generosity, and gratitude, are rich sources of pleasure to the agent; and pleasure is also communicated by sympathy. Again, excess of any kind of affection is unpleasant; an exaggerated love of life creates a painful state of fear, and leads one to overlook that life in certain circumstances may not be worth living. Excess in resentment and appetite lead respectively to revengefulness and sensual cravings, and both of these are painful states of mind. The satisfaction of anger is not a positive pleasure, but a mere relief from torture. By using these and like arguments, Shaftesbury concludes that "the Wisdom of what rules and is first and chief in Nature has made it to be according to the private interest and good of everyone to work towards the general good."

Shaftesbury's system may be summarily described as a attempt to prove by empirical observations, and from a hedonistic standpoint, that Plato's conception of social Justice—which "moral sense" informs us is the highest good—is altogether coincident with Justice as realised in the individual soul.[1] But the proof is naïvely optimistic, as the intelligent reader will see. Besides, Shaftesbury does not establish a real identity between public and private good; the opposition between these as motives of action still remains, and the idea of moral obligation has not yet been clearly analysed. The doctrine is not a real answer to Exclusive Egoism, but only to the artificial social psychology of Hobbes, who tried to reduce social affection to forms of self-affection. Shaftesbury points out that social and moral affections are direct sources of pleasure apart from considerations of self-interest; but he fails to recognise that the immediate gratification of social feelings, even of sympathy, may be purely egoistic, if not accompanied by the consciousness that the good of another is my good.

Hutcheson.

Moral Sense.—Francis Hutcheson [2] develops Shaftesbury's theory of moral sense, and in his most im-

[1] See Plato, *loc. cit.* Plato's defence of Justice was not hedonistic ; Justice (individual or social) is good in itself, and the rulers must sacrifice their private pleasures for the sake of the state.

[2] 1694-1747, born in Ireland, a schoolmaster in Dublin, afterwards Professor of Moral Philosophy in Glasgow.

portant work (*System of Moral Philosophy*, 1755) he
was also influenced by Butler's doctrine of Conscience.
He insists that the moral sense is affected by *objective*
distinctions—so far agreeing with the Rational
Intuitionists—and compares it in this respect with
the aesthetic sense: " As in approving a beautiful
form we refer the beauty to its object; we do not
say that it is beautiful because we reap some little
pleasure in viewing it, but we are pleased in viewing
it because it is antecedently beautiful," so, "when we
admire the virtue of another we are pleased in the
contemplation because the object is excellent, and
the object is not judged to be therefore excellent
because it gives us pleasure." In the same spirit he
rejects Hume's teaching that moral distinctions arise
from education, custom, and the subjective associations
of ideas and feelings of pleasure and pain, for he
holds that these factors cannot produce *new* ideas
like those of morality.[1] Hutcheson admits that
moral sense does not give an unconditional knowledge
of its objects; like the sense of beauty and other
perceptions, it improves with wider experience[2]—a
fact which explains the difference between moral
standards in different nations and in different periods
of history.

The Three " Calm Determinations." — Hutcheson
agrees with Hume[3] in teaching, in opposition to the
Rational Intuitionists, that Reason is purely theoretical;
at the most it can only direct to means or compare two

---

[1] This doctrine is partly due to Locke, who asserts that all simple
irreducible ideas are given by Sense, whether inward or outward.

[2] See Aristotle, p. 72.

[3] See Chap. IV. The anti-rationalism in Hutcheson's *System* was
probably due to the influence of Hume, whose *Treatise* was published in
1739-40.

ends, but it does not *per se* provide motives to action.
The Will, so far as it acts deliberately, is determined
to action by Self-love, Benevolence, or Moral Sense.
Of these three "calm determinations" Nature unites
the last two, but Religion alone[1] renders the three
harmonious. The germs of Utilitarianism are to be
found in Hutcheson; the objects of the moral sense
are indeed affections of the will, but they agree in the
general character of "tending to the happiness of
others and the moral perfection of the mind possessing
them." Moral perfection consists apparently in a
constant desire to produce such happiness:—"When
the moral sense is in its full vigour it makes the
generous determination to public happiness the supreme
one in the soul." The end which the Deity has in
view is to produce the "greatest sum of universal
happiness," and He has given us the moral sense as
the source of our approval of this end and to make
us work for it.

Hutcheson's description of moral sense is inconsistent
and wavering. He gives it various names—"perception," "taste," "instinct"—all suggesting that it
is a merely passive faculty, capable of being affected
by objects external to the soul. But he also regards
it as equivalent to moral approbation, which, since it
expresses a judgment, is more than a mere feeling or
sense, and involves a rational or cognitive element.
A judgment is always about an object, or about an
action regarded as objective. It is one thing to
feel and act instinctively as the feeling prompts,
and another thing to *judge* that this action is good
or bad and *ought* to be done. Influenced, no doubt,

[1] Here Hutcheson differs from Shaftesbury and agrees with Butler.

by Butler, he speaks of its "commanding nature," but he fails to make it clear whether it has supreme authority over all our actions; indeed a special sense could not have such authority.   It will be seen in Chapter III. that Butler describes conscience—which corresponds in some degree to moral sense—in terms which make it impossible to regard it as a merely passive feeling; it is the authoritative voice of the true inward self, *passing judgment* on its own actions and on those of other persons; it is not an artificial "taste" attached to certain actions by the Deity; it is indeed the voice of God, but His voice speaking, not *to* the soul, but *from* the soul.

There is nevertheless a permanent truth in the "moral sense" theory of Shaftesbury and Hutcheson. In all judgment as to the goodness or badness of a particular end there is an intuitive or immediate element involved.   Even if the worth or particular ends were always judged by general principles, this would be the case; the highest general principles must be accepted intuitively, since *qua* highest, they are not further reducible;   this was recognised by the Rational Intuitionists, especially Clarke.   But the necessity for an intuitive judgment, which, indeed, is often unreliable, is still more conspicuous in practical life, in those numerous cases where careful reflection is impossible.   Further, the direct apprehension or enjoyment of any particular good, whether it be pleasure or mental activity or anything else, is an intuitive act.   Good is *for* personal consciousness.   The very idea of "good"—something satisfying in itself—implies that it must sooner or later be directly apprehended as a source of immediate satisfaction either to one

person or to several. From this point of view the
moral sense theory may be regarded historically as a
reaction against the error, to which Cudworth was
especially liable, that good is merely an abstract
universal, which is never apprehended in particular
concrete experiences.

C. SYMPATHETIC INTUITIONISM

Adam Smith [1] recognises that moral judgments are
impartial; we apply to ourselves the same standards
as we apply to others. He describes the psychological
process through which this takes place as follows.
Our first moral criticisms are passed on the characters
and conduct of other people according to the way in
which we are directly affected. To approve of the
conduct of another is, primarily, to sympathise with
the motives or affections from which it proceeds.
But we soon learn that other people criticise our conduct,
and sympathy then compels us to judge ourselves by
the same standard. Approval or disapproval of our
own actions is thus possible only in society. But it
is not dependent on the criticisms of any particular
person. Through frequent intercourse with others,
we form the general idea of an imaginary " impartial
spectator" who passes judgment on our own actions.
This imaginary spectator is a kind of " second self,"
whose judgments influence our actions by the force of
sympathy. In criticising my own conduct " I divide
myself, as it were, into two persons," the imaginary
spectator who is the judge, and the agent who is

[1] 1723-1790, a professor at Glasgow; author of the *Wealth of
Nations*.

judged.   The judge is described by Smith as the "man within the breast," or "conscience."   He has to be kept awake by frequent intercourse with the "man without the breast," that is, with particular persons. He is only a "demi-god," and is liable to error; he is set up by Nature, and his verdicts are subject to the higher tribunal of the Judge of all the world.

There is a good deal of inconsistency in Smith's treatment of this subject.   At first sight his method seems to be a naturalistic attempt to derive morality from sympathy after the manner of Hume,[1] to whom he owes much.   And are we to infer that the "impartial spectator"—who appears to be a representative of the rest of society—imposes on us the impossible task of adjusting our conduct to the feelings of every one we meet? If sympathy were the infallible guide, the magistrate would be equally justified in releasing or in punishing a convicted criminal.   In the one case, he would act from sympathy with the criminal, and with those who desired his release; in the other case he would act from sympathy with the rest of society.

Smith, however, was really an Intuitionist.   Like Hutcheson, he taught that the Creator aims at the maximum quantity of happiness; to secure this end He delegates His authority to "the demi-god within the breast," who judges our conduct according as it agrees or disagrees with our intuitive perceptions of virtue and vice.   It is thus "moral sense" combined with self-judgment.   In emphasising the idea of self-judgment, Smith's doctrine is superior to Hutcheson's,

[1] Hume's *Treatise* was published in 1739 (see next note).   Probably Hume and Smith influenced each other.

and more akin to Butler's.[1]   The "man within the breast" does not seek the praise of others, but what is worthy of their praise.   He is not a mere representative of the feelings of other persons, but is the better or true *self*, stimulated, but not controlled, by the criticisms of others.   It is therefore not fair to interpret Smith as deriving morality from sympathy, though, as we have seen, his language leaves him open to the charge of inconsistency; he confounds the naturalistic and intuitional methods in Ethics, and divides himself "as it were into two persons."   What he really effected was to give a psychological explanation of the force which conscience is able to exert by means of sympathy.   But he did not appear to recognise that sympathy can only have a right effect in a community of persons of fully developed moral sense.   The judgment of another should only influence my actions so far as I recognise it as objectively right.   Though the feelings of others have to be considered, the final verdict must be given by our own inward consciousness of what is right. This point is brought out clearly by Butler.

[1] It should be remembered that Smith's *Theory of Moral Sentiment* was published in 1759, Hutcheson's *System* in 1755, and Butler's *Sermons on Human Nature* in 1726.

CHAPTER III

D. AUTONOMIC INTUITIONISM—BUTLER

Method.—The most famous and the most practically profound of the eighteenth century English Intuitionists was Joseph Butler.[1]   Though he admits the validity of the *a priori* rational method of Clarke, his own method is chiefly inductive; he wishes to base pure Ethics—so far as it can be considered without reference to revealed religion—on the observed facts of human nature.   In addition to facts given by observation he uses the principles that the end for which man is intended can be discovered from such observed facts, and that his true happiness will be found in working towards that end.[2]   Butler holds that observation, when directed inwards by

---

[1] 1692-1752.   Bishop of Bristol 1738, of Durham 1750.   The substance of his purely ethical doctrines is to be found in his *Sermons on Human Nature* (1726, preached in the Rolls Chapel, London) and the *Dissertation on the Nature of Virtue.*   The quotations in this chapter are from the *Sermons* unless otherwise stated.

[2] In the *Sermons*, which do not form a systematic philosophical work, Butler does not clearly exhibit the grounds for assuming these principles. But he appears to base them tacitly on the postulate that the Author of Nature is intelligent, since He adapts means to ends, and benevolent, since He instructs man as to the actions which he is intended to perform, and allows him to attain happiness in performing them.

reflection, proves that the nature of man is not merely that of a being who commonly acts according to certain laws, but rather that of one who *ought* to act according to certain ideal principles, whether he does or not. The consciousness of moral obligation is a fact of human nature, and this consciousness is conclusive evidence that moral obligation is an objective reality.

Butler owes much to Shaftesbury, especially the doctrine that society is *naturally* an organic whole or system, whose parts cannot work separately. He thus rejects the Hobbist view that society is merely the product of artificial compacts between self-seeking units. But he differs from Shaftesbury in the stress which he lays on moral obligation——which he generally regards as having higher authority than self-love, ——and in refusing to admit that social and private happiness are altogether harmonious in the present life.[1] At the same time he allows that there is less opposition between present and future happiness than is commonly believed.

The Social Nature of Man.——Hobbes taught that society is a mechanical adjustment arising from compacts between individuals who are not naturally adapted to an organised social life. In opposition to this Butler argues that if each individual acted according to his true nature, society would become a perfect organic structure, with its parts working in harmony for the good of the whole. " There are as real and the same kind of indications in human nature that we were made for society and to do good to our fellow-creatures, as that we were intended to

[1] See p. 154 *sq.*

take care of our own life and health and private good." [1]
There are three distinct lines of proof of this proposition. First, there is a natural principle of
Benevolence in man, which aims *directly* at the good
of others and finds its satisfaction only in attaining
that good. It expresses itself, for example, in friendship, compassion, paternal and filial affection, and it
is essentially *disinterested*, seeking the good of another,
just as Self-love seeks the good of self. These observations are particularly directed against Hobbes, who
tried to reduce such affections to interested motives.
Secondly, there are certain passions and affections in
man—distinct both from Benevolence and Self-love,
and contributing just as much to public as to private
good. Examples of these are, the desire of esteem,
contempt and esteem of others, love of society, and
indignation against successful vice. These are called
public affections or passions, since they work towards
social harmony. They differ from Benevolence in not
seeking directly the good of others, and from Self-love
in not seeking directly the good of self; they aim
directly at the attainment of certain definite objects,
but indirectly they tend to increase the general
happiness. The love of society, for example, is not
a desire for the happiness of others, nor a desire for
the agent's own happiness; it is a natural interest in
a particular kind of activity, but its satisfaction in
due degree is indirectly beneficial to others as well
as to the agent. Thirdly, Conscience, or the " principle
of reflection," by which a man " approves or disapproves
his heart, temper, and actions," urges men to public
good as much as to private, and may compensate for

---

[1] In this discussion " good " means almost the same as " happiness."

the want of spontaneous benevolence. Duty, for
example, may cause a man to relieve distress where
the sentiment of compassion might be too weak.

These, with other observations, prove that mankind
is a corporate organism, not a mere collection of
individuals, and that it is not possible for any one
to distinguish sharply between his own interests and
those of society. Some, indeed, want natural social
affections, but in like manner some want natural
regard for their *own* interests. The normal nature of
man is not to be judged by the exceptions.

The Moral Nature of Man.—The Stoics made
virtue to consist in following nature, and St. Paul
said, " the Gentiles do by *nature* the things contained
in the law." Butler accepts this view in the sense
intended, but points out that the word " nature," as
applied to human actions, may have three different
meanings. First, any human motive of action may
be called natural, whether anger, affection, or any
other ; in this sense two natural tendencies may contradict each other. Secondly, the strongest passions
are sometimes called natural, but by this interpretation, man is *vicious* by nature, since the strongest
passions are usually immoderate. Thirdly, by man's
nature we may mean that principle in man which
has the highest *authority*, though that authority be
not always effectual ; this is Conscience. " There is
a superior principle of reflection or conscience in
every man, which distinguishes between the internal
principles of his heart, as well as his external actions ;
which passes judgment upon himself and them ; pro-
nounces determinately some actions to be in themselves just, right, good ; others to be in themselves

evil, wrong, unjust; which without being consulted,
without being advised with, magisterially exerts itself,
and approves or condemns him the doer of them accordingly; and which, if not forcibly stopped, naturally
and always of course, goes on to anticipate a higher
and more effectual sentence, which shall hereafter
second and affirm its own." Thus Conscience has
a natural supremacy, not of strength but of authority,
and actions in obedience thereto are in the highest
and most proper sense natural. Conscience provides
us with a rule of right and puts us under a direct
obligation to obey it.

Man is a Law to Himself.—The obligation to obey
Conscience is not imposed from without, but from
within; it is by this faculty that man is "*a law to
himself.*"[1] It does not require to give evidence of
its claim to supremacy, for "it carries its own
authority with it that it is our natural guide, the
guide assigned to us by the Author of our nature."
Butler speaks of Conscience as a "faculty," but,
strictly speaking, it is the man himself regarded as a
moral agent. It is this inwardness that distinguishes
Conscience from the "moral sense" of Hutcheson,
which, as its name implies, is a faculty by which we
get information from without. Conscience, in fact, is
the "true self" which Aristotle identifies with Reason.[2]

Human Nature a System.—Butler's conception of
the human soul is very similar to Plato's in the
Republic,[3] and he likewise compares it to a civil
constitution. For as the idea of a civil constitution

---

[1] On this account I have called Butler's Intuitionism "Autonomic."
"Autonomy" means "self-legislation."

[2] Compare Butler's doctrine with Aristotle's, p. 77.

[3] Cf. p. 46 *sq.*

implies that each citizen and each part of the State have their special functions, and all are rightfully subordinate to the central government, so the idea of human nature consists in this, that all passions and affections have their due right to gratification within the limits prescribed by the supreme authority of Conscience. The conception of human nature has thus become less abstract; Conscience is now conceived as the regulative principle that *ought* to secure a harmony between the concrete active principles of our nature. This harmony is to be attained by seeing that all these active principles (compassion, self-love, resentment, etc.) are exercised in such a way that they will promote, and not oppose, the end for which they have been given to us.

The System of Active Principles.—The doctrine that human nature is a system under the authority of Conscience implies that all the elements of that nature have a special function ; they have individual rights and duties as members of the State of which Conscience is the supreme ruler. The active principles are divided by Butler into the following classes: (1) *Particular appetites, passions, and affections*, which aim at special objects appropriate to them, and in which they find satisfaction. Thus the object of hunger is food; of compassion, the relief of the sufferer's pain; of resentment, to hurt the offender. Butler, in opposition to Hobbes, insists that these active principles are not forms of Self-love; by this he means that they do not aim either at immediate pleasure or at the permanent happiness of self,[1] with both of which

---

[1] This may be regarded as Butler's criticism of Psychological Hedonism (the doctrine that all desire is for pleasure).

they may conflict. The importance, in Butler's Ethics, of this principle is due to the support which it gives to his doctrine that a regard for the good of others (Benevolence) is an active principle in human nature; it is no more extraordinary than hunger or resentment, since, like these, it finds satisfaction in its appropriate object, viz. the welfare of others. (2) *Self-love* is a deliberate and regulative principle of action, seeking the permanent happiness of self. It differs from the *particular* affections, etc., just mentioned, in pursuing a general enjoyment extending through the whole life. It uses particular active principles as a means to secure this end. As a co-ordinating and harmonising principle it has naturally, so long as it is reasonable, an authority higher than any special affection. Self-love is unreasonable and contradicts its own end when it allows some particular passions to destroy the general harmony which is essential to permanent happiness. (3) *Conscience*, or the "principle of reflection," is, like Self-love, a deliberate and regulative principle of action, but it possesses supreme authority. It delegates its authority to the other principles, especially to reasonable Self-love. It also enjoins special duties to society, which may not be directly enjoined by Self-love. While conscience has supreme authority over particular affections and impulses, it is nevertheless dependent on them, for "Reason alone [*i.e.* Conscience] is not in reality a sufficient motive of virtue in such a creature as man"; it is only directive, and cannot by itself always exert a force proportional to its authority. On this account it has to ally itself with the affections and to encourage their cultivation in an appropriate degree. In fact it balances them against each other, having enough weight to turn the scales in its own favour. Hence both Self-love and Conscience are opposed to asceticism; the former because happiness consists in the normal satisfaction of desires; the latter because it is right that desires should be normally gratified, and because affections, when properly cultivated, tend to regulate each other.

Applications.—The functions of some " particular affections and passions " are considered from the point of view just mentioned. Butler now constantly uses a teleological method, *i.e.* he inquires into the natural end or purpose of these affections or passions. These ends are to be determined by their observed effects—on the agent or on others—of their normal exercise. Such exercise is then justified by showing that all the particular ends harmonise with the general ethical end, viz. the increase of the happiness of the agent and of the rest of society, in accordance with the principles enjoined by Conscience.

Butler pays special attention to *compassion* and *resentment*. The final cause of compassion is to relieve and prevent suffering, in cases where Reason alone would not be a strong enough motive for action. To the objection that compassion really increases pain by transmitting it, Butler replies that normal or natural compassion is only just painful enough to stimulate our active help, and that excessive compassion, being both unnatural and ineffectual, should be discouraged. Moderate compassion is moreover inseparable from that gentleness of heart and delicacy of sentiment which are essential to the full enjoyment of the pleasures of life. On the whole it increases the happiness of society, even when the apparently superfluous transmitted suffering is taken into account.

Resentment has the peculiar characteristic that its gratification necessarily involves the suffering of others, and this gives special importance to the question, what is its function in human nature ? Resentment is of two kinds, *sudden* and *deliberate*. The final cause of the former is the protection of self against sudden physical harm inflicted by others either accidentally or deliberately ; it makes no inquiry into motives, being only a form of the self-protecting instinct of all living creatures.   Deliberate resentment, on the other hand, is directed against *intentional* injury either to the self or to other persons.   Its final cause is to prevent and remedy injury, and the consequent miseries, by inflicting just punishment on the offender ; it thus prevents mutual aggression and co-operates with justice.   Resentment is quite consistent with good-will and forgiveness of injuries, since in its natural exercise it will not seek to inflict more pain than is required to prevent or remedy the offence.   A careful check should be kept on resentment, which tends to propagate itself and so to defeat its own end, the increase of general happiness.   No degree of resentment should destroy our benevolence.

Any further consideration of Butler's applied ethics would lead into natural and revealed religion.   He holds that the present life is only a state of probation for a future one, and that our business here is "improvement in virtue and piety, as the requisite qualification for a future state of security and happiness." [1]

----

[1] *Analogy* I, v.

Conscience and Reasonable Self-love.—Though the inward law of Conscience is obligatory, it is, on the whole, in conformity with the law of Self-love. Both require the subordination of violent passions, and the exercise of benevolent and other social affections. This doctrine shows the influence of Shaftesbury,[1] who asserts that there is a perfect harmony between virtue and self-interest in the present life. Butler, however, while admitting that duty and interest are " for the most part " coincident in this life, holds that the harmony may not be complete unless the future life is taken into account. Meanwhile we are under a strict obligation to obey Conscience, " even upon supposition that the prospect of a future life were ever so uncertain." This emphasis on a moral obligation that transcends self-interest in the present life is the chief distinction between Shaftesbury's Ethics and Butler's. At the same time Butler is forced to admit that " though virtue or moral rectitude does indeed consist in affection to, and pursuit of, what is right and good, as such ; yet when we sit down in a cool hour, we can neither justify to ourselves this or any other pursuit till we are convinced that it will be for our happiness, or at least not contrary to it." It appears, then, that Conscience must be regarded in some sense as a guide to general happiness in which our own is included by the arrangement of a beneficent Creator.

CRITICISM

In Butler's Ethics we find that the two following principles are constantly in opposition :—

[1] pp. 154, 155.

(1) Conscience is the supreme inward lawgiver in human nature; its commands ought to have prior authority to those of Self-love, if there should happen to be any conflict between them. It follows that virtue of character and conduct is, as the Stoics said, of the highest worth, and better than the greatest conceivable quantity of pleasure.

(2) Man cannot reasonably justify to himself any actions contrary to his own permanent interests. This being admitted, the supremacy of Conscience must yield to that of Self-love if there is a conflict, and the supreme authority of Conscience is destroyed. Here Butler follows Shaftesbury, who, in turn, unconsciously follows Hobbes in regarding self-interest as the only possible ultimate and rational motive of action. The existence of sympathetic and philanthropic tastes does not—as Shaftesbury and Butler seemed to think—affect the question of ultimate motive.

The above contradiction would disappear if it could be shown, first, that the actions approved by Self-love and Conscience are *necessarily* coincident, and, secondly, that they are really identical motives. To both of these propositions Butler assents; in the third Sermon he says: "Duty and interest are perfectly coincident, for the most part in this world, but entirely and in every instance if we take in the future, and the whole; for this is implied in the notion of a good and perfect administration of things." As regards the second, he says [1] that "veracity, justice, and charity, regard to God's authority and to our own chief interest, are not only all three coincident, but each of them is, in itself, a just and natural motive or principle of action." He

[1] *Analogy*, Part I. chap. v.

has not however proved this coincidence from the observation of the inward nature of man, but has deduced it from the theological principle that a benevolent, all-powerful Creator could not have given such natural strength to both Conscience and Self-love if He did not mean them to be harmonious both in motive and effect. On the other hand, how are we to reconcile the identification of Self-love and Conscience with Butler's teaching that "ill-desert" has a real meaning, that moral wrong *per se* deserves punishment apart from the curative effects of the penalty? It is superfluous, if not meaningless, to say that imprudence (a disregard for our own interests) *ought* to be punished, if its viciousness consists in nothing but the fact that it *will* be punished in the natural course of events.

Butler's system was really eclectic; a fact which explains many of his inconsistencies. He strove to combine the teleology of Aristotle and the nature-theory of Stoics with Christian Theism, Egoism with moral Purism,[1] Platonism with Hedonism, and all of these with conventional theories of morality. Moral Purism, however, admits no rival; it must either rule or be banished. Kant showed this by exhibiting its true form in the most uncompromising manner.

Relation of Butler to the Greeks.—The "idea of human nature" is the same as Plato's "Justice in the individual," and the Shaftesbury-Butler conception of society as an organised system is a generalisation—familiar to the Stoics—of Plato's conception of social

[1] By moral Purism I mean the doctrine that a regard for duty and a regard for own chief interest are two entirely distinct motives (though their effects may ultimately coincide), and that the former *ought* to regulate our actions in every instance (see chap. v.).

Justice.[1] Doubtless Shaftesbury and Butler were influenced by the Platonist, Cudworth, who had a profound knowledge of Greek philosophy. Butler himself regards his doctrine of conscience as equivalent to the Stoic teaching that virtue consists in following nature, and the kernel of this doctrine is to be found in Aristotle's identification—to which I have already referred—of the "true self" with the moral self or Reason.[2]

It is however worthy of note that Butler's conception of the relation between the soul and its Well-being is in one respect quite different from, and inferior to Aristotle's. When Aristotle said that the true self is Reason, he meant that rational activity is Well-being. Butler, on the other hand, distinguishes between right action and its rewards; like other eighteenth-century intuitionists, he uses theological principles to remove the apparent opposition between virtue and happiness (a life of pleasure). According to Aristotle, Well-being, which he does not identify with the passive enjoyment of pleasures,[3] is the perfect activity of the soul. Butler's language would lead us to infer that Well-being is something external to that activity; that it is a reward (happiness) bestowed by the Creator on those who exercise their faculties in the way for which they were intended. So long as this view is taken, either the opposition between duty and self-interest must remain, or one of them must be excluded as an ultimate motive.

Individualism and Responsibility.—The best results of English Intuitionism are to be found in Butler.

[1] Plato had already effected this generalisation, and indeed he regarded the whole universe as an organised system (pp. 62, 63).
[2] p. 77.   [3] Cf. pp. 77, 78.

He recognised and partially solved the most important ethical problem of his age—to reconcile individualism with moral responsibility. He taught that the individual has a right to pursue his own highest Well-being, and that he has the right freely to judge and to determine his own conduct. He saw that those rights involve responsibility to society, of which the individual is in his very nature an integral part. We have seen, however, that his solution of the problem was incomplete and inconsistent. The inconsistency was due to the vain attempt to reconcile Hedonism with moral Purism. He implicitly identifies personal Well-being—the end sought by Self-love—with pleasure; and, as we shall see, no consistent philosophy of ethics can be based on this assumption

CHAPTER IV

THE problems discussed by the Intuitionists were treated by David Hume [1] by the naturalistic method, which, while accepting as psychological facts the ordinary moral judgments and feelings, endeavours to explain them as being the effects of natural laws having originally no moral significance. [2] This method is concerned more with describing and analysing moral beliefs than with the intuitionist's problem of determining the *true* nature of the good, and the rational ground of moral obligation. It resembles the method of the physical sciences, for it seeks to determine some of the laws according to which men act, rather than the laws according to which they *ought* to act. Hume's psychology was superior to that of Hobbes, for he was able to use the results obtained by the intuitionists; thus he accepts without dispute the existence and operation of social feelings and sympathies, and of the consciousness of moral obligation. He regards our moral beliefs as complicated products of self-interest, custom, and sympathy. On the whole he tends to treat sympathy [3] as the

---

[1] 1711-1776, born at Edinburgh. [2] See p. 119 *sq.*
[3] By sympathy Hume meant pleasure or pain arising directly from the consciousness that another person is pleased or pained.

ultimate source of our feelings of social obligation, and for this reason his system may be described as "sympathetic naturalism." The phrase emphasises the chief distinction between his system and that of Hobbes. Like Hobbes, he discusses all philosophical problems with the free and independent spirit which characterises the best types of Naturalism. The following account of Hume's theories is derived chiefly from his *Treatise on Human Nature*.[1]

Impressionism.—Hume, following Bacon and Locke, held that all our knowledge is derived from experience, and that this experience consists either of impressions received by the senses from external objects, or of ideas, which are "copies" of impressions, and differ from them only in being weaker and less lively. Reason only combines ideas but gives no knowledge of reality. Feelings or passions are "secondary impressions." They arise either directly or indirectly from pleasure and pain, and are the motives of all our voluntary actions. This "impressionism" colours Hume's Ethics as well as his psychology, and is the chief defect in both. It leads him to the conclusion —which makes fictitious the ideas of personal knowledge and personal good—that the Ego is merely a "bundle" of impressions and feelings, possessing no real unity.

Morals a Science.—Hume insists that morality is capable of scientific treatment, since characters, as well as material systems, are subject to uniform laws which may be ascertained by observation.

Reason and Passion.—Passion,[2] and not Reason,

[1] 1739.

[2] "Passion" is here equivalent to what is now usually called "feeling."

is the source of voluntary actions, for Reason only combines and compares ideas, and tells us of truth and falsehood.[1] "We speak not strictly when we talk of the combat of passion and of reason. Reason is and ought only to be the slave of the passions, and can never pretend to any other office than to serve and obey them." "'Tis not contrary to reason to prefer the destruction of the whole world to the scratching of my finger. 'Tis not contrary to reason for me to chuse my total ruin to prevent the least uneasiness of an Indian or person wholly unknown to me; 'tis as little contrary to reason to prefer even my own acknowledged lesser good to my greater." This is opposed not only to Rationalism, but also to the doctrine of Hobbes that only Exclusive Egoism is reasonable. Hume holds that the proper contrast is between calm passions and violent. He admits, however, that "Reason and judgment may be the mediate cause of an action by prompting or by directing a passion," but he means that Reason is here used as a passive instrument by some passion desirous of satisfying itself. Reason is also useful in Ethics because it helps, by comparison of individual instances, to determine the real motives of action.

In the preceding criticisms, Hume appears to regard Reason as the faculty of grasping the meaning of general principles and of deducing correct conclusions from them. The question is whether Reason is also the original source of our knowledge of the truth and falsity of such principles, or whether it is only an instrument for retaining them in the mind and deducing their consequences; in other words, can we

[1] A criticism of the Rational Intuitionists. (See p. 148 sq.)

ever directly cognise the truth or falsity of a general
proposition as soon as we know what it means ?   The
passages just quoted express the views of the English
empirical school (Bacon, Locke, Hume, Mill), on this
question.   The empiricists teach that our knowledge
of general principles is not direct, but derived by
induction from particular sensible and emotional experiences; the function of Reason is therefore only
to co-ordinate and to retain, not to discover; it can
test the correctness of *inferences* from premisses, but
it cannot guarantee the truth of those premisses.[1]
The Rational Intuitionists, following Plato, hold the
opposite view, namely, that there are general propositions—*e.g.*, mathematical and moral axioms—whose
truth is intuitively known as soon as we apprehend
their meaning, and that the evidence of particular
experiences is both superfluous and insufficient.

Hume, applying the empirical method to Ethics,
concludes that emotional states are the only possible
sources of our knowledge of good and bad; the
qualities of these states even constitute the distinction
between good and bad, a pleasant feeling being good
and a painful feeling bad.

Moral Sense and Virtue.—Hume fully recognises
that morality is capable of influencing actions.   This
being so, it cannot spring from Reason, but is " more
properly felt than judged of," and moral distinctions
are derived from a *moral sense.*   " To have the sense
of virtue is nothing but to feel a satisfaction of a
particular kind from the contemplation of a character."
The immediate pleasure or pain which the contemplation of an action, sentiment, or character gives us " from

[1] See Mill's *Logic*, Bk. II. chap. iii.

the mere survey " is the sense of its virtue, just as the
immediate pleasure in the contemplation of a picture
is the sense of its beauty.[1]   But this moral pleasure
does not rise directly from self-interest.   The quality
of *disinterestedness* is what distinguishes it from other
pleasures yielded by the contemplation of actions or
characters.   " The good qualities of an enemy are
hurtful to us, but may command our esteem and
respect.   'Tis only when a character is considered in
general, without reference to our particular interest,
that it causes such a feeling or sentiment as
denominates it morally good or evil."

Motive and Moral Approbation.—But Hume is not
satisfied, as Hutcheson was, with " moral sense " as an
explanation of the approbation given to right action ;
he holds that moral sense is derived from some more
fundamental feelings in human nature,[2] which serve
both as motives to right action and as the ground of
moral approbation.   These more fundamental feelings
arise from self-interest, sympathy and custom, combined in different ways, as follows.—

Following Locke, Hume identifies good with
pleasure and evil with pain, thus using pleasure as
the ethical standard for valuating actions (Ethical
Hedonism).   He can give no better reason for this
than the experienced fact that men use this standard.
But we must distinguish the pleasures and pains
which are the remote results of actions from the
immediate pleasure or pain which an action raises in
the mind through the moral sense.   This immediate
pleasure *is* moral approbation or disapprobation.   The

---

[1] Cf. Shaftesbury and Hutcheson (pp. 154, 157).
[2] On this account Hume is described as a naturalist. but Hutcheson as
an intuitionist.

pleasure which *is* moral approbation is either (*a*) originally derived from direct sympathy with the pleasure which an action tends to give to particular persons (*e.g.* a spontaneous act of generosity) or (*b*) it is a complex product of feelings created by the associations of custom and tradition (*e.g.* the approval of justice and honesty) combined with a general vague sympathy for human welfare. Sympathy is a fundamental tendency of human nature, and as general conceptions, according to Hume, are vague ideas arising from frequent particular experiences, so general indefinite sympathy arises from frequently sympathising with particular persons. The associations of custom and tradition originate with education, and they continue to operate in society, partly because of the influence they naturally possess, and partly because it is generally felt that virtues like justice and honesty are of advantage to every person in the community. Thus they are supported by self-interest as well as by sympathy of a vague kind.

Natural and Artificial Virtues.——The two sources of moral approbation, both agreeing in being forms of pleasure, correspond to a distinction between two kinds of virtues : (*a*) The *natural* virtues, as generosity, clemency, moderation, temperance, prudence, equity ; these please instinctively, usually from sympathy with *particular* persons who benefit from the exercise of these virtues, but often for no assignable reason ; (*b*) the artificial virtues, which give immediate pleasure (*i.e.* are approved) partly owing to custom and tradition, partly owing to *general* sympathy with man as man. The artificial virtues (*e.g.* justice) arise in society because they benefit all its members. Through education they permeate our customs and traditions, which again create new feelings that yield them immediate approval.[1]

Obligation.—Hume does not clearly distinguish between obligation and the actual *motives* to virtuous action that exist in human nature. For *artificial* virtues there are (*a*) the *natural* obligation of self-interest and (*b*) a *moral* obligation due to sympathy; *e.g.* we may put ourselves in the place of a person who is the victim of an unjust act, and this leads us to condemn it; there is also a general but weaker sympathy for humanity. Public praise, education, and custom co-operate to strengthen moral obligation, but sympathy is the main root. The obligation to natural virtues is also sympathy due to the pleasure their exercise gives to those around us.

Motive to Justice.—Justice is the most important type of an artificial virtue. What is its motive? Not public interest, for this is " a motive too remote and sublime to affect the generality of mankind "; and in general " there is no such passion in human minds as the love of mankind, merely as such, independent of personal qualities, of services, or of relation to ourself," for sympathy does not extend to every one. Nor can "regard to the interests of the party concerned " be the motive, for I may hate a person to whom I act justly. In fine, the sense of Justice and Injustice

---

[1] Hume's distinction between natural and artificial virtues is unsatisfactory. It seems to be based on the erroneous idea that men were once in "a state of nature," when there was no custom, tradition, or education, and that virtues in that state were natural as being spontaneous. But clearly custom, tradition, and education can give rise to spontaneous virtues. The distinction is dropped in the *Enquiry Concerning the Principles of Morals*, where Hume remarks that all disputes about the meaning of "natural" and "artificial" are "merely verbal" (*Enquiry*, p. 258, note).

is artificial and not natural; the immediate motive
to just action is the passion which is produced by
custom and education. By artificial, however, Hume
only means the product of a complicated social
machinery, and by natural, the opposite of this. But
Justice, he holds, is inseparable from the species, and
so "natural"—in another sense of the word—and its
laws may be called the "Laws of Nature."

Origin of Justice in Society.—In the preceding
argument Hume meant to prove that a knowledge
of the ultimately good or pleasant effects of just
actions is not a sufficient motive to act justly,
because such a *generalised* feeling would commonly
be too weak to control opposing passions. This is
only one form of the Aristotelian doctrine that the
force of good habits is required to supplement
knowledge. But Hume recognises that there must
be ultimately a *natural* reason for the establishment
of Justice in society by custom and education. This
reason he finds, like Hobbes, in self-interest, which he
terms the *natural obligation to Justice,* in distinction
from the artificial *motive* which operates in particular
cases. But in wholly rejecting the theory that all
men are exclusively selfish, and in recognising the
universal existence and operation of disinterestedly
kind affections, he shows more knowledge of human
nature than Hobbes. At the same time he asserts
that selfishness, as well as the natural preference for
friends and relations, produces an opposition of passions
and interests which is dangerous to society. Compacts
are therefore made to the advantage of every one;
thus there arise the three laws of justice called by
Hume "the three fundamental laws of Nature."—

that of the stability of possession, of its transference
by consent, and of the performance of promises. On
these the peace and security of human society depend.

Pleasure, Sympathy, Utility.[1]—According to Hume,
"the chief spring or actuating principle of the
mind is pleasure or pain" (practically Psychological
Hedonism). A virtuous quality is one giving pleasure
by the mere survey, and this pleasure (moral approval)
is made possible by *sympathy* with the persons, real
or imaginary, whom the virtue tends to benefit by
giving them pleasure. Custom and education only
strengthen this sympathy and give it force. Sympathy,
becoming generalised by thought, yields *public utility*
as the first universal standard of morality. Reflection on the tendencies of actions to produce happiness determines "all the great lines of our duty."
Thus Hume may be regarded as the founder of that
form of Utilitarianism which bases its arguments on
Psychological Hedonism.[2]

Criticism

Impressionism. — The word "Reason," even in
technical philosophical systems, has various meanings.
To give definiteness to Hume's criticisms,[3] we have
attributed to him a special use of the word. But
we may now consider the question from a wider point
of view, and regard Reason as either (*a*) *concrete* or
(*b*) *abstract*. Reason is sometimes described as (*a*)

---

[1] In this paragraph the distinction between artificial and natural
virtues is neglected.
[2] The general tendency comes from Locke, who said that uneasiness
determines the will, and identified the good with pleasure.
[3] See p. 179.

the unifying faculty of Mind, the power of grasping a totality, of apprehending the one in the many and the many in the one, of recognising that truths, both theoretical and practical, are not isolated but form a connected system. This faculty (*Concrete Reason*) man undoubtedly possesses in some degree, but its scope is narrow, owing to the limitations of time-experience, the defects of memory, and in general, the finitude of human knowledge. If Concrete Reason had full scope, we should be able to understand the significance of all details and their positions in the whole scheme of the Universe. The bounds set to our power of grasping details compel us to use (*b*) *Abstract Reason*, the faculty of having general conceptions, or of apprehending general principles, by which isolated experiences and objects are brought together in thought, without attention being directed to each particular detail. This power, according to Locke, distinguishes man from the lower animals. We may regard Concrete Reason as striving to realise its ideal of the co-ordination of truth with the aid of Abstract Reason.

Now it is clear that the deliberate pursuit of a good which cannot be realised now, or by me alone, involves Reason in both of these senses, and implies, further, that Reason, in the first sense at all events, is capable of influencing our actions; for I must be able to conceive (dimly, no doubt) good as a *totality*, including within it the particular good ends realised in a number of different experiences of myself and of other persons, before I can deliberately reject a present gratification for the sake of a higher good. Accordingly self-control, the refusal to be governed by momentary feelings that might interfere with permanent private or social interests, involves Reason. We can now see the force of Aristotle's doctrine that the true Self is Reason.[1] We can also see how close is the relation between speculative and practical Reason, since they both pursue the ideal of truth as a totality.

These considerations reveal the error, so far as Ethics is concerned, of Hume's doctrine that the Ego is merely a " bundle " of impressions, ideas, and feelings. The doctrine means that the ethical Self is identical with the passions and feelings of the moment, that it changes every instant and possesses no permanent substantiality; this is equivalent to saying that Reason, the power of looking beyond the feelings of the present moment and of the individual, has no power to influence our actions. No doubt it is true—and so far Hume's criticism of the Rational Intuitionists is justified—that a merely abstract conception of general good is too vague to influence conduct; present desires are required to give a motive force. But the satisfaction, in due degree, of these desires, is included in the total good pursued by Reason, which is thus the true inward Self—a Self both permanent and social. Reason is not, as Hume said, the rightful " slave of the passions," any more than the whole body is the slave of its different members, or than an organised society is the slave of the individuals composing it; it is more properly regarded as the regulative principle, and Butler fitly describes it as the rightful sovereign in human nature. The impressionist theory of the Ego is indeed refuted

[1] p. 77.

by the experience to which it appeals, since a regard
for remote good is a phenomenon of present consciousness, even if it is not always effectual. To overcome
the temptation of the moment is much the same
thing as to prevent the collapse of the Ego into a
" bundle " of isolated feelings.[1]

Psychological Hedonism.—Hume generally assumes
that pleasure and pain affecting the self, are practically
the only motives of voluntary action (Psychological
Hedonism).   As Butler pointed out,[2] this is not true.
Appetites, passions and affections aim commonly at
their appropriate objects, not at the pleasure of self-
gratification. Hunger, for example, urges one to eat, not
merely towards the pleasure of eating. And—what is
particularly important at this stage of the history of
Ethics—the *consciousness of duty* is a practical motive
quite apart from pleasure, as Butler and Kant have
shown.

The Defect in Naturalistic Methods.—Naturalistic
methods tend either to degenerate into Exclusive
Egoism, or to regard conscience as an unreasonable
and inexplicable instinct. Hume's Ethics illustrates
the first of these defects, and to some extent the
second, since he can give no reason why some natural
virtues are approved.   We have seen that his psycho-

---

[1] The impressionist argues that memory, expectation, fear, and
sympathy are *present* impressions or feelings leading us to adapt our
actions to the future or to the welfare of other persons. But these elements,
when—as is the case with developed intelligences—they are not merely
blind instincts, but links consciously connecting the present with the
past and future, and the self with other selves, presuppose the rational
conceptions of a permanent self and of other permanent selves whose good
is objective.   The sceptic may argue that this presupposition is an
illusion, but surely the natural and the most satisfactory explanation is
that it is justified.

[2] p. 168.

logy was superior to Hobbes', in that he recognised that pure sympathy and moral feelings are active forces in society. But in deriving all ultimate motives from the feeling of pleasure in the agent, he relapses unconsciously into Exclusive Egoism;[1] this impressionist theory of the Ego is, in fact, consistent only with the " monochronistic " hedonism of the Cyrenaics. He fails to recognise that the good of another must be immediately accepted by a clear thinker as objectively good,[2] and that this acceptance *is* the obligation which may or *ought* to lead to action, quite apart from the pleasure felt by the agent in such actions.[3] The attempt to reduce the power and authority of the consciousness of social obligation to other motives, must always fail. This consciousness is an ultimate intuition, as the intuitionists have recognised, so far as they were consistent.

Moral obligation, as ordinarily understood, is therefore meaningless in Hume's system ; we cannot be under an obligation to do anything except to follow the pleasure of the moment, and we *must* do that. On this point Kant represents the critical reaction against Hume, asserting that moral obligation provides a motive that can and *ought* to transcend all feelings, and that it is a product of Reason, not of Sense.

The growth of modern Ethical theory was thus influenced by Hume in two ways ; the negative reaction against his doctrines led to Kantian Purism ; the positive development of his theory of utility led to Utilitarianism.

Hume is, moreover, the progenitor of the " genetic "

---

[1] See criticism on Shaftesbury (p. 156).
[2] Cf. Clarke (p. 150 *sq.*).
[3] Cf. Hutcheson's criticism (p. 157).

method in Psychology and Ethics, the method which seeks to explain the present condition of anything by tracing its past history. Thus he holds that the universal approval of the artificial virtues is partly explained by the fact that it is a gradual product of custom, tradition and education.[1] The method is, in fact, the central method of Naturalism, and through the influence of Darwin and Spencer it has been freely applied to every sphere of inquiry.

[1] This idea has been fully worked out in a work of great interest—Westermarck's *Origin and Development of the Moral Ideas* (1906).

CHAPTER V

MORAL PURISM——KANT

Relation to Preceding Systems. —— The ethics of
Immanuel Kant [1] is connected very closely with the
forms of English Intuitionism described in the fore-
going chapters. He differs from all preceding
Intuitionists and Naturalists alike, in regarding duty
and self-love as two eternally distinct motives; [2] at
the same time he admits that duty, if made the
supreme motive, will ultimately lead to the highest
happiness. His system is partly a development of
Rational Intuitionism; he agrees with Clarke and
Cudworth in recognising that the rightness of actions
is objective, and therefore cannot be apprehended by
Feeling—which is purely subjective and peculiar to
the individual—but only by Reason.[3] He differs from
these writers in points too numerous to mention; but
in the present connection it is important to notice
that his superior critical power led him to recognise——
what they failed to see——that practical and speculative

[1] 1724-1804 ; born, lived, and died at Königsberg, where he taught as
a University Professor.

[2] On this account I have called his doctrine Purism (see note, p. 174).
It is distinctly a form of Intuitionism.

[3] The source of this doctrine is in the Stoics, Aristotle, and Plato, but
we must recognise that the English Rational Intuitionists presented it to
Kant in a more definite form.

Reason cannot be hastily identified; he held indeed that for man, with his present limitations, they are distinct, though perfect knowledge would establish a radical connection between them.[1]

Whether Kant was, or was not, directly influenced by Butler, he was certainly familiar with the thoughts current in the English Ethics of the eighteenth century, of which Butler was the most important intuitional representative. Kant's treatment of moral obligation and autonomy may therefore be regarded, historically, as a development of Butler's less rigorous analysis of Conscience as the supreme authority over the soul, and the faculty by which man is a "law to himself."

Kant's system, in short, combines Rational and Autonomic Intuitionism. Its form is largely determined by opposition (a) to Hume's derivation of morality from feelings of pleasure and pain; and in lesser degree (b) to Aesthetic Intuitionism, which, while recognising the objectivity of good, inconsistently derives our knowledge thereof from a purely subjective feeling or taste (moral sense).

Kant does not attempt to prove the existence of

---

[1] Reason (*Vernunft*) is used with less ambiguity by Kant than by preceding writers. He regards it in general as the faculty for apprehending unconditional or ultimate principles. Speculative Reason in beings whose knowledge, like man's, is limited to Time and Space, cannot attain its end, viz. the knowledge of the unconditioned principles of existence. These principles, if known, would provide an explanation of the whole universe that would perfectly satisfy the intellect. Practical Reason, however, attains its end in man; it apprehends the unconditionally obligatory principles of action; these principles are morally right, and ought to influence all our actions. The Existence of God, the Immortality of the Soul, and the Freedom of the Will, cannot, according to Kant, be proved by merely speculative Reason; but they are necessary postulates of practical Reason, since, without them, the notion of duty would be self-contradictory. We shall consider these later.

morality, or to justify moral conduct; he assumes that every rational being has the conception of moral obligation, and that the only business of ethical philosophy is to analyse its nature, in order to prevent that conception from being corrupted. He may be regarded as starting with the postulate that every man has a conscience (in Butler's sense) which "carries its own authority with it."

The Good Will; Motive and Effect; Duty and Inclination.—The only absolutely good thing, says Kant, is the good will. External effects, pleasure, and even the happiness[1] of sentient beings are only relatively good; they have *moral worth* only so far as they assist the action of the good will. A will, therefore, is good, not because of its *effects,* but in itself and for its own sake. It follows that the morality of an action lies in the *principle* with which the will consciously identifies itself, in other words the *motive.* The only good motive is a consciousness of duty. For example, a man may act honestly or tell the truth because he finds that it assists him in his business by securing the confidence of others,[2] or he may live temperately because health is a source of pleasure. But, according to Kant, if the consciousness of duty is not the ruling motive, such actions are merely prudent, and have no moral worth. Even a lie told with the intention of preventing a murder is

---

[1] By "happiness" (*Glückseligkeit*) Kant means the constant satisfaction of desires as they arise. He regards desire as belonging to the sentient and non-rational part of our nature, and appears to assume, with less than his usual insight, that all desire is for pleasure. (See the criticisms of the Stoics and Butler on this view.) In this chapter, therefore, "happiness" and "self-love" may be regarded as having the same meaning as they have for Butler and the Utilitarians. (See p. 24.)

[2] Cf. Hobbes' "Laws of Nature."

unconditionally wrong, because the effects of the lie have nothing to say to its morality. All motives except duty are morally worthless since they are forms of inclination ; they are desires for pleasure or private happiness, or for some transient pleasure-giving effect. We have thus a sharp contrast between motive and effect; and, within the sphere of motives, another sharp contrast between duty and inclination as generically distinct motives. The characteristic of the moral motive is that it has its worth in itself; all other motives derive their worth or worthlessness from the effects that follow.

The Categorical Imperative.—The doctrines just stated follow from the analysis of the popular notion of morality. From the philosophic point of view the antithesis between duty and inclination is expressed by saying that the moral law is *unconditionally* binding on all rational beings ; it admits no exceptions ; it forbids the interference of motives arising from particular inclinations or desires for particular effects ; none of these have unconditional—but only relative— worth, depending on the taste of the individual and the circumstances of the moment. Thus the moral law is not dependent on the special characteristics of the individual or even of the race. It is the law that *ought* to be obeyed by all rational beings, under all circumstances, and for its own sake. Its form is therefore universal, and this fact makes it binding on rational beings only, since they alone are capable of conceiving universal laws, and acting in accordance therewith.[1] From these considerations Kant deduces the formula of the *Categorical Imperative*—"Act only

[1] See footnote, p. 192.

on that maxim whereby thou canst at the same time
will that it should become a universal law." The
"maxim" here only means the principle of action
adopted by the agent, as distinct from the law which
is independent of the agent. Kant tacitly assumes
that self-love and duty provide all possible maxims.
The Categorical Imperative may be paraphrased as
follows in order to show its application : " If the
maxim of your action cannot be given universal
validity without coming into opposition with itself,
then it is not moral."

Illustrations.—All applications of this consist in
determining whether self-love is a moral motive.
Suppose the question arises whether I may, when in
distress, make a false promise with the intention of
breaking it. The source of the maxim is plainly
self-love, but perhaps it is moral nevertheless. But
if this particular maxim were universalized it would
mean that all persons in distress should make false
promises, which would come into opposition with
self-love for two reasons ; first, because the utility of
promises would be abolished, and *I* should be likely to
suffer with the rest of society ; secondly, if I were the
person to whom the promise was made, my self-love
would desire it to be kept. In like manner it may
be shown that self-love is not a morally right motive
for refraining from philanthropic actions ; from which
it may be inferred that we are in general bound to
practice philanthropy, since only self-love could forbid this. Similarly also, self-destruction from selfish
motives is wrong ; and it is also wrong to refrain from
cultivating one's talents from selfish motives.[1]

[1] The point of Kant's illustrations is often missed by commentators

The Categorical Imperative, the general formula of which has just been stated, is expressed by Kant in three special forms all equivalent to each other and to the general form. The first special form is " Act as if the maxim of thy actions were to become by thy will a universal Law of Nature." This is almost the same as the general form, and need not detain us.

Humanity an End in Itself.—The second special form is derived from the consideration that the will is determined by some *end*, and that the will of a rational or moral being, so far as it is good, must be determined by an end having absolute worth and good in itself; for no end having merely relative worth could give rise to the Categorical Imperative, which commands unconditionally and universally. Only rational nature is such an end;[1] it is the sole reality that has intrinsic worth (or dignity). The moral law

(*e.g.* J. S. Mill). He did not mean that every principle that can be logically universalized is moral ; for example, there would be no contradiction in universal self-destruction, or universal self-seeking, or universal distrust of others. Nor did he mean that self-immolation (as *pro patria*), or inflicting pain on others (as for their good), or refraining from cultivating all our talents (perhaps with the motive of perfecting *one*), is never morally justifiable. His point was that such actions are never justified by self-love ; *they may, however, be justified by duty.* It is clear, then, that we cannot use the Categorical Imperative as a criterion of the positive nature of duties, but only as a negative principle showing that self-love is *not* the universal criterion of morality. Nor did he mean that self-love is *never* coincident with the dictates of a morally right motive ; on the contrary it is our duty (he held) to seek happiness under the restraints imposed by everyone else seeking theirs, and by the obligations we are under to help them. Only the form, not the matter, of our duties is given in the Categorical Imperative, and as Doctor Abbott says, "practically its value consists, like that of the Golden Rule, in the elimination of inward dishonesty " (*Memoir of Kant*, prefixed to Abbott's translation of Kant's *Theory of Ethics*).

[1] The language of Kant is somewhat unusual in this connection. An end (*Zweck*) generally means something to be realised, but Kant applies it to something whose existence and worth ought to determine our actions. To treat rational nature as a means only, is to ignore its *dignity* or absolute worth.

orders us to treat personality [1] as of absolute worth.
Thus suicide is wrong because it treats a rational being
as a means of avoiding pain instead of treating him as
an end in himself.   Disinterested benevolence is right
because it agrees positively, not merely negatively,
with the maxim that each man is an end in himself.
The second special form is then " So act as to treat
humanity, whether in thine own person or in that of
any other, in every case as an end withal and never
as means only."   There are great difficulties in the
full exposition of this formula, but it may be enough
to say that the formula expresses at least, that every
person, *qua* rational, has certain absolute rights which
should never be violated.

Autonomy and the Kingdom of Ends.—The third
special form of the Categorical Imperative expresses
that the will of every rational being, *qua* rational,
is to be a universally legislative will, or, in the
language of the other forms, Act as if the will of any
other rational being, *qua* rational, were the legislator
of thy actions.   This follows from the consideration
that the Reason in one individual gives the same
laws of conduct as Reason in any other, since these
laws being universally and unconditionally binding
do not derive their authority from the special
characteristics of any one individual.   Or, otherwise,
the condition that each person is to be an end in
himself, determining the actions of all others, is
equivalent to saying that his will, *qua* rational, is to
be universally legislative.   Kant thence derives the
conception of a Kingdom of Ends consisting of a

[1] A person is, according to Kant, an individual possessing Reason, a
moral agent.

community of rational beings, each rightfully subject to the laws of his own making. Morality therefore leads to a necessary harmony between all rational beings; one quite distinct from the artificial and negative harmony of the Hobbist State, since it is not the resultant of a number of opposing wills, but the expression of the inward unity of all rational wills.

Autonomy.—The third form of the Categorical Imperative is the principle of Autonomy (self-legislation) expressing that the Reason of each person is itself the author of the laws which he ought to obey. This form is clearly the same as the third; for it makes no difference whether I take my own rational will or another's as universally legislative, since all rational wills originate the same laws. Herein Kant finds what he regards as the final solution of the opposition between Egoism and Morality; there can be no difficulty in understanding how a man can voluntarily obey a law that conflicts with his inclinations, when it is recognised that his true (*i.e.* rational) self is the author of that law.[1] He holds that all previous ethical systems failed to overcome this difficulty because they were heteronomic; they strove to derive moral obligation from some principle external to the self, such as the command of God,[2] or feelings of pleasure and pain, or a moral sense peculiar to the individual. It is important to re-

---

[1] Butler had a similar conception (p. 167), but he did not follow it out consistently. Sometimes he speaks of Conscience as the true inner self; at other times he regards it as a faculty not essential to the person, but given to him by the Creator to induce him to perform certain actions.

[2] Kant holds that obedience to the commands of God is justified only so far as they are recognised to be right, *i.e.* by an autonomic motive. Fear of the punishments that He may inflict is a heteronomic motive.

member that Kant regards Reason and not Feeling as constituting the essence of the self, which explains his regarding Egoistic Hedonism as a heteronomic theory.

Connection between the Three Forms.—Three conceptions are prominent in the three different forms of the Categorical Imperative; these are Unity, Plurality and Totality. The first form expresses the *unity* of the Moral Law; there is one law which all are to obey. The second emphasises that there is a *plurality* of rational subjects, each of which is to be treated as having absolute worth. The third form follows at once from the condition that there can be no contradiction between the first two forms; there is not a different law arising from the absolute worth of each person, but only one law (Totality = Unity in Plurality).

Free-Will.—Freedom, considered negatively, means that the will is independent of external compulsion;[1] positively it signifies autonomy or self-determination, which we have seen is equivalent to morally right action. Kant's proof that the will is free is thus based on the consciousness of moral obligation,—" we ought, therefore we can." On the other hand, morality is essentially dependent on freedom of the will, without which it would have no meaning; but we are directly conscious not of freedom, but of moral obligation.

Free-Will and the Laws of Nature.—The difficulty

---

[1] Kant does not, of course, mean that the body cannot be moved by external compulsion, but that the will (the rational self) is capable of resisting, absolutely, all *motives* outside itself, external movements being regarded as *effects* differing from the motive. Such external motives are pleasure, avoidance of pain, fear, etc., which Kant attributes to physical Nature. The negative element in Kant's Freedom is very similar to the resistive element in Fortitude as described by Plato (pp. 44, 45).

in admitting the freedom of the will arises from its apparent contradiction with the natural law of cause and effect, which asserts that all changes, including those in our own minds and bodies, take place according to necessary physical principles and are determined by preceding physical events. How then is there room for a cause which is not physical but rational (the moral will)? Kant holds that we cannot give a satisfactory *speculative* answer to this difficulty, the true answer being practical—the consciousness of duty. Speculative philosophy can, however, show that there need be no contradiction. Briefly and in rough outline, the argument is as follows.— As members of the world of sense (phenomena in space and time) we are subject, like the rest of Nature, to the laws of cause and effect. But as members of the supersensible rational world, transcending space and time, we *may* be free, and the consciousness of duty proves that we are free. The apparent contradiction is removed, Kant thinks, by his speculative philosophy, in which he argues that the laws of Nature are themselves, as regards form, created by the understanding; there is, then, no contradiction in supposing that this creative understanding is one with the free ego; an event, it would appear, may have two heterogeneous causes, one the event preceding it in Time, the other a cause outside the series of events in Time.

Happiness and Virtue; the Three Postulates of Morality.—Moral virtue, consisting in conformity to the moral law, is the only intrinsically good quality of character; it is the *Supremum Bonum*, and gives to other qualities what worth they have. Now the moral law demands that happiness should be distributed in exact proportion to virtue; and this proportionate distribution is the *Summum Bonum*. We ought to cultivate virtue, and happiness ought to be given to us in proportion to our virtue; practical Reason assures us of both of these truths, and to avoid contradiction, we must assume that what ought to be realised can be realised. Kant is thus led to the three Postulates of morality :—

       (1) The Existence of God.
       (2) The Freedom of the Will.
       (3) The Immortality of the Soul.

By a " Postulate " of morality he means a necessary condition of the fulfilment of a requirement of practical Reason. The grounds for postulating the freedom of the will have been given.[1] We must postulate the existence of an intelligent all-powerful Author of Nature as a condition of realising that exact proportion between virtue and happiness in which the *Summum Bonum* consists. Physical Nature, since its laws work mechanically, cannot secure this exact proportion ; in fact " motives "—which constitute the whole morality of actions and of personal characters—are ignored by physical Nature. What is required, therefore, is a Being Who is conscious of the wrongness or rightness of motives and Who has the power to reward or punish them. The immortality of the soul is postulated in the rational obligation we are under to strive towards perfect holiness, an ideal realisable only in an infinite length of time.[2]

---

[1] p. 199.

[2] The approach towards perfect holiness is described as " asymptotic." An asymptote is a line which constantly approaches a curve, but never meets it, or, as the saying is, it meets it at infinity.

H

Good and Moral Law.——Kant holds that all systems that deduce morality from the conception of good,—defined as that which satisfies desire—are heteronomic; the moral law determines what is good, what ought to be done; but this is not true of desires. Goodness is an attribute of actions conforming to the moral law, and is independent of the desires of the individual. His argument is that the good, if it were determined by desires, would depend on particular desires of particular persons, and could not give a universal law or one unconditionally binding.[1]

Particular Duties.——Kant held that particular duties as well as the general principles of morality can never be doubtful—they are known by rational intuition. That this was his view may be inferred from his asserting (*a*) that we *can* do what we *ought* to do, which would be impossible if we did not know what we ought to do; (*b*) that a conflict of duties is impossible; and (*c*) that it is the *motive* and not the effects that determines the morality of the actions. Clearly if the effects of an action determined its morality for the agent, we could never be certain what actions are right, since these effects are infinitely complex.

CRITICISM

Formalism.——Kant has set in its clearest light the conception of a moral obligation independent of feelings and desires. His system, except as regards the *Summum Bonum*, is Stoicism rendered formally exact. The truth, expressed however baldly, by Hobbes—and admitted even by his opponents, Shaftesbury and

---

[1] On Kant's use of " desire," see footnote, p. 193.

Butler—that a man cannot deliberately act contrary to his own permanent interests, Kant strove to make room for by the principle of the Autonomy of Reason. But logical consistency was achieved at the cost of identifying the essence of the true self with a purely formal Reason, and of regarding feelings and desires as merely transitory accidents in self-consciousness. Here Kant's psychology was wrong, for the individual self, as Plato and Butler [1] in particular recognised, includes feelings and desires as constituents. What is left in human nature when these are gone? The result of such abstractions was a one-sided formalism. We cannot be under an obligation to obey an abstract law of conduct merely for its own sake, since the worth of such laws is determined by the ends they tend to realise. These ends again must in some way appeal to the feelings and satisfy the desires of conscious beings. Here the Utilitarians are right and Green—who is in many other respects a follower of Kant —recognises this. Moral obligation consists, not in the suppression of inclinations in favour of an abstract law, but in the suppression of those that interfere with desires whose satisfaction is known to be more complete and more permanent. The obligation to act for the good of others depends on the conception which the agent actually has of their good as *his* good; without this conception he has no motive for deliberate altruistic action.

Virtue and Happiness.—Kant attempts to escape from the formalism of his primary doctrines by the conception of the *Summum Bonum*—happiness in proportion to virtue. But he has given no proof from

---

[1] See pp. 46 *sq.*, 61 *sq.*, 168 *sq.*

the moral law that happiness ought to be proportional to virtue. Such a proof one has a right to expect, because he bases morality on Reason alone; but on that very account, the proof is impossible, since happiness involves Feeling. He tacitly assumes that happiness is good, if united with virtue, and that virtue is not unconditionally good, unless it is rewarded by happiness. Thus moral excellence, regarded as a quality of will, becomes a subordinate, though indeed an essential, element in the highest good; the satisfaction of desires and feelings is found to be also essential; the moral law remains binding only because God rewards those who obey it. Hence obedience to a universal abstract law, without reference to concrete ends, is no longer the supreme ground of obligation; it is not the supreme end, it is only a part of that end.

But this view is inconsistent with Kant's starting point. He first tells us that obedience to the law is unconditionally good, apart from its effects; he is then driven to conclude that the highest end must include happiness, and receives part of its worth from the satisfaction of desires and feelings. The inconsistency is due to a primary abstraction; if we once separate the idea of Duty from that of the Well-being of the agent, they cannot be philosophically re-united.[1]

Motive and Effect.——We have seen that Kant taught that morality of an action depends only on the motive, and is entirely independent of the effects either on the agent or on others. Now it is true that

---

[1] This abstraction, as we have seen, was the source of many of the eighteenth-century ethical discussions.

the morally best action under given circumstances is the one to which conscience directs us; for we have no guide but our own convictions; the morally best is always the best within our power to perform deliberately, and this means practically that it is morally right for the agent to perform the actions he *believes* to be best.[1] In this sense, therefore, the motive determines the morality. But it is an error to infer that the motive is independent of the foreseen effects upon the character and happiness of the agent or of other persons. Duty usually requires men to ascertain these effects, so far as this is possible with the leisure and knowledge at their disposal. It is the duty, for instance, of a politician to investigate the probable effects of a bill before speaking publicly in its favour; and of a doctor to consider the effects of his prescriptions. But Kant appears to have assumed that the morality of an action is, so to speak, stamped on its face—a doctrine very akin to the "moral sense" theory—and that its effects may be left to the Deity. He argues, for example, that it is intrinsically wrong to deceive a would-be murderer, even with the intention of preventing the murder. In such a case (he held) the deceiver would be responsible for all the bad effects possibly following the deception; but if he told the truth he would not be responsible for any subsequent bad effects! Here the extreme of Moral Purism defeats itself, for the prevention of the crime might have the effect of saving the self-respect and moral character of the would-be murderer. even if his happiness and that of

---

[1] This is quite consistent with the truth that conscience is capable of improvement.

his victim and of those dependent on both, is of no moral consequence, as Kant's doctrine logically implies.[1]

The theory of the *Summum Bonum* is Kant's way of escape from these obvious difficulties. Actions are ultimately rewarded by the Deity in exact proportion to the morality of their motives. So long as we ignore happiness and pursue virtue only, we shall ultimately attain happiness; if we cast our bread upon the waters we shall find it after many days, provided we do not look for it! But the difficulty cannot be removed in this artificial way. Either happiness is a worthy object of pursuit, or it is a morally indifferent end; and, in the latter case, virtue cannot be improved by rewards. The only solution of this problem lies in a return to the Greek position;[2] the true Well-being of a man must actually *consist* in morally right action. A good man finds his highest satisfaction in right action; and the assertion that a bad man *ought* to change his conduct, means, amongst other things, that such a change would, from the start, yield him higher satisfaction, and that the satisfaction would be more permanent. This truth, so clear in Aristotle, was revived in Rational Idealism.

Nature and Freedom.—Kant scarcely faced the full consequences of his attempt to reconcile free-will

[1] Kant's doctrine is really a protest against Hedonism. It amounts to saying that there are no *moral* effects of actions, and therefore, if effects are to be estimated, the standard can only be hedonistic; morality is an attribute of the will, and the will acts morally only when it is self-determined (autonomous). A moral act is therefore never the effect of anything outside itself, though it may be the cause of physical and mental effects morally indifferent.

[2] Kant was fully aware of the Greek view, and deliberately rejected it. See *Dialectic of Pure Practical Reason*, chap. ii., Abbott's translation (p. 207).

and natural necessity. If the soul can act freely in agreement with natural laws, because it, *qua* understanding, created these laws [1]—and this is what his doctrine implies—then surely all the phenomena of Nature are the actions of each autonomous Ego, since they follow necessarily from these laws.[2] All such actions are therefore moral, and immoral acts are physical impossibilities—a conclusion wholly rejected by Kant. On the other hand, if the soul is not the author of the necessary laws of Nature, it can never violate them, and the consciousness of duty can produce no effects that would not have followed without it, unless that consciousness is itself the natural product of preceding events.

But in fairness to Kant we must admit that he virtually recognises that the problem is insoluble. For practical purposes it is better to use the elementary conception of freedom as a limited power of realising ends that we conceive to be good.[3]

PERMANENT INFLUENCE OF KANT

Just as the development of Hobbes' doctrine really led him to refute the exclusive Egoism with which he started,[4] so Kant, by his thorough logical analysis,

[1] This interpretation of Kant may be objected to, but I believe his speculative philosophy is inconsistent with any other.

[2] This thought in fact formed the basis of Fichte's philosophy, which arose as an attempt to reconcile the practical and speculative philosophy of Kant.

[3] See p. 11.

[4] See p. 139. It is interesting to note that Kant and Hobbes are extremists who have gone to opposite extremes. For Hobbes the only rational end I can act for is the gratifying of my own particular desires. For Kant not even the happiness of others, but only obedience to a universal law is an unconditionally rational motive.

has unconsciously refuted his original position, by exposing the contradiction involved in saying that mere law is the ultimate ground of morality. If obedience to a universal law—*qua* universal—is alone moral, there can be no particular end worthy of pursuit, and we have no reason for doing one thing more than another. The source of moral obligation must therefore be some concrete end. The Utilitarians and Green endeavoured to express this. Negatively, then, Kant's analysis has pointed to the need of moving in this direction—towards a concrete determination of the highest end.

Kant's most important positive contributions to ethical philosophy are (1) the analysis of the conception of autonomy and its relation to freedom, (2) his insistence with the Rational Intuitionists on the idea of universality contained in all morally right action, and (3) his connecting this idea with that of unconditional obligation.

The principle of universality is to be interpreted as enjoining impartiality in the distribution of concrete goods, not merely obedience to a formal law. It requires me to recognise the good of others as objectively good, and therefore good for me. The validity of the principle is assumed by the Utilitarians—unconsciously, except in the case of Sidgwick—by the Rational Idealists, and even by Spencer (in the formula of Justice).[1] It implies also that goodness is consistent with itself, and we have thus another interpretation of the Socratic dictum that " Virtue is one," and of the saying of Aristotle that there are many ways of going wrong, but only one way of going right.

[1] See chapter on Spencer.

Unconditioned obligation, again, is involved in the very definition of moral good, for the morally good is the best attainable end.[1] But we are not to infer that the satisfaction of particular feelings and desires and interests have no worth; what is meant is that particular interests, etc., are to be judged and to be subjected to selection. Reason or Conscience is to regulate our desires, which, as Aristotle says, are naturally subordinate to Reason. And the nature of this regulation can seldom be determined by abstract rules, but only by a sagacious consideration of the particular circumstances.

Links between Kant and Subsequent Systems.—In Kant, Reason and Will were never fully reconciled, and this gave rise to two opposite movements. (1) German Rational Idealism (Fichte, Schelling, Hegel) taught that self-conscious Reason or Mind is the ultimate reality, and endeavoured to express Will in terms of this reality. The result was a form of Optimism —the truly existent is essentially good. (2) The Voluntarism of Schopenhauer is a direct negative of this position; he taught that unreasoning Will, for the most part unconscious, is the ultimate reality, and that Reason is merely a superficial phase of Will. The result was hedonistic Pessimism—life is essentially miserable.

The following systems were also influenced by Kant, either directly or indirectly. (*a*) Utilitarianism appears in Bentham and Mill as a reaction against Moral Purism; it insists that the morality of actions is determined neither by their motives nor by abstract law, but by their pleasant and painful effects. These

[1] See p. 9.

writers waver between Naturalism and Intuitionism. The later Utilitarianism of Sidgwick is more in sympathy with Kant and the Intuitionists, the idea of the rational universality of the good being given a prominent position. (*b*) The Evolutional Naturalism of Spencer recognises the existence and power of the consciousness of moral obligation, but regards this consciousness, not as an idea of Reason having a true object, but as an irrational instinct arising partly from the individual's past forgotten experiences of pleasure and pain, and partly through heredity; an instinct which owes its prevalence to the fact that it is favourable to the life of the race. (*c*) The Rational Idealism of T. H. Green (closely akin to the German type) accepts the Kantian idea of rational universality and teaches that the moral law is unconditionally binding; but he holds—in opposition to Kantian formalism—that the moral law is determined by its end, a *concrete* good which yields the highest and most permanent satisfaction, and that virtue is not mere conformity of the will to an *abstract* law.

CHAPTER VI

GERMAN RATIONAL IDEALISM

THE most remarkable developments and criticisms of Kant's philosophy, both theoretical and practical, took place in Germany, in two opposite directions. The first, Rational Idealism, strove to represent Reason and Self-consciousness as the ultimate explanation; the second, Voluntaristic Pessimism, treated irrational Will as the source of all reality. Of these two developments the first claims most of our attention. Practical philosophy in this movement is so much bound up with speculative, which seeks to give a general world-view, that the account here given must be regarded as a summary of results, rather than a complete analysis. This applies especially to the references to the systems of Fichte and Schelling, but I hope that the analysis of Hegel's more complete and more satisfactory system will be found not altogether inadequate.

A.

FICHTE

The idealistic movement initiated by Johann Gottlieb Fichte [1] appears at first, so far as Ethics is concerned, as an attempt to overcome the Kantian opposition

---

[1] 1762-1814 ; Professor at Jena, and first Rector of Berlin University.

between theoretical and practical Reason, or to reconcile the freedom of Mind with the necessity of
Nature.   Autonomy, he teaches, is the essential
characteristic of Mind and belongs to the knowing, as
well as to the acting, intelligence.   The infinite Ego,
self-consciousness, pure intelligence, is the fundamental
reality, and it is essentially free or self-determining.
Individuality, which gives rise to a plurality of finite
egos, is an incomplete but necessary manifestation
of self-consciousness; a person only transcends his
finitude, and knows what he really *is*, when he has
recognised his identity with the infinite Ego.

Perhaps the most remarkable characteristic of
Fichte's Ethics is the doctrine that moral action is
the solution of all theoretical difficulties; that mere
theory is an abstraction and that practical Reason is
the explanation of speculative.   If the Ego were
merely theoretical it would not be the fundamental
reality, since the merely knowing Ego presupposes an
object of knowledge different from itself.   By the
action of rational will the object, the so-called non-
Ego or Nature, becomes assimilated to the Ego, which
thus becomes free, for it is no longer controlled by an
alien object.   The freedom of the infinite Ego appears
to us as a process of development, but this is a limited
view, due to the conditions of time-experience.   Time
in fact is the form adopted by the infinite Ego to
express its nature.

The Ego then is not merely consciousness, it is
also will, and the two sides are inseparable.   The end
of finite rational nature is to acquire or preserve
freedom in thought and action.   The "independence
of freedom" is the highest good.

The moral life is a progressive struggle with Nature, and freedom can be obtained only by such struggle and opposition. The external world is the sensuous material of our duty. Nature only exists in order that individuals may acquire freedom; it is, indeed, created by the infinite self-consciousness as a means for the realisation of freedom by individuals.

Freedom is possible only through knowledge; right action and knowledge are the same; we cannot err as to our duty, for every man has his own proper position and knows what it is.

Though the moral life is a process of development it is not therefore incomplete; the different moments of time form parts of a perfect system; in determining the right path of duty, it is therefore necessary to take the historical conditions into account.

As individuals in their truth are manifestations of the infinite Ego, it follows that Exclusive Egoism, in the Hobbist and Epicurean sense, is impossible for any one who really knows what he *is*, *i.e.* for a self-conscious person as such. All duties have reference to the whole; each man has his own special place. State and Church, Art and Science, Industry and Commerce are forms of the moral life of the whole community.

B.

SCHELLING [1]

Schelling's philosophy was largely based on Fichte's, but a fundamental difference soon became apparent. Both regarded knowledge as an agreement or assimilation of the object with the thinking subject; but

---

[1] Friedrich Wilhelm Joseph Schelling (1775-1854); Professor at Jena and taught afterwards at other German Universities.

whereas Fichte subordinated the object to the conscious subject, Schelling sought for a higher unity the *Absolute*, in which subject and object are united. The problem of philosophy is to show how object and subject are united, and this means, to show how the unconscious becomes conscious (the Philosophy of Nature) and how consciousness necessarily involves the existence of a complex of objects outside itself (Transcendental Philosophy). Schelling rejects the Fichtean doctrine that Nature only exists as a field for moral activity; he claims that it has a truth and objectivity of its own. Speculative knowledge therefore cannot be subordinated to practical, for it is an end in itself; in fact the knowledge of the Absolute is the highest end both of thought and action. In the consciousness of the self as a part of the Absolute, all difficulties disappear, and the necessity of Nature and the freedom of Consciousness are seen to be inseparable.

In his earlier philosophy Schelling taught that the unity of subject and object is most perfectly represented in Art, which takes Nature for its model, and idealises with the freedom of Consciousness. Art then is higher than Philosophy and its productions are the greatest works of man. In his later works he became more mystical and taught, in the manner of the neo-Platonists, that the highest end is the immediate vision of God, the Absolute, as He *is*; such vision is higher than merely reflective knowledge.

C.

HEGEL [1]

Introductory

Hegel lays much stress on method in philosophy; he holds in fact that it is an essential part of philosophy and that no true position can be reached without it. His method may be briefly described as follows. Thought first takes up a position which further reflection shows to be abstract and incomplete and therefore self-contradictory when taken by itself. Thought then adopts the opposite position, but the truth is to be found only in combining these two positions or "moments" into a higher unity. There are thus three "moments" of which the second is the negation of the first and the third is the unity of both.[2]

This "dialectic process," Hegel teaches, is not to be regarded as a way of arriving at the truth by a series of blunders; it is the necessary way in which Reason finds expression. And it is not merely an artificial method in philosophy; it represents the actual path of development in the history of philosophy; and in the history of social institutions this development is the manifestation of self-conscious Reason. The three moments are illustrated in the growth of Rational Idealism from Fichte through Schelling to Hegel. Fichte starts with the principle that Self-consciousness is the ultimate reality; Schelling rejects this view on the ground that knowledge is an agreement between object and subject, and therefore involves a higher

---

[1] Georg Wilhelm Friedrich Hegel (1770-1831) was Professor at Jena and Heidelberg, but delivered his most influential lectures at Berlin.

[2] The reader who is interested mainly in Hegel's Ethics may pass on to p. 222.

unity than either (the Absolute). The Absolute, however, as conceived by Schelling, is for Reason a mere abstract unity, something that is indifferent as to whether it becomes subject or object. Now Hegel accepts the view that self-consciousness is the final reality; not, however, *particular* self-consciousness (as Fichte taught), but rather Reason, which embodies universal ideas. The Absolute again is the unity of subjective and objective, but it is not a mere abstract unity; it contains differences within its own unity. The apparent abstractness and indifference of the Absolute, as described by Schelling, are, according to Hegel, due to his want of proper method. Schelling states dogmatic conclusions about the Absolute without exhibiting the rational order which Reason spontaneously follows in moving towards these conclusions.

In working out his system Hegel divides Philosophy as follows. It must be remembered that he regards this division not as a merely convenient method, but as determined by the inward movement of thought from one position to another.

1. *Logic.*—Thought is primarily universal; hence Logic deals with all conceptions regarded merely as *universal, e.g.* Quantity, Cause, Judgment, Will, etc. Logic begins with the most universal and abstract conception — Pure Being. Moving in determinate order from the simple to the complex, it ends with the Absolute Idea, which embraces all these conceptions in a complex totality, and contains the truth of each without their one-sidedness. The position of Logic taken alone is subjective, inward, and merely universal.

2. *The Philosophy of Nature.*——If thought remained a merely abstract universal, it would contradict itself, for particularity and number are categories immanent within it.   It therefore *externalises* itself, and loses its unity by breaking into a plurality of particulars. Nature is the idea in the form of externality or mere objectivity.   Considered merely as such it is a *congeries* of lifeless atoms.   But Nature really contradicts its primary atomism; and this contradiction is just due to the fact that Nature is a partial expression of the Absolute Idea, and therefore contains the principle of unity concealed.   The principle of unity strives to assert itself in inanimate nature, in living organisms, and is at last successful in man, who is the highest product of Nature; he is a rational intelligence in whom Mind, working in Nature, has at last freed itself from the bondage of mere externality.

3. The *Philosophy of Mind* expresses the truth of both the previous positions, and abolishes their onesidedness.   Only Mind *is* in the full concrete sense; the universal conceptions of Logic, the particular objects of Nature, are both——though in opposite senses ——too abstract to stand alone, to exist.   But concrete Mind is free and self-determining, and as such it is the beginning and end of all actuality.   Nature thus receives its true meaning when it is recognised, not as mere externality, but as a part of the process in which Mind expresses itself, asserts its own freedom.

The Philosophy of Mind

In its inward movement towards the Absolute, which is Mind as the perfected unity of subject and

object, Mind passes through certain necessary but
incomplete positions, the transition from one position
to another being due to the abstraction and contradiction in the former.   Mind is

I. Subjective.

II. Objective.

III. Absolute.

I. *Subjective Mind.*

Mind is primarily subjective; this expresses its
character in opposition to the mere externality of
Nature.   It is (*a*) Soul, (*b*) Consciousness, and (*c*)
Subjective Mind in its completeness.

(*a*) The Soul is, first, the natural soul which only
is, and is not conscious; this is physical life as such,
the life of lower organisms, of cells, of nutritive and
other unconscious organic processes; secondly, we have
feeling or sentient soul; and, thirdly, actual soul, the
unity of body and feeling in a single subject.

(*b*) Subjective Mind as Consciousness is, first,
consciousness as such, with awareness of objects
which are abstractly regarded (in sense-perception) as
different from the self (the position of common-sense
realism).   *Understanding* now appropriates the object
as something belonging to itself, and in this way we
reach, secondly, self-consciousness, which, by identifying
the object with the subject, really annihilates the
former (the position of pure idealism).   Thirdly,
Reason combines realism and idealism into a wider
whole by abolishing the partiality of each, and
preserving what is true in both.   It is self-consciousness, for which its own determinations are objective,

universal, and expressing the very essence of things. The objective and subjective are united, yet both factors stand out distinct.

The transition from self-consciousness to Reason takes place as follows.—Self-consciousness is primarily desire or appetite, which expresses the contradiction arising from the subject and the object not yet being united. The subject is not yet objective, and the object is not yet subjective, and desire is a movement of Mind towards overcoming this disagreement with its true character as unity of subject and object. But the satisfaction of desire is only *particular*, since other egos are not satisfied in my satisfaction. Self-consciousness is therefore still at war with itself. Hence it becomes, secondly, *recognitive*; other egos outside myself are recognised as existing independently of me. At this stage there is a battle between this recognition and the self-assertion of the particular ego.[1] The result is the relation of master and slave, and the origin of States by force. The contradiction —the inward strife of self-consciousness—disappears in the third stage, universal and objective self-consciousness or *Reason*. Here the self is identified with other selves. Reason, in this sense, lies at the root of all true spiritual life, in family, friendship, or public life.

(c) Mind as Reason has itself for object. It is, in the first place, Theoretical Mind or Intelligence. At this stage it *finds* itself determined,—*e.g.* intuition, representation, including imagination and memory,— but as *knowing* it appropriates what it finds as its own. This appropriation takes place by means of

[1] Cf. Hobbes.

thought, which thinks particular intuitions by means of universal conceptions. The truth of an object is the thought which it embodies, and this implies that Mind as thought determines its own content. Secondly, therefore, when Mind becomes aware that it is capable of determining the content of its knowledge, it is Practical Mind or Will. As such it steps into actuality, and indeed *creates* it by its own autonomous activity; thus freedom is its characteristic trait. Will is, first, practical feeling, but this does not adequately express its true nature. Different feelings, impulses, and desires conflict with each other. Will, as free and thinking, separates itself from these particulars, as choice. But the sphere of choice is still limited to the satisfaction of a multiplicity of particular desires. Hence Will sets before it the ideal of Happiness, an abstract and unrealised unity of particular satisfactions. Happiness, however, thus conceived, involves a contradiction, for it consists of particular satisfactions of the desires of particular individuals, and, on the other hand, restrains each desire for the sake of something beyond.[1] Happiness, moreover, regarded as the satisfaction of all desires is only imaginary; it is conceived as something which ought to be but is not. It cannot, therefore, express the true nature of Mind.

We now find a contradiction between theoretical and practical Mind, or between Intelligence and Will. Intelligence has found that self-knowing universal Mind is its own object, and that truth does not lie beyond it; but Will seeks at first to reach this universality by a merely imagined and contingent ideal of universal

[1] Notice the criticism of Hedonism.

happiness. This contradiction is at once resolved by the consideration that Will is itself free and self-determining.[1] Thirdly, therefore, we reach the position of Free Mind, which is the unity of Intelligence and Will. As free Intelligence, Mind knows what it really *is* in its universal nature; in conformity with this, as Will, it puts into a subordinate place the satisfaction of particular desires and the imaginary and contingent idea of the happiness of particular individuals. Its practical goal is now to realise its own inner essence, not as a particular subject, but as a universal object, which is likewise subject and is manifested in different individuals. Free Mind is Mind as it actually *is*, self-knowing and self-determining. Historically, the freedom of actual Mind was first recognised by Christianity, which teaches that each individual as such has infinite value.

II. *Objective Mind.*

Objective Mind is free Mind in the presence of external conditions, *e.g.* personal needs, inanimate objects, and different individuals. Though Mind is timelessly free, and is indeed, as such, the very truth of existence, its freedom under these conditions is expressed as a development in time. It is however questionable whether Hegel meant it to be regarded

---

[1] Mind as Intelligence cannot accept anything except that which *is* or *must be* ; Mind as Will (at this stage) seeks happiness, the hedonistic ideal, which is only something which *ought* to be, but may never be realised. But when Mind finds that the true ideal is the realisation of its own nature, not the impossible gratification of all particular desires, the opposition between that which *is* (in the non-temporal sense) and that which *ought* to be disappears, since Mind *must* realise itself. Thus Will becomes harmonised with Intelligence, and Mind in this harmony becomes consciously free or self-determining.

altogether as a time-development; it is essentially an inward movement of self-determining Mind from one position to another; but, provided this is remembered, it will fix our ideas to regard it at least subjectively as a time order; *we* think in time, and our thoughts move from one position to another in time order. For the purposes of this work it will be convenient to describe it as ethical development, though Hegel does not thus describe it.

Ethical Development.

The actuality of freedom consists in the unity of the universal Will with the individual will. Ethical development moving in this direction passes into three positions as follows:—

(*a*) *Legal Right.*—At this stage Mind is the individual limited by external conditions and by relations to other individuals. Surrounded by these conditions the freedom of Will takes the form of the possession of property, subject to the authority of Law. In submitting to the equitable execution of Law the individual claims his own rights, and at the same time recognises the rights of others; he regards himself and others as persons. In this sphere freedom is merely liberty to possess and exchange property. But the complete idea of freedom is only latent. The freedom of a particular person to possess property may contradict true freedom if his will, *qua* particular, sets itself against the like freedom of others by violating their legal rights. Hence arises Wrong. The idea of Wrong, for Hegel, is an irrational contradiction, since the Law of Right cannot really be superseded. The contradiction is removed in punishment, which is thus essentially rational, and is by no means merely corrective (as *e.g.* the Utilitarians afterwards said [1]). The criminal ought to be punished, he has indeed a *right* to be punished, so far as he is a subject of true freedom. But the coercion involved in punishment shows that the legal position *per se* is contradictory and abstract; the individual objects to being punished, and thus the unity between his will and the universal Will is broken.

(*b*) This contradiction leads to the second position of Objective Mind, *Morality*. [2] The criminal as a merely particular will may object to being punished, but so far as he possesses conscience he approves of it. The distinction between the legal and the moral position is, that in the first the obedience to the Law of Freedom is ensured only by external compulsion— and is not real obedience,—in the second it is justified by a free inward verdict. In Morality there are three "moments." (*a*) The Purpose, the agent's immediate aim, for which alone he regards himself as responsible. (β) The Intention, which looks to the more important particular effects of the action, including the agent's own well-being, to which he has a right. Now these elements are often contradictory; a crime may be committed with a good intention,— *e.g.* a person may steal to provide food for his children, —and the particular ends in which I place my well-being may conflict with each other or with the well-being of other persons. (γ) The third moment is Good and Evil. By the contradictions in the second moment we are led to the idea of an essential good,

---

[1] Cf. Bentham (Chap. VII.)   [2] *Moralität.*

as a concrete totality to which all other ends are to be subordinated. It is the duty of an agent to realise this good both in motive and effects. There must therefore be a universal principle to determine what is good. But here again a contradiction arises. If the agent submits his will to one abstract universal law, he negates his own freedom. But if he pursues his own well-being and satisfies his own interests as a free subject, the freedom which he realises is, as we have seen, only particular; particular interests (as Kant pointed out) ought not to be the motives. The particular interests and the universal law *ought* to be in harmony, but it is a mere accident whether they are or not. The expression of this contradiction is Evil. Evil in its pure form is exclusive egoism, self-assertion; the agent *qua* free sets up his own particular will against the universal Will. Evil and the *abstract* goodness of mere morality both arise from the same source—the contingency of the subjective will in the presence of an "ought" that is not actual, and may as well not be as be. The subject *qua* particular, is conscious of a choice between abstract good and evil, and thus contains two opposing factors, Conscience and Evil. So long, therefore, as we remain at the position of mere *Morality* (in Hegel's sense) Evil expresses an essential element in freedom, —the right of the subject to assert himself,—an element which is ignored by Conscience, because it conceives the good as a merely abstract universal. [1]

(c) *Social Ethics.* [2]—The contradiction just exposed is due to the individual regarding himself as a

[1] This paragraph is to be regarded as a criticism of Kant.
[2] *Die Sittlichkeit.*

particular subject, and the moral law as *abstractly*
universal. In Social Ethics this contradiction is
removed. The Mind of a society is the ethical substance. It is conscious of itself and thus admits the
principle of subjectivity which is essential to freedom ;
but this subjectivity is no longer evil for it is
universal, and is not the consciousness of one
individual to the exclusion of others. It is the
one Mind in every individual who is truly a member
of the society. The performance of duty is no longer
a merely contingent " ought," but expresses what the
agent *is,* so far as he has identified himself with the
Mind of society. Good is no longer abstract and impersonal, for the individual finds his own well-being,
his true freedom, in the actual performance of his
social functions, including a due regard for his own
welfare as an individual, and for his own special
interests. The practical operation of freedom is a
natural unforced observance of the established moral
customs and manners of the society. Here, finally,
there is a unity between freedom and necessity ; the
individual attains freedom by identifying his will
with the universal Will, and when he has done this he
must act accordingly, for otherwise he would contradict his own being. His acts are both autonomous
and necessary ; autonomous, because they proceed from
conscious Reason, which alone is free self-determining ;
necessary, because there can be nothing arbitrary or
contingent in the way in which Reason unfolds its
true nature.

The ethical substance takes three forms. First,
the Family ; the characteristic here being an inward
unity of interests in which, however, Mind appears

only as a natural feeling of love.   The family is only
a single person, and this brings us, secondly, to Civil
Society, a plurality of families and individuals bound
together into an external unity by a system of adjustments, *e.g.* the division of labour, judicial administration
and police.   Here particular active interests assert
themselves and are the prominent characteristics.
Thirdly, the State, the self-conscious ethical substance,
is the unity of the Family principle—in which love
is the chief feature—and of the principle of Civil
Society—in which the particular interests of individuals are secured.   Here there is an *inward* unity
between the interests of one and all.   The State is
one living Mind, not figuratively, as with Spencer and
others, but literally.   To the question, who is to
make the constitution of the State, Hegel replies that
it cannot be made by a particular person or group of
persons; it is the expression of the true Mind of a
nation, and arises by necessary rational development.

The State again, as self-conscious Mind, contains
three factors.   First, it is an inward single constitution.
Secondly, the external differences between particular
States give rise to a system of international customs
and laws.   Thirdly, the unity of the two preceding;
each particular State and Constitution, as embody-
ing some essential principle, is a stage in the World-
History, the movement of Mind—in Time, and subject
to physical conditions—towards its own freedom.
This development is founded on a necessary and
rational end, which is and will be realised—popularly
described as the plan of Providence.

III. *Absolute Mind.*

Absolute Mind is the unity of Objective and Subjective Mind. Mind is no longer to be regarded— like merely Objective Mind — as moving in an external world over against it; it has asserted its own supremacy over this world, not by abolishing it, but by making it a fit vehicle for the expression of subjectivity. We cannot enter into the details of Hegel's treatment of this, but for the sake of completeness we give the names of the three stages of Absolute Mind: (1) Art, (2) Revealed Religion, and (3) Philosophy, which is the unity of the first two.

D. REMARKS ON THE ETHICS OF GERMAN RATIONAL IDEALISM

Hegel's Philosophy may be regarded as the consummation of Fichte's and Schelling's. It is impossible to give an adequate estimate of his doctrines without considering the whole of this great system, and the following remarks are only intended to show the relation of some of his ethical theories to previous and subsequent doctrines.

In the first place he openly and consciously identifies the ethical ideal with the truly existent, in the manner of Plato.[1] He cannot therefore be classed either as an Intuitionist or as a Naturalist. Only the rational is good and only the rational exists; evil is an incomplete and contradictory, though a necessary, stage in the movement of Mind. The same thing applies to the idea of a moral obligation that

[1] See pp. 58, 59.

can be evaded; a duty that may be shirked does not exist except contingently. What duty *is* can only be known by a person who is conscious that he must perform it, and this consciousness arises when he finds his own freedom, by identifying his will with that of the Mind of society. The universal Mind *is* the good and true, and there is nothing outside it.

Now, it may be remarked that the majority of men, including philosophers, are at the imperfect stage at which evil appears to be a reality, and if this be merely an illusion surely that illusion is itself an evil. For them at all events the practical problem of Ethics is not yet solved. The notion of moral obligation (as an unpleasant feeling of an unpleasant duty) since Hegel's time has indeed taken a secondary place in philosophy; but it has been replaced by the practical problem, "What is the content of duty?" We have seen Hegel's solution; but, admitting for the moment its validity, the question still remains, how am I to identify my mind with universal self-consciousness; and, secondly, having done this, can I tell the direction in which its development takes place? If not, it seems that I have not yet fully identified myself with it, and my obedience to it is faith not knowledge. And this is really the practical issue of Hegel's ethics. The individual is to submit his will to the existing order of things; the Positive Morality of the society in which he lives is to be the guide of his conduct.

We have noticed[1] that the earlier English Intui-tionists, and, in some degree, Kant, were unable to unite rationally the ideas of duty and personal Well-

[1] pp. 175, 204.

being. This was partly because they identified the
latter with pleasure. For the Greeks this opposition
did not exist, perhaps they did not fully recognise it.
Autonomy really contains the secret of the reconciliation, which was effected by Hegel in the doctrine that
man finds his own freedom, and therefore his good, in
the free performance of his functions as a conscious
member of society. Hegel, however, tends to crush
individualism and to treat pleasure and pain as of
little consequence; thus Hedonism was the inevitable
reaction, though, as we shall see, one full of hopeless
contradictions.

Rational Idealism, Naturalism, and Intuitionism.—
In a previous chapter it was remarked[1] that the
Rational Idealists cannot properly be classed with
either Rationalists or Intuitionists; not with the
Naturalists, for they teach that external Nature is
only a one-sided and incomplete expression of Mind,
and, moreover, they unanimously reject the descriptive
or empirical method in philosophy, seeking everywhere
for *a priori* reasons. And they cannot be classed
with the Intuitionists, because the distinction presupposed by Intuitionism between good and evil
as two different realities, becomes meaningless when
evil is identified with negation and a partial view
of things. In this respect the Rational Idealists
resemble Spinoza, whom, however, I have described
with some hesitation as a Naturalist; owing, first, to
his relation to Hobbes, and, secondly, to the fact that
his view of Nature is half mechanical, since he does
not regard it as an expression of Mind, but treats
Mind and Nature alike as two different parallel

[1] p. 123.

attributes of one Substance.[1]   Again, there is no doubt
that the Intuitionists of the eighteenth century regarded Spinoza as a bitter enemy because he constantly asserted that the distinction between moral
good and evil is purely subjective.   The eighteenth-
century opposition between Naturalism and Intuitionism is due to the fact that neither side made any
attempt to understand the relation of Mind to Nature.
That Mind is in some way immanent in Nature is
the permanent result obtained by Rational Idealism
whatever may be thought of its methods.   And this
truth which was *thought* by them was *felt* by the
great poets of the earlier half of the nineteenth
century; thus Wordsworth says in a well-known
passage :—

> I have felt
> A presence that disturbs me with the joy
> Of elevated thoughts ; a sense sublime
> Of something far more deeply interfused,
> Whose dwelling is the light of setting suns,
> And the round ocean, and the living air
> And the blue sky, and in the mind of man,—
> A motion and a spirit, that impels
> All thinking things, all objects of all thought,
> And rolls through all things.

*Relation of Rational Idealism to Positivism and
Subsequent Systems.*—(1) Whereas Rational Idealism
regards knowledge as the *inward* free development
of Mind, the Positivism of the French philosopher,
Auguste Comte,[2] teaches that knowledge comes *from
without*, from the positive or given data of the senses
and feelings.   The co-ordination of knowledge was an

---

[1] This Substance resembles Schelling's Absolute, the unknown unity
of Subject and Object.
[2] 1798-1857.

ideal common to Comte and Hegel, as well as the
doctrine that the history of mankind is a development,
but for the former that development is determined by
mechanical laws of psychology and physics, not by
self-unfolding Mind. In Ethics Comte teaches that
Well-being consists in the satisfaction of feeling, and
that the social feelings, in the course of intellectual
and moral development, tend to overcome the egoistic.
Comte regards humanity as one great feeling organism,
constituted from the social feelings of its different
members. The unity which Hegel found in the self-
conscious Reason of society, Comte sought in Feeling.
Modern Utilitarianism and the Spencerian ideas of
social evolution[1] are due largely to Comte. What
we specially owe to Comte is his insistence on the
ethical importance of physical science as a means of
increasing human Well-being.

(2) Voluntaristic Pessimism is the direct negative
of Rational Idealism. Fichte endeavoured to reconcile
freedom and necessity by the theory that Nature is
itself the expression of the free Ego, and the Rational
Idealists in general regarded conscious Reason as the
ultimate reality. Now Schopenhauer's[2] philosophy
started from the following criticism of Fichte's position.
I am unconscious of the creation of Nature by my
own Ego, therefore the creative Ego cannot be always
conscious of its own actions. Further, Nature shows
many signs of being unreasonable, as in the war
between living things. Schopenhauer inferred that
the fundamental reality, which is both substance and
activity, is blind, irrational *Will*, which acts for the

[1] Comte, however, rejected the Darwinian doctrine of the evolution of
life from a common stock.

[2] Arthur Schopenhauer (1788-1860), born at Danzic.

most part unconsciously, though it strives to become conscious. Reason and Feeling are merely superficial and impotent phases of Will. In the sphere of Ethics this doctrine, united with Schopenhauer's own restless and passionate disposition, led him to hedonistic Pessimism. In man Will becomes self-conscious, and he is ever driven forward by the blind relentless " Will to live." But this only leads him to un-happiness; the pain of life far exceeds the pleasure, for all desire is painful, and pleasure, the satisfaction of desire, is nothing positive, but only the removal of the pain of want. The only escape from unhappiness is to renounce the Will to live. But Schopenhauer does not appear to recognise that this advice is inconsistent with his fundamental principles, since it implies that deliberate rational choice can affect events. Schopenhauer's philosophy, as the negation of practical Reason, is, strictly speaking, the negation of Ethics. Well-being, however, he placed in feeling, and thus his Ethics is really hedonistic.

The relation between Schopenhauer's doctrines and the Evolutional Naturalism of Spencer is to be found in the fact that the blind Will can only be conceived as a mechanical force. Spencer, assuming that Nature is a mechanical system, nevertheless endeavours to show that its purely mechanical evolution will lead to the realization of the hedonistic ethical ideal. His system, starting from the same mechanical view as Schopenhauer, curiously enough leads to hedonistic optimism.

(3) The Evolution Naturalism of Spencer adopts the Hegelian notion of necessary development, and even holds that this development proceeds towards

ethical perfection (though hedonistic).   But the vital difference is that Spencer teaches that the development is determined by the *external* mechanism of Nature, not—as for the Rational Idealists—by the *inward* movement of self-conscious Mind.   The ethical ideal for Spencer was utilitarian.

(4) The Rational Idealism of T. H. Green may be described as an Oxford expression of the Ethics of the German movement, but there is more attempt to emphasise the importance of regarding the good as including the satisfaction of each individual.   And Mr. F. H. Bradley shows still more clearly, in his doctrine of "self-realisation," that the Hegelian Ethics is quite consistent with Individualism.

CHAPTER VII

UTILITARIANISM

UTILITARIANISM is the doctrine that the "greatest happiness [1] of the greatest number" provides the ultimate ethical standard. It attempts to combine the theory that pleasure is the final good with the law of impartiality, according to which all persons have an equal right to a share of the pleasures available; on this account Sidgwick calls it "Universalistic Hedonism." It is peculiarly characteristic of English Ethics, being foreshadowed in Bacon and Hobbes, and appearing in various forms in the eighteenth century. Shaftesbury, Hutcheson, and occasionally Butler, assume that the Deity uses the utilitarian standard, but that man has to follow conscience or moral sense to guide him in the same direction. The last two, with Paley,[2] extend the sphere of pleasures and pains to the future life. Hume, on the other hand, struggles towards establishing a naturalistic basis for Utilitarianism. But the first to give definite shape and aim to the principle of utility in an ethical system was Jeremy Bentham,[3] who was followed by John Stuart Mill[4] and Henry Sidgwick.[5]

[1] See p. 24.
[2] 1743-1805. [3] 1748-1832. [4] 1806-1873. [5] 1838-1900.

234

A. EGOISTIC UTILITARIANISM—JEREMY BENTHAM

" Nature," says Bentham,[1] " has placed man under the governance of two sovereign masters, pain and pleasure. It is for them alone to point out what we ought to do, as well as to determine what we shall do." Upon this foundation is based the " principle of utility," which " approves or disapproves of every action whatsoever according to the tendency which it appears to have to augment or diminish the happiness of the party whose interest is in question." This " party " is, in general, the community, and its interest is the " sum " of the interests of its members. An action that *ought* to be done is one conforming to the principle of utility, and moral obligation has no other meaning. All other standards of morality are wrong if taken as ultimate; in any case there would be no motive for obeying them. Asceticism, sympathy, moral sense, duty, the Will of God, the love of esteem—all these are *per se* impotent as ultimate motives; though they may operate as external sanctions, since they are connected with pains and pleasures.

The question now arises, How are pleasures and pains to be measured, what is the principle of the hedonic scale? Bentham answers that the *personal* value of pleasure depends on its (1) intensity, (2) duration, (3) certainty, (4) propinquity, (5) fecundity (tendency to be followed by other pleasures), and (6) purity (freedom from accompanying or following pain). The value for the community depends further on (7) the extent, *i.e.* the number of persons who share the

---

[1] *Introduction to the Principles of Morals and Legislation* (1789).

pleasures. From the last Bentham is led to the principle of impartiality, or equity; in distributing pleasures, " every one is to count for one, and no one for more than one." But he fails to show that any individual can have a motive for preferring equitable distribution to increasing his own pleasure. He appears to have held with Shaftesbury,[1] that there is a perfect harmony between public and private interests. The individual, however, Bentham implies, can pursue only his own pleasure; thus the doctrine is to some extent akin to Hobbes', and on this account I have named his system *Egoistic*.

Virtue, Motive, Punishment.—The ordinary moral virtues (honesty, temperance, justice, veracity, etc.) are prized by the utilitarians as being types of character that tend on the whole to the greatest social happiness. Though the morality of an act is primarily dependent on its hedonistic effects, yet motives, intentions and dispositions are subjects of praise and blame and deserve rewards or punishment, because good motives, intentions and dispositions *tend* generally to increase social happiness, though in particular cases they may not be successful. In like manner bad motives and dispositions deserve punishment, because they tend towards a decrease of general happiness.

Bentham's doctrine of punishment appeals strongly to the merciful feelings of mankind. Punishment, he holds, is essentially bad, and must only be used to avoid greater evil in accordance with the principle of utility. Herein the utilitarians differ widely from the purists, *e.g.* Kant (and Butler in some of his moods), who held that wrong motives *deserve* punish-

[1] p. 155.

ment apart from its remedial effects.[1] We must agree with Bentham in admitting that the *remedial* criterion of punishment is the proper one for men to use in their dealings with each other, even if the retributive doctrine be correct, because we are incapable of judging the worth of other men's motives except by their effects.

B. SYMPATHETIC UTILITARIANISM—J. S. MILL

Bentham was unable to find a *motive* in human nature for obeying the utilitarian law, and thus the objections raised by him against other moral standards apply to his own. Mill endeavoured to get over this difficulty, but was unable to overcome it, because he, like Bentham, adhered to Psychological Hedonism, which assumes that pleasure is the motive of all actions.

Proof of Utilitarianism.[2]—Since all desire is for pleasure, it follows, according to Mill, that pleasure or happiness (an extended sum of pleasures) is alone desirable or good; for there can be no proof that anything is desirable beyond the fact that people actually desire it. A further inference is that the greatest happiness of the greatest number is the most desirable end. "Each person's happiness is a good to that person, and the general happiness, therefore, a good to the aggregate of all persons." Hence follows the utilitarian doctrine, that tendency to produce general happiness is the sole moral criterion of the goodness of actions, characters, or motives.

The Sanctions of Utilitarianism.—Mill's " proof '

---

[1] Cf. also Hegel, p. 223.
[2] The quotations are from Mill's *Utilitarianism* (1863).

tacitly assumes the Kantian principle, that the good is objectively and universally good, that what is really good or desirable for another is a desirable end for me to pursue. Now the advocate of Utilitarianism ought to explain *why* I should seek the general happiness, since if this is a good end for me I must have a motive for seeking it. In the proof, however, Mill has burnt his boats, because he based that proof on the principle that all desire is for pleasure, not for the general happiness. The only escape would be to show, in the manner of Shaftesbury, that the individual will get greatest pleasure by the course of action that tends most to multiply the pleasures of others. Mill, however, takes a different line; he abandons Psychological Hedonism. In answer to the question, What are the sanctions of Utilitarianism?— *i.e.* What are the sources of the obligation to adopt it instead of following private pleasure?—Mill replies that these sanctions are to be found in the conscientious feelings of mankind, in the consciousness possessed by every one that he is an integral part of society. This feeling is natural and operates in every mind of well developed feelings, "in proportion to the sensitiveness and thoughtfulness of the character."

Quality of Pleasures.—Mill differs from Bentham in admitting that the worth of pleasures depends on quality as well as on quantity. There are higher pleasures and lower, and those who have experienced both consciously prefer the higher, which proves that they are essentially more desirable. This preference of higher pleasures to lower, Mill attributes to a "sense of dignity," which makes a man choose rather to be Socrates unhappy than a pig satisfied. It has often been argued that Mill's recognition of a qualitative distinction in pleasures is inconsistent with mere Hedonism, which estimates the worth of pleasures by their quantity or intensity alone. The inconsistency was concealed from Mill by his ambiguous use of the word pleasure. He sometimes identifies pleasure with any desirable or desired state of consciousness, and he regards one pleasure as greater than another when it is desired more ; and the example of Socrates and the pig shows that the objects desired may be something more than passive feelings. At other times, speaking as a strict hedonist, he appears to regard pleasure as a special kind of feeling, for the most part sensuous, or at least passive, and not deriving any conscious worth from the nature of the object causing the feeling.

Self-Sacrifice and Conventional Morality.—Mill is particularly anxious to show that Utilitarianism is consistent with the ideals of self-sacrifice and the nobler forms of Stoicism. " In the golden rule of Jesus of Nazareth we read the complete spirit of the Ethics of utility. To do as one would be done by, and to love one's neighbour as oneself, constitute the ideal perfection of utilitarian morality." And he does not wish to be regarded as a radical in reference to conventional morality. The end to be pursued is not one's own pleasure, but public happiness. This explains why certain secondary moral rules are to be obeyed ; for example, though it may often be to a man's interest to tell a lie, Utilitarianism enjoins veracity as the " principal support of all present social well-being " ; though occasional exceptions may be allowed, as is acknowledged by most moralists.

Virtue as an End.—Mill admits that virtue, though primarily only a means to happiness, is nevertheless often desired for its own sake. His views on this subject were similar to Hume's, but inferior in psychological subtlety; so far as they can be expressed without inconsistency, they were somewhat as follows.—Certain cultivated and sympathetic persons happen to find pleasure in increasing the general sum of human pleasures, *i.e.* they *desire* this increase. Now virtue is that habitual quality of character which prompts actions tending to increase the general sum of pleasures; it is therefore an indispensable means for attaining this desired end. The means, being constantly thought of in connection with the pleasantness of the end, become associated with pleasure, and in this way give immediate pleasure, apart from their effects. Hence virtue—since everything pleasant is desired, and all desire is for pleasure—becomes an end desired for its own sake by cultivated and sympathetic people, but not (it would seem) by other persons. In the same way money, power, and fame, are originally conceived as means of increasing pleasure, but, becoming mentally associated with the pleasantness of these effects, they are often desired for their own sakes.

Criticism of Bentham and Mill.

Psychological Hedonism, a doctrine criticised in connection with Hume,[1] was the chief source of the inconsistencies in Bentham and Mill. Before the time of Spencer (who recognised the existence of

[1] p. 188.

powerful non-rational instincts differing from the desire for pleasure) Naturalists generally accepted this doctrine; but its inadequacy was brought into special prominence through the fact that Bentham and Mill confound it with Ethical Hedonism,— which asserts that pleasure *ought* to be the end of our actions. Hume was an open Naturalist; he is not so liable to the charge of inconsistency, since he recognised that the naturalistic method can only decide what motives actually have influenced mankind. But Mill, in laying down the "greatest happiness of the greatest number" as the end which *ought* to be pursued, uses the intuitional principle of impartiality, which requires every one to regard the good of others (in this case pleasure) as equally desirable with his own good. The *obligation* to accept this principle cannot be deduced; it is either an ultimate ethical law, or it has no meaning. Pure Naturalism can only treat moral obligation as a feeling sometimes producing effects, but Intuitionism regards it as an objective fact which *ought* to dominate our feelings. Bentham and Mill fail to recognise, that if every one desires his own pleasure, it must be shown that actions which tend to increase general happiness must seem to the agent to increase his own happiness, before he can regard the greatest happiness of the greatest number as the most desirable end. But the proof would not be valid except for those already possessing enough "sensitiveness and thoughtfulness of character" to make them feel most pleasure in increasing general happiness. Clearly Psychological Hedonism can only lead back to Hobbes; for though it be true that pleasure is, metaphorically speaking,

communicated through sympathy, it is also true
that one person's pleasure is actually distinct from
another's.

These criticisms prove two things: first, that
Utilitarianism cannot be based on Psychological
Hedonism; and secondly, since it claims to set up an
ethical standard demanding obedience, it cannot be
proved by naturalistic methods, since these are only
concerned with what *is*, not with what *ought* to be.
As Sidgwick recognised, it involves the axiom of
impartiality, and a denial of the theory that every
man can only desire his own pleasure.

C. INTUITIONAL UTILITARIANISM—SIDGWICK

Problem and Methods of Ethics.—Henry Sidgwick [1]
defines Ethics as the study of " what individual beings
ought, or what it is right for them, to do or to seek
to realise by voluntary action." [2]   All ethical methods
are either Hedonism or Intuitionism,[3] but these
methods are not mutually exclusive. The first
regards happiness as the ultimate end; Egoistic
Hedonism teaches that the agent must, or ought to,
pursue his own happiness exclusively; Universalistic
Hedonism regards universal happiness as the end.
According to the intuitional view, conduct is held
to be right when conforming to certain precepts or

---

[1] 1838-1900 ; Professor in Cambridge.

[2] All the quotations are from Sidgwick's *Methods of Ethics.*

[3] The meaning of "intuitionism" as used by Sidgwick must not be
identified with the meaning given to the same word in other parts of
this work (see p. 119). It happens, however, that the systems we have
described as intuitional are also so described by Sidgwick. Our definition
is chiefly appropriate in classifying English Eighteenth Century systems ;
it has reference to the question whether good is objective. Sidgwick is
thinking more of the source of our *knowledge* of right and wrong.

principles of duty, intuitively known to be un-conditionally binding. Any method which takes perfection or excellence of human nature as the ultimate end "will *prima facie* coincide to a great extent" with the intuitional view; but Sidgwick holds that the intuitional method is somewhat wider, and that when strictly applied it leads to Universalistic Hedonism, which regards happiness, not perfection, as the end.

Kant's system, moreover, though intuitional in the above sense, cannot *prima facie* be identified with the "perfection theory," since he denies that it is my duty to take the perfection of others as my end.

There are three forms of intuitional morality. *Perceptional Intuitionism*, the common - sense view of conscience, holds that the rightness or wrongness of every particular action can be determined by direct intuition ; this view is unphilosophical, since it ignores the existence of general principles. Secondly, *Dogmatic Intuitionism* accepts common-sense morality and endeavours to express in abstract form the general principles underlying it. Sidgwick appears to regard the systems of Butler and Hutcheson as types of this theory, since they treat the moral sense or conscience of the ordinary man as a completely satisfactory guide to conduct. Thirdly, *Philosophic Intuitionism* accepts provisionally, but in a critical spirit, the morality of common-sense, and it "attempts to find for it a philosophic basis which it does not itself offer." The ideal philosophic basis is a system of self-evident axioms. Here Sidgwick confessedly follows Clarke,[1] whom he takes as one of the

[1] p. 150.

best examples of the method. The philosophic differs from the dogmatic view in claiming the right to transcend, and if necessary, to correct, the unmethodical judgments of common-sense. *The philosophic Intuitionism which Sidgwick adopts leads him to Utilitarianism.*

Criticism of Common-Sense and Dogmatic Intuitionism.——The axioms or fundamental principles of Ethics, if it is to be an exact science, possessing the highest possible degree of certainty, must satisfy four conditions:——The terms used must be clear and precise, the axioms self-evident, mutually consistent, and accepted by experts in the subject. Common-sense or traditional morality is open to criticism when judged by these conditions. The analysis of popular conceptions of Justice, for example, shows that the word is used in different and conflicting senses. Sometimes Justice is regarded as Gratitude systematised, but it is not decided whether the benefit received or the trouble exerted by the benefactor is to be the just measure of the benefactor's claims. In determining what is just, various other principles are used, *e.g.* requital of desert, distribution according to the recipient's capacity for enjoyment, production of the maximum of freedom for all members of the community, conformity to positive law, fulfilment of natural expectation; all of these may conflict with each other. The ambiguities in the popular theories about other virtues (*e.g.* Chastity or Veracity) lead Sidgwick to conclude that a philosophic science of Ethics cannot be derived from the analysis of common-sense morality. Dogmatic Intuitionism cannot therefore be accepted as satisfactory.

Philosophic Intuitionism.

Many philosophic principles are useless as ethical axioms because they are tautological. This criticism applies to the maxims identifying right action with reasonable action, or with obedience to the higher parts of our nature; to Plato's theory of Virtue as a harmony; to Aristotle's doctrine of the Mean, and to the Stoic or Butlerian injunction to "follow Nature." All these maxims, Sidgwick holds, are useless because they try to solve the problem by expressing it in different language.[1]

The Rational Axioms of Ethics.—A useful Philosophic Intuitionism is nevertheless possible, for there are certain absolute self-evident practical principles which are not tautological, though by themselves they are too universal and formal to determine particular right actions. These are—

(1) The axiom of Justice or Equality: "that whatever action any one of us judges to be right for himself he implicitly judges to be right for all similar persons in similar circumstances." In Law this takes the form of "impartiality in the application of general rules."

(2) The axiom of Rational Self-Love, "that one ought to aim at one's own good *on the whole.*" The italicised words emphasise that the pursuit of my own good is to be impartial. I am not to sacrifice the present to the future, nor the future to the present.

---

[1] Apparently Sidgwick means that these maxims, regarded as *isolated* propositions, are tautological. But the chapters on the systems mentioned show that the ideas suggested by the maxims were fully developed, and received complex meanings not capable of being expressed in a few abstract axioms.

(3) The axiom of Rational Benevolence, which is, strictly speaking, a product of two rational intuitions : —(a) " that the good of any one individual is of no more importance from the point of view . . . of the universe than the good of any other," and (b) " that as a rational being I am bound to aim at good generally, so far as it is attainable by my efforts, not merely at a particular part of it." It follows that I am bound to seek impartially the good of all individuals, including myself. This axiom, with (1), Sidgwick regards as equivalent to Kant's Categorical Imperative, and to Clarke's axioms.[1] Taken together they are exact expressions of the golden rule, " Do unto others as you would that they should do unto you."

The Proof of Utilitarianism.—" Philosophic Intuitionism" leads, according to Sidgwick, to Utilitarianism, which he maintains to be a logical inference from two distinct principles. The first is the axiom of Rational Benevolence, which is intuitively apprehended and neither requires nor is capable of proof. The second is the principle resulting from analysis, and also incapable of strict proof—that the only ultimate good is the pleasure of some sentient being. This maxim of Hedonism emerges from the following considerations. All personal qualities are only valuable " on account of the desirable conscious life in which they are or will be actualised." Now consciousness is either Cognition,[2] Feeling, or Will; but Will and Cognition

---

[1] pp. 150, 194.

[2] This psychological division is adopted by Höffding (*Psychology*, chap. iv.) and other psychologists, but Stout's division (*Groundwork of Psychology*, chap. iii.) into Cognition and Interest (including Feeling and Conation) seems preferable, since it regards Feeling and Conation as indissoluble. This being so, Sidgwick's argument falls to the ground, or is at all events seriously weakened.

are neutral in respect of desirability, and desirable Feeling is the same thing as Pleasure. From these two principles it follows that we are to direct our actions towards impartially increasing the happiness of sentient beings.[1]

Utilitarianism and Common-Sense.—Sidgwick holds that Common-sense morality is, on the whole, an unreflecting and unmethodical Utilitarianism. Both recognise that virtues like generosity, self-sacrifice, scrupulousness, etc., are of the highest value as expressions of the axioms of Rational Benevolence, but that in exceptional cases they may require to be restrained owing to their painful consequences; hence both condemn quixotism, over-scrupulousness, and fanatical self-sacrifice. Common-sense, again, while approving of benevolence, recognises that the individual's private interests should occupy his chief attention—a conclusion consistent with Utilitarianism, since a man has more power to increase his own happiness than that of others. And though impartiality is an essential feature in Utilitarianism, the duties arising from the narrower social relations, such as those implied in gratitude, family affection, and patriotism, are recognised by Utilitarianism, as well as by Common-sense, because pleasure on the whole would be greatly diminished by ignoring them. The different and often conflicting elements in Common-sense conceptions of Justice appear to spring from utilitarian considerations, since each of these elements

---

[1] Lower animals are included. This suggests a serious practical obstacle to applying the utilitarian theory ; it is seldom possible to estimate the pains and pleasures of men, to say nothing of the lower animals. This, however, is not in any way a proof that the utilitarian theory is false, but only that it is unpractical.

if properly applied, tends to the happiness of society; but all should be regulated and controlled by the strict utilitarian standard.   Veracity, again is a utilitarian duty; and the exceptions allowed by common-sense are also utilitarian, *e.g.* deception of a criminal to prevent crime or of an invalid for his own good, or verbal inaccuracy for reasons of courtesy.   In like manner other virtues are considered.

Applications, Positive Morality.—Systematic Utilitarianism is, however, required to correct and improve Common-sense Morality, to resist the tyranny of mere custom and tradition, by insisting that there is only the one unconditional standard of right action. But on the whole the utilitarian will be very cautious about interfering with the Positive Morality[1] of his age and country, for two reasons.   First, Positive Morality is a great force for social happiness, and is sanctioned by the power of custom and tradition, which would be wanting in the case of new rules of conduct, even though these were intrinsically better; thus a theoretical improvement might practically result in anarchy.   Secondly, Common-sense is offended by radical exceptions to its code, and the hasty reformer may lose all influence for good.   The utilitarian seeks to reform *gradually*, but on the whole he will uphold traditional morality.

In actions lying beyond strict duty, Utilitarianism will lay less stress than Common-sense on the negative virtues of self-restraint and will recommend conduct giving positive pleasure.

Egoism and Altruism.—The axiom of Rational Egoism is the great stumbling-block for strict

---

[1] Positive Morality and Common-sense Morality are much the same.

utilitarians, since they insist on impartiality in the distribution of pleasures. To establish a harmony between this axiom and the axiom of Rational Benevolence is, according to Sidgwick, " the profoundest problem of Ethics." The ultimate harmony between these two motives is to be regarded as " a hypothesis logically necessary to avoid a fundamental contradiction in one chief department of our thought." If there be any objective good which the individual can recognise as such, then he is bound to regard the good of others as ethically equivalent to his own. Sidgwick says, almost in the manner of Descartes, " I find that I undoubtedly seem to perceive, as clearly and certainly as I see any axiom in Arithmetic and Geometry, that it is ' right ' and ' reasonable ' for me to treat others as I should think that I myself ought to be treated under similar conditions, and to do what I believe to be ultimately conducive to universal good or happiness." This is the " clearest and most certain of our moral intuitions." It abides though the harmony of goods cannot be empirically established by sympathy or by religious sanction ; not by the former, since sympathy is often partial; nor by the latter, since we cannot tell with certainty what actions the Deity wishes us to perform.

D. General Criticism of Utilitarianism

Sidgwick, on the whole, follows in the lines laid down by Bentham and Mill, but he may be regarded as the most philosophical representative of Utilitarianism, since his logical analysis is far more thorough. He recognises that the *impartiality*, which is vital to

the theory, is incompatible with the assumption that
private pleasure or sympathy provides the sanctions.
In this respect he was deeply influenced by Kant, and,
if the phrase were not a misnomer, he might be called
a " Kantian Hedonist."

In the analysis [1] which leads Sidgwick to conclude
that pleasure is the ultimate good there are two
distinct principles involved.   The first is that the
final good is some form of conscious life, whose worth
is apprehended along with its content; it is *intrinsically* desirable, and contains its own ethical justification,
as an inseparable part of its being.   The Greeks, [2] on
the whole, recognised this primary self-evident axiom
of individual ethics, and it has never been expressly
denied.   It was obscured, however, by the Stoics and
Cynics, who laid undue stress on the active and
resistive elements which, under the conditions in which
man is placed, are indispensable to the realisation of
the good, but do not constitute its whole nature ; and
by Kant, [3] who subordinated good to Duty, thereby
inverting the proper order.

Ethical Hedonism.—The second principle referred
to is, that, of the three psychological elements, cognition
and will are ethically indifferent, and that desirable
consciousness is the same thing as desirable feeling,
i.e. pleasure.   Reasonable men will admit that neither
cognition nor will, *per se*, is intrinsically desirable, but
it seems to be equally true that feeling *per se* is
seldom, if ever, the only desirable element in consciousness. [4]   Cognition, feeling, and will are usually bound

[1] p. 246.
[2] Especially Aristotle, who insists that Well-being is an activity of the
soul, complete-in-itself, p. 68.   [3] pp. 202, 203 *sq.*
[4] Cf. Plato, p. 60, and Aristotle, pp. 77, 78.

up so closely in a concrete mental experience that we regard the *whole* experience as intrinsically desirable or undesirable. In admitting, with Plato, that an experience is not intrinsically good unless it is also pleasant, we do not imply that pleasure is the only constituent that makes the experience good.

The arguments used by Sidgwick in favour of Ethical Hedonism are, as we have seen, based on the division of mental experience into Feeling, Cognition, and Will. Now such divisions—as psychologists are well aware—are abstractions and are therefore liable to mislead. We know that none of these three elements ever occur in isolation, and, therefore, we cannot directly conclude that any particular element alone gives its value to an experience. Feeling, in fact, is a quality of a mental state which cannot exist apart from other elements any more than colour or shape can exist without matter. Feelings can only be remembered and identified by the characteristic elements which accompany them, including sensations, cognitions, and interests of specific kinds. It is not too much to say that we cannot be conscious of *mere* feeling, and, when we speak of feelings being valued or compared ethically we are referring to complex states of mind containing far more than pure feeling.

The controversy is, however, partly verbal. If the feeling of pleasure in a mental experience *means* the desirableness of the experience (which of course includes the consciousness of the desirableness), then it is a mere truism to say that things are desirable in proportion to the pleasure they give ; but it must be recognised that the desirableness is an intrinsic element in the experience, and inseparable therefrom.

But the hedonists do not appear to mean this; they mean that pleasure is something detachable from the elements of an experience; if a man can feel equal pleasure in staring at a stone wall as in looking at a beautiful landscape, then, they say, the experiences are equally good.

If, then, the feeling of pleasure is regarded as a particular separable mental element in experience, the conclusion that pleasure is the essence of its desirableness is shown to be false by direct experience. For example, my conscious approval of a landscape or play is based on the perception of certain features in the landscape or play. The pleasure may, to a large extent, be bound up with the approval, but it is not the object approved.[1] Even if we agree with Hume's questionable doctrine,[2] that the pleasure *is* the approval, it is absurd to say that the object approved of is the approval! To take another example: When a scientist or mathematician discovers a new law or fact, the source of his immediate pleasure is the conviction that he has discovered the truth; it is the truth which he judges to be good, not his pleasure in finding it. If the law turns out to be false, he even disapproves of his false beliefs and of the pleasure he originally felt in its discovery. This again shows that the object of his approval is truth, not pleasure.

The hedonistic argument is based on the fallacious logical inference that pleasure, because it is essential to the complete desirableness of an experience, must constitute the essence of its desirableness. The same misleading form of argument has been used in turn to prove that the essence of matter is extension

[1] Cf. Hutcheson, p. 157.   [2] p. 181.

since all matter is extended, that it is motion
since all matter is in motion, and that it is im-
penetrability since all matter possesses this quality
in some degree. From "all good contains pleasure"
it is inferred that good and pleasure are identical.
As Plato showed, this would imply that good is a
self-contradictory conception, since different pleasures
may clash with each other.[1]

The ideal experience is then not mere feeling, but a
complex state in which knowledge and feeling are fully
exercised and the will moves forward without restraint.

The Quantification of Happiness.—Utilitarianism is
also open to the objection that its fundamental formula,
"seek the greatest happiness of the greatest number,"
has an illusory appearance of exactness. The conception of a quantity of happiness will remain obscure,
until it is shown how happiness is to be measured
with practical accuracy. And this difficult problem
has not yet been solved. Neither has it been shown
how the above formula is to be combined with the
Benthamite formula of impartiality,—"Every one to
count for one, and no one for more than one,"—and
it is conceivable that these two formulae might
practically conflict. Possibly, however, these defects
may hereafter be partially removed by the discovery
of some new formula of social distribution, without
abandoning the spirit of Utilitarianism.

A permanent truth in the doctrine that good may
be quantified seems to be that there are in this life
degrees of social good, that the present state of society
may be improved; and that, though a Best is here

---

[1] See p. 60. I think Plato used all the best arguments against
ethical Hedonism.

unattainable by merely human effort, a Better may
nevertheless be realised. Thus social good possesses,
it would seem, one attribute which may be expressed
by number and quantity, namely *order*; if A, B, C
are three real or imagined social conditions, in saying
that A is better than B, and B than C, we arrange
these three in a scale, just as numbers naturally
fall into a scale. Again, number certainly has much
to say to the general good of a social group. If
the welfare of one or more members of the group
advances without interfering with the welfare of the
other members, it is self-evident that the general
welfare of the group advances, and that this advance
is *pari passu* with the number of persons sharing
the improvement. But if the welfare of some
members is sacrificed in order to increase that of
others, we have no means of determining whether
there is a general advance in welfare, whether the
change is objectively good. We cannot subtract
the adversities of one person from the prosperity of
another and say whether the resultant prosperity is
plus or *minus*, or fix its degree otherwise. Indeed if
prosperity is good and adversity is bad, then the change
is both good and bad; and this suggests—what we
shall now consider more fully—that the utilitarian
conception of good is self-contradictory, in the forms
in which it is presented to us by its chief supporters.

Logical Defect in Utilitarian Idea of Good.—
Sidgwick, we have seen, regards the axiom of Rational
Self-love as self-evident. It must be noticed that
this is an *intuitional* [1] axiom, expressing a real obligation that is sometimes evaded; it is not a mere

[1] In our sense of the term as well as Sidgwick's (p. 242, note 3).

assertion that each man must seek his own good. Now Sidgwick recognises that there is no final dogmatic solution of the possible opposition between self-love and benevolence. He is too cautious to assert that the need felt by practical Reason of harmonising the two is a proof that such a harmony is possible, and he is not willing to accept as self-evident or necessary the solutions offered by Shaftesbury, Butler, and Hutcheson, or Kant.[1]

This difficulty, which Sidgwick fully recognised, surely proves that the axiom of Benevolence is inconsistent with the axiom of Self-love, *so long as good is identified with pleasure*; this identification is, in fact, the source of the contradiction in the " Idea of the Good " as described by the Utilitarians. Even if we accept Shaftesbury's proof that the actions most pleasant to the agent are those that tend most to increase the general happiness, the harmony established by this proof is merely external and accidental. The harmony does not differ widely from Hobbes' political harmony, since it consists merely in this, that Nature has arranged by means of sympathy and social feelings that conflicting interests will not clash. There is however no inward and true harmony of interests.

We might resolve the logical difficulty by rejecting the axiom of Self-love; but this would be a practical absurdity, since, in recognising that a good is worthy of pursuit, I appropriate that good and regard it as mine; besides, to exclude my own good would be inconsistent with the principle of impartiality, and would lead to a form of inverted Egoism. If good

[1] See pp. 156, 158, 172, 201.

is identical with pleasure, the goodness of an
end is, for the agent, proportional to the pleasure
which its realisation gives him. But one person's
pleasure, though loosely described as communicable
by sympathy, is always distinct—as a feeling—
from another person's pleasure. Ethical Hedonism, in
short, is really equivalent to Egoistic Hedonism, and
leads back to Epicureanism, unless the axiom of Self-
Love is given a subordinate place.

At this point the logical value of the Platonic
doctrine of the Unity of the Good becomes very clear.[1]
Good, if identified with pleasure, does not possess logical
unity, that is, it contradicts itself, since my pleasure
is not another person's pleasure. This contradiction
appears in all the eighteenth-century intuitional
systems, since they regard virtue and general happiness as two distinct ultimate ends, both equally good.
The distinction is not removed by the dogma that
virtue always leads to happiness either in this
world or the next. If we once sever Self-love from
Benevolence and Virtue they cannot be re-united.
What is required is a return to the simplicity of
the Aristotelian doctrine that the Well-being of
an individual *consists* in apprehending and realising
objective good; that Well-being is not merely an
external reward of good actions; it *is* those good
actions; as Spinoza said, "*Beatitudo non est virtutis
premium sed ipsa virtus.*" [2]

But if this doctrine is to avoid Egoistic Hedonism,
it must be shown that the idea of an "absolute and
common good" is a possible one. This was the
problem which Green attempted to solve.[3]

[1] See p. 60 (par. 2).   [2] *Ethica*, v. 42.   [3] See Chap. IX.

CHAPTER VIII

EVOLUTIONAL NATURALISM—DARWIN AND SPENCER

Historical Position. — Modern ethical Naturalism began with Hobbes. We have seen that he regarded self-preserving and self-gratifying impulses as the ultimate principles of action in all living things, and attempted to reduce to these all so-called benevolent and social affections. This exclusive Egoism was corrected by Butler, who pointed out in the first place—following Shaftesbury—that *unselfish* social affections and impulses are actual constituents of human nature, and, secondly, that Conscience, though not always obeyed, yet provides a motive tending to urge a man to sacrifice his own immediate interests for the public good. In the second doctrine he was supported by Kant, who insisted that the consciousness of duty is capable of overcoming personal inclinations. Auguste Comte [1] went further, and maintained that individual happiness was best secured by the complete subordination of egoistic to altruistic sentiments, thus asserting an identity between self-seeking and other-seeking motives. From a rationalistic standpoint Fichte and Hegel taught that the individual can realise his true

[1] 1798-1857.

self only by identifying his interests with those of the larger whole of society.

These results explain why the starting-point of Evolutional Naturalism is quite different from that of Hobbes. The former assumes, as acknowledged data, the existence and operation of purely altruistic (race-preserving) motives and impulses as well as the purely egoistic (self-preserving), and it attempts to explain the value and origin of both by a new principle, that of natural *evolution*.

Evolution. — In its widest sense, " evolution " signifies the unfolding or development of the manifestly complex from apparently simple forms. The seed, for example, in its evolution becomes a tree, though to human eyes it is a far less complex structure; and the modern State is " evolved " from simpler and more primitive forms of government. A follower of Aristotle might describe evolution as the transition from the " potential " (*i.e.* what exists only in germ or possibility) to the actual; the seed, for example, potentially contains the fruit, which is the actuality of the seed. The idea of explaining by tracing development is of course not new,[1] but as a comprehensive philosophic method it was probably first used systematically by Comte and by Hegel, though in very different senses. Comte traces the historical growth of the sciences; he claims that the simple precedes the complex, each stage making use of the results already reached. He urges that the Sciences should be taught in this order which is the natural one. Comte's method is chiefly *empirical*

[1] *E.g.* the Ionics, the first Greek philosophers, had some idea of tracing the origin of everything from one fundamental substance, such as water or air.

or descriptive. Hegel's, on the other hand, is *rational*; he endeavours to show that the actual development of knowledge and of social and moral institutions is the necessary order in which Reason finds expression; the development is the manifestation of Reason or Mind.

The term "evolution," as used by Darwin and Spencer, includes "growth," but also emphasises the idea that growth is not the creation of new forms, but the necessary outcome of what already exists; it also suggests that *growth is not merely of individuals but of races and institutions*, and even of material systems. What is required to give precision to the term is to state some *principle* by which growth takes place; and such principle may be either a law, working mechanically (*e.g.* "survival of the fittest") or an ideal end at which Nature or the Mind in Nature aims. Unless some working method or end of evolution is implied, the word evolution can mean little more than change.[1]

A. DARWIN

Natural Evolution.—The empirical hypothesis of Natural Evolution, though foreshadowed by Comte in the sphere of knowledge, and by others in biology, is specially associated with the name of Charles Darwin,[2] who first collected the facts required to

---

[1] A number of different views as to the meaning of evolution and its applications will be found in the essays collected under the title *Darwin and Modern Science* (1909). What is still required is a systematic exposition of the connecting links between these different meanings.

[2] 1809-1882. His most famous works are the *Origin of Species* (1859) and the *Descent of Man* (1871).

give it support. With him it signified the principle
that all living species, plants, animals, and men,
originally sprang from less developed forms of life;
that species have become differentiated through the
survival of those endowed with organs and faculties
adapted for life in the environment in which they
happen to be placed. Thus the "survival of the
fittest"[1] is the mechanism by which evolution is
said to take place, and the process is described by
Darwin as a "struggle for existence," carried on by
each individual, partly with the inanimate environment, and partly with other living creatures; the
result being that only those survive who possess
the appropriate armour for the struggle.[2] The
process by which the unfit are eliminated and the
fit survive is metaphorically called "natural selection"
by Darwin. In order to apply the principle to
explain the survival of races it is necessary to assume
as an additional mechanism—whether original or
accidentally evolved—some kind of *heredity*, by which
life-preserving organs or aptitudes are transmitted
from parent to offspring.

Darwin was chiefly interested in the physical
evolution of species, but he drew attention to the
possibility of explaining the existence of moral
instincts in the same way, and the subject was fully
worked out by Herbert Spencer; who, however, took

---

[1] This term was first used by Spencer, not by Darwin.

[2] That the fittest survive and the unfit are eliminated are truisms,
since possessing fitness to survive and actual surviving are the same from
the naturalistic standpoint. As an abstract principle the theory gives
no information, but it is of use when taken in conjunction with the
empirically observed fact that certain qualities—*e.g.* strength, agility,
fleetness, endurance, and intelligence—help individuals in the struggle for
existence.

up the idea of evolution quite independently of Darwin, and endeavoured to apply it, not only to Ethics, but to all human institutions and customs.

B. HERBERT SPENCER [1]

The End imposed by Nature—Life.—Evolution is applied by Spencer not only to the physical growth of organisms (Biology) but also to the moral growth of humanity (Ethics) and to the development of societies (Sociology). The Darwinian conception of evolution as a differentiation of species is accepted, but generalised, so that evolution is regarded by Spencer as a process from the homogeneous to the heterogeneous, from the simple to the complex. In every case there is a transition from elementary and comparatively few adjustments to needs to complex and more numerous ones, necessitated by the struggle for existence, in which increased power of adaptation to circumstances is always an advantage. The objective end imposed by Nature is *life*—the life of the individual organism and, through it, of the race. Life is defined by Spencer as the " continuous adjustment of internal relations to external relations."

The Subject of Ethics.—In the course of evolution through survival of the fittest, organisms acquire the useful power of adapting their actions to various ends, such as the acquisition of nourishment or the avoidance of danger. Such adaptation of actions is Conduct. Conduct again evolves further, for, as the ends sought become more numerous and various, life increases in

---

[1] 1820-1903. The *Data of Ethics* and *Justice* contain the fundamental principles of Spencer's Ethics.

breadth and intensity as well as in length. The evolution of conduct takes place in three directions, since the immediate end may be the preservation of the individual (the agent), of the offspring, or of the race. As we ascend in the scale increased security is given to life in all the senses mentioned. Now Ethics has for its subject-matter that form which universal conduct takes during the last stages of its evolution, and this stage is represented by the human race.

Good and Bad.—These terms generally have reference to some prescribed ends; thus a "good knife" is one that cuts well, a bad umbrella is one that leaks— and so forth. With animate beings the same thing is true; here the terms are used of conduct, and the end tacitly assumed is life. Applying this to the three divisions of conduct, we find that actions are called good or bad, according as they tend to further or to hinder the complete life [1] of self, offspring, or fellow-men.

The Ethical End—Pleasure.—A difficulty now arises that occurs in all forms of Naturalism. The end imposed by Nature is life; but life may be undesirable for the conscious subject, and, therefore, ethically objectionable in the ordinary sense. The pessimist asserts that life is not worth living and is therefore under an obligation to destroy life. The optimist, however, holds that life is essentially desirable. Spencer holds that optimists and pessimists agree in the doctrine that "life is good or bad according as it does or does not bring a surplus of agreeable feeling." [2]   Spencer is himself a hedonistic

---

[1] *I.e.* life in length, breadth, and intensity. Breadth consists in the fullest possible exercise of different aptitudes.

[2] Notice the questionable doctrine that every standard of Ethics is hedonistic.

optimist; he holds that all opposition between the
"biological" and "ethical" conceptions of good and
bad tends to be removed in the course of Evolution.
As soon as sentiency appears amongst living creatures,
only those survive who, on the whole, take pleasure
in life-preserving acts.

Spencer on the Evolution of Conduct.

This is considered by Spencer from four points of
view, the physical, the biological, the psychological,
and the sociological. In each case moral conduct
stands at the highest point of development.

(1) *Physically*, the evolution proceeds from the
indefinite and incoherent to the definite and coherent.[1]
Corresponding to this, moral conduct follows fixed
principles; immoral or indifferent conduct is fickle
and inconstant.

(2) The "physical view" is purely formal, but the
"*biological view*" considers conduct with reference to
its natural end—breadth and length of life—and thus
provides a test of moral actions. The moral man is
one whose functions "are all discharged in degrees
duly adjusted to the conditions of existence."[2] "The
performance of every function is in a sense a moral
obligation."

The "biological view" introduces a consideration
of the *causal connection between feeling and function*.
Sentient beings strive to exercise functions that give
pleasure, and to avoid those that give pain. It follows
that "sentient existence can evolve only on condition

[1] Compare with the "widest sense" of "evolution," p. 258.
[2] Cf. Plato's conception of "Justice in the individual" (p. 46), and
Aristotle's doctrine of the Mean (pp. 70, 71).

that pleasure-giving acts are life-sustaining acts."
Thus, that Nature tends to produce a harmony between
her end (life) and the human ethical good (pleasure)
follows *deductively* from the evolutional principle.
Experience verifies this inference, by showing that
pleasure as such increases the vital powers and so
prolongs life, whereas pain lowers vitality.[1] Pleasure
is essentially good, both biologically and ethically,
though its indirect consequences may sometimes be
injurious to life.   In the course of evolution these
occasional injurious consequences tend to disappear,
and pleasure-giving, self-preserving, and race-preserving acts will ultimately coincide.

(3) In the "*psychological view*" of the evolution of
conduct, Spencer assumes that feelings and sensations
are the ultimate elements of consciousness.   Feelings
may be either immediate sensations or ideal (representative) feelings, referring to a possible future
(*e.g.* expectation, hope, or fear).   In the course of
development immediate simple sensations become subordinated to the more complex ideas of sensations to
come.   This power of looking into the future is on
the average favourable to the preservation of life, and
thus the psychological view coheres with the biological.
A remote good becomes now more valued than an
immediate one, and there thus arises the sense of
obligation (the felt need for repressing an immediate
impulse), of the *authority* of one motive over another,
and of a scale of worth.   From this point of view
moral feelings are at the highest level ; honesty and
truthfulness, for example, restrain the desire for
immediate profit.   Spencer insists, however, that the

---

[1] Cf. Hobbes (p. 129 and note 2).

authority of a remote good is not unconditional; it would be absurd and suicidal to sacrifice the present to the future on every occasion, since the fruition of good is in the present, and is only postponed in order that it may be realised in another " present."

The *sense of duty* or *moral obligation* is not an isolated representative feeling; it is the idea attached to all representative feelings that possess the two elements of authority and coerciveness. The sense of compulsion proceeds from an anticipation of the natural consequences of transgression, and is increased by the associated ideas of legal penalties. Spencer holds that " the sense of duty or moral obligation is transitory, and will diminish as fast as moralisation increases." He means by this that, as evolution proceeds, morally good actions will tend to be performed spontaneously, through the immediate pleasure they give to the agent.

(4) The " *sociological view* " of the evolution of conduct investigates the natural laws of right living for human societies. For any particular society or State, these laws are to be determined by the condition that the lives of each of its members may be " the greatest possible, alike in length and breadth." Spencer appears to assume that Nature aims at the preservation of the type rather than of the individual, and that, therefore, " the life of the social organism must as an end rank above the lives of its units." On this account the individual is often required to sacrifice his welfare or life for the sake of the community, as, for example, in war with other communities. But here we are met with the difficulty that the ultimate end is the welfare of

K

individuals, and that social communities only arise because on the average the individual profits by living with others. The type, moreover, exists only in individuals. *Evolution solves this contradiction by gradually removing the opposition between individual and social good.* This takes place in two ways: First, by the improvement in the mutual relations of different States, by which war will gradually die out; secondly, by improvement in the relations between members of the same State.

The Limit of Social Evolution.—The advantages of social life are shared by each member of the society concerned, and arise from co-operation. The essential requirements are absence of mutual aggression and mutual fulfilment of contracts. But the " limit of evolution " is not reached until spontaneous and disinterested Benevolence is added to Justice. The natural source, both of Justice and Beneficence, is Sympathy, which, therefore, tends to increase through survival of the fittest races. This is only a special application of the general principle that the end imposed by Nature (life) and the ethical end approved by man (pleasure) must move towards harmony if the race is to survive. Spencer concludes that " pleasure will eventually accompany every mode of action demanded by social conditions." This ideal is the limit of social evolution.

Egoism and Altruism.—Egoism is biologically prior to altruism, since, if there were no self-preserving impulses, altruism would be meaningless and all would lose their lives. But egoism is ethically, as well as biologically, prior to altruism, since the individual is the ultimate seat of happiness. Moreover, the exercise of special faculties generally conduces to the happiness, not only of the agent, but of the society around him. " The pursuit of individual happiness within those limits prescribed by social conditions is the first requisite to the attainment of the greatest general happiness." A strong, healthy, and cheerful constitution is the most valuable bequest a parent can give to a child, and this is secured only by the parent taking care of his *own* health and happiness. Good health and good spirits tend to produce happiness in those around us, often more than directly altruistic actions. Again, the egoistic individual retains those powers and energies that make altruistic action possible. Moreover, unselfishness carried to extremes tends to increase selfishness, partly through the fact that it cannot be exercised without evoking the selfishness of the recipient; and partly because unselfishness as such tends to lower vitality, and in the long run, through natural selection, to diminish the number of the altruistic.

Altruism, as well as egoism, is essential to the preservation of a species. The " spontaneous fission " by which the more elementary types multiply is a form of physical altruism. In general the life of the offspring is secured by sacrifice on the part of the parent. Self-sacrifice may take the form of instinct (as with birds), or it may be conscious or deliberate (as often with man). But in any case parental altruism, whatever its motive, is essential to the life of the race. Unduly egoistic and unduly altruistic individuals alike tend to disappear from the race.

Parental altruism advances by degrees into social

altruism, the effects of which are best seen in the human race. Spencer shows, after the manner of Hobbes, that a universal recognition of the laws of Justice (abstinence from mutual aggression, and fulfilment of contract), and of honourable dealing, is an advantage to each member of the community, and that this fact provides an *egoistic* motive for preserving those laws intact. Further, the well-beings of different members of a community are closely interdependent; physical strength and mental talents and skill, in individuals, tend to benefit all the members of the social group; the same is true of moral qualities like social truthfulness (*e.g.* in recommending servants). There are therefore egoistic motives for looking after the physical health and the mental and moral education of other people. Moreover unselfishness and sympathy reap more direct rewards, by creating mutual regard and prompting unstinted return of favours. Altruism, besides, often has an immediate egoistic value arising from the joys of sympathy and kindly action. The pleasures of Art depend to a large extent on the power of sympathising with joy and sorrow and other human feelings. On the whole an egoism that ignores the welfare of others defeats its own end, and would produce social dissolution,[1] if it became universal, or grew beyond a certain limit.

On the other hand, pure altruism is an untenable moral ideal, for it likewise defeats itself. We cannot gratify the pleasures of others unless they have *egoistic* pleasures. The pleasure of sympathy cannot exceed the direct pleasure of the person sympathised with;

[1] Compare the discussion in this paragraph with Shaftesbury (p. 155).

the pleasure of giving is inferior to, and dependent on, the pleasure of receiving the gift. The mere altruist feeds on the egoistic pleasures enjoyed directly by others.

Compromise.—The maxims, "Live for Self" and "Live for others," are both wrong. What is required is a compromise between egoism and altruism. *But a complete reconciliation cannot be secured by an artificial attempt on the part of all to seek the greatest happiness of the greatest number.[1] It must be left to the forces of natural evolution, which are constantly working towards a more and more perfect adaptation of egoistic to altruistic requirements,* partly through the deepening of sympathy and partly through the adjustment of social conditions.

Spencer's Theory of Justice.

Justice in general is concerned with the causal relations that ought to subsist in a community between acts and their pleasant or painful consequences to the agent or others. Justice is an evolutional ideal tending necessarily towards realisation, and its form is to be determined by considering what laws in this sphere tend to increase the "length and breadth" of the life of the species. Spencer assumes that Nature's end is the preservation of the type, and of the individual only in so far as his preservation tends to ensure that of the type.

"*Sub - human*" *Justice.*—Any living species, to survive, must conform to two laws. First, the helpless

[1] Spencer, however, does not reject Utilitarianism. He insists that it is of little use as a practical guide owing to its indefiniteness and to its tendency to degenerate into mere Altruism.

offspring must be preserved; and here the rule is that " during immaturity benefits received must be inversely proportional to capacities possessed." Secondly, after maturity, " benefit must vary directly as worth—worth being measured by fitness to the conditions of existence." If the first law were violated the helpless young would not survive, and the species would disappear. The second law leads to the law of sub-human justice, which applies to all living species: " Each individual shall receive the benefits and the evils of its own nature and its consequent conduct." Spencer holds that this " law of relation between conduct and consequence " is the chief condition that the principle of the " survival of the fittest " may operate, and is therefore " the primary law holding of all creatures." It works most freely with solitary animals, since amongst gregarious animals it is restricted by the condition that each individual is to be restrained from impeding the conduct by which others in like manner receive the benefits or evils of their own actions. Punishments arise from the need for preventing transgression; a " rogue " elephant is banished from the herd; the idle drones, when useless encumbrances, are killed by the other bees. A second modification of the primary law arises amongst gregarious animals by the occasional need for individuals to sacrifice or endanger their lives for the sake of the community, as in the protection of the females and young by the males among various animals.

Human Justice. The Formula of Justice.—As human life is a development of sub-human life, so human justice is a development of sub-human justice, and its formula is essentially the same. In order

that the fittest may survive, " each individual ought
to receive the benefits and the evils of his own nature
and consequent conduct." As an actual law Justice
becomes more pronounced among higher animals, and
is most influential in the human race; evolution tends
to increase its efficacy, and to realise it in society.
In order that Justice may operate generally, transgression must be prevented, and in this way is
evolved the custom of inflicting punishments by the
community as a whole. A modification arises from
the fact that in human races the need for the sacrifice
of individuals in defence of the species assumes large
proportions. Spencer claims that such sacrifice is
justified only in defensive war, and even this will
ultimately die out, since it hinders human welfare.
Since conduct is the expression of the individual will,
the formula for Justice, containing both a positive
and a negative element, may be expressed as follows:
" Every man is free to do that which he wills, provided
he infringes not the equal freedom of any other."
This is not to be taken as justifying retaliation; its
meaning, as interpreted by the condition that " the
greatest sum of happiness is the remote end," is that
" the sphere within which each may pursue happiness
has a limit on the other side of which lie the similarly
limited spheres of action of his neighbours."

*Development of the Sentiment of Justice and of the
Idea of Justice.*—The *sentiment* of Justice passes
through three stages, the egoistic, the " pro-altruistic," [1]
and the altruistic. (1) the egoistic sentiment of
Justice is rooted in the universal love of freedom

---

[1] A " pro-altruistic " sentiment apparently means a sentiment coming
before the genuine altruistic sentiment, or perhaps a *substitute* for the
latter.

possessed by all living things, the desire of each individual to retain control over his own natural powers. (2) The "pro-altruistic" sentiment is partly egoistic, and depends on fear. There is the fear of retaliation, of adverse public opinion. Again, when political authority is established for the good of the tribe, the warrior chief punishes mutual trespasses in order to prevent his tribe from being weakened by dissension. Finally the dead chief is deified, his commands are accepted as divine sanctions, and infringements are punished. (3) But it is mainly through the *sympathy* which develops in gregarious animals in proportion to their intelligence that the "altruistic sentiment of Justice" is able to evolve. Sympathetic Justice leads men to feel for the rights of others, and thus presupposes the existence of the egoistic sentiment of Justice, and, in addition, a developed imagination and a power of mental representation. Its full development is possible only in a permanently peaceful state. Finally, *the Idea of Justice* is a much later development, since it calls into play the highest powers of abstraction, whereas the sentiment is only evoked instinctively in particular cases. The Idea of Justice is the recognition of the universally binding force of the Formula. It is a generalisation of the altruistic sentiment of Justice.

Error of Communism.——The communistic theory of Justice as *equality*, in the sense that every one is to receive an equal share of the results of human activity, is contrary to the formula of Justice. It violates the principle of the survival of the fittest, and is thus injurious to the race as a whole. Justice is equality only in the sense that equal opportunities for action are to be given to all, and that each agent is to receive the benefits and evils of his own actions. But it is inequality in the sense that these benefits and evils vary, because the capacities of individuals vary.

The Authority of the Formula of Justice.—Spencer holds that the formula of Justice, as regards its authority, is derived in the first place from a direct intuitive *a priori* belief. It is the "principle of natural equity," and is equivalent to the Golden Rule, to Kant's Categorical Imperative,[1] and to the Benthamite principle that all men have an equal right to happiness. But the law of Justice has also an *a posteriori* justification, based on the observation of the natural laws of life, since its operation is the condition of the maintenance of life in general, and, in particular, of social life. The belief in it is "but a conscious response to certain necessary relations in the order of nature." "No higher warrant can be imagined." The law of equal freedom is in fine an "ultimate ethical principle having an authority transcending every other."[2]

Applications.—From the principle expressing the right to equal freedom Spencer deduces various practical corollaries relating to the Right to Physical Integrity, to Property, etc., the Rights of Women, the Duties of the State, etc. He shows, for example, that the State is a machinery that has evolved naturally for enforcing the law of equal freedom by preventing aggression from without, and securing justice within the community.

---

[1] p. 194 *sq.*

[2] *Justice,* vii. 35. Compare Sidgwick on the Axiom of Rational Benevolence, which is equivalent to Spencer's formula (p. 246).

Criticism of Spencerian Ethics.

The Fittest to survive are not necessarily the Ethically Best.—The principle of the survival of the fittest is, when considered alone, a truism, and occupies in Biology the same position as the Law of Contradiction in Logic.[1] It receives a concrete meaning only when it has been determined, by inference from experience, what general types of life tend to survive. The claws of a tiger, the swiftness of an antelope, the wings of a bird, the instincts which lead beavers to build their houses in a stream, and spiders to spin webs to catch flies, the higher intelligence of men—all these are " biologically good," because they help the survival of the types possessing them. But even if it could be proved—and Spencer has not proved it—that actions biologically good and actions ethically good coincide in the limit of evolution, the two conceptions are yet radically different. The biological view makes life *per se* the end, and prefers one type of life to another, only if it is more permanent; thus the character or type of life has only a secondary value. Pigs and cows and corn are biologically as good as man, because they are likely to survive as long as the human race, unless, indeed, the " limit of evolution " for man is cannibalism, or starvation, or feeding on minerals. But for Ethics it is the character of life, not life *per se* that is good or bad. Life cannot be the ethical standard, for the worth of any type of life has to be judged by an ethical standard.

Ethical Judgment is Free not Mechanical.—If " ethically good " has a meaning, it must be predicated

---

[1] See footnote 2, p. 260.

of some ideal type of life of which thinking beings approve and are able in some degree to realise *through that approval*. It may be said that Nature compels men to approve of certain types and actions, but this is meaningless if the approval is free and ultimate; as, for example, in the case of pleasurable feeling, or in the case of the authority of the Law of Justice, which Spencer himself holds is given by direct intuition. The power of conscious ethical judgment may emerge in living creatures at a definite period of time, but, when it has appeared, it acquires a *freedom* to direct external Nature in some degree towards ends intrinsically desirable for conscious beings. That conscious choice actually produces effects at which it aims is a matter of experience, since, within a certain sphere of action, it is constantly followed by these effects, which (as, for instance, the building of a house) are never caused without the presence of conscious choice preconceiving the end.[1] It is not easy to say how far the deliberate pursuit of ethical good can determine the course of social evolution; but that it has some efficacy is undoubtedly true, and we may therefore conclude that it is of practical importance to determine the true character of ethical good. But this cannot be done if we adhere too closely to Naturalism, which is not concerned with the true worth of ethical ideals, but only with their origin, and with their possible effects in prolonging or shortening the life of the human race.

Confusion between Naturalism and Intuitionism.—— Had Spencer admitted that conscious judgment of what is intrinsically good is either impossible or

[1] See p. 141.

inefficacious, he could not be open to the charge of inconsistency, and his work might be regarded as a purely naturalistic or descriptive theory of the origin of moral beliefs and instincts that operate mechanically towards the prolongation or destruction of life, but are not to be regarded as judgments about what is really good.   But a prominent difficulty in estimating the ethical meaning of his work arises from his constant confusion between ethical considerations and descriptive biology, sociology, and anthropology; or—to express it otherwise—a confusion between intuitional and naturalistic methods in Ethics.[1]   Preservation of certain types of life is the only end that can be attributed to Nature; what these types are can only be determined by observing what types have so far survived, and which are likely to continue.   But, as we have seen, we cannot argue that the ethically best types are those most fit for physical life, if ethically good means that which is apprehended by consciousness as intrinsically desirable.

Spencer, recognising to some extent the opposition between the natural "end" and the ethical idea, strives to overcome it by introducing two new conceptions.   (1) "Breadth of life" is introduced as a connecting link between biology and Ethics, for it indicates a principle of natural selection other than that of mere fitness for organic life.   By "breadth" Spencer refers to the *variety* of functions which a higher animal is capable of exercising; and he assumes that "breadth" is favourable to the type by increasing the power of adaptation to unfavourable circumstances. This is exemplified by intelligence, and the corre-

[1] See p. 122.

sponding complex nervous structure. But it would seem that prolific multiplication, rapid migration, minuteness (to avoid the notice of enemies), and an adaptable digestive structure, would afford a mechanism more suitable for the preservation of the type than the complex brain structure found in man and higher animals. Moreover, certain lower forms of life—such as edible animals and fruits—which man requires for *his* life, must survive as long as he (otherwise he would starve), and are therefore as *good* according to the biological meaning of good. The "breadth of life" that is ethically good—namely, a variety of interests and tastes and means to gratify them—is clearly not synonymous with the "breadth of life" which is biologically good, and it is conceivable that it might hinder the preservation of the type. (2) Spencer argues that the ethical good, which he identifies with immediate pleasure, will in the limit of evolution accompany every action tending towards the natural good, the preservation of the life of the type. But during the many generations that must be born and disappear before this elysian state is reached, before

> Love is an unerring right
> And Joy its own security,

how is man to guide his actions if there happens to be opposition between pleasure-giving and type-preserving actions? Is he to seek his own pleasure or to sacrifice it for the mere physical life of future races? Spencer might reply, that a man should seek his own pleasure, and that the life of future races must be left to Nature. If his own pleasures happens to be biologically good, he will have the satisfaction of knowing that his type of character will survive. If his pleasures are biologically bad, he will die young, his type will be eliminated, and future races will reap the hedonistic benefit of his self-immolation.

Hedonism and the Limit of Evolution.——Assuming for the moment that the ethically good is pleasure, can we infer that Nature, in the " limit of evolution " will necessarily realise general social happiness, by preserving only those whose pleasures are life-preserving? Surely not. There are many powerful instincts and impulses quite different from the desire for pleasure,[1] and Nature might secure her end by eliminating, not those who find pleasure in life-destroying actions, but those whose instincts and impulses are too weak to resist the allurements of pleasure towards actions possibly injurious. There might arise, then, by natural selection, a race of Stoics whose sense of duty would unconsciously lead them to race-preserving conduct, not yielding the maximum of pleasure even in " the limit of evolution." Experience further shows that only *moderate* pleasures are good for the health, and that excessive feelings of any kind are attended by injury to the individual and to the race, and this law seems likely to survive in the race. Nature points, therefore, to temperance, as being more biologically desirable than pleasure; and if, as Spencer asserts, pleasure is the supreme ethical good, the contradiction between the natural and the human good is never completely removed. Can any one believe that the human race is moving towards a state in which excessive and indiscriminate indulgence in pleasure will be *good*, even in the biological sense of the term?

[1] Cf. p. 168.

In Spencer's treatment of Justice the futility of attempting to deduce strictly ethical principles from the biological law of survival is still more marked. It is a truism to say that types survive if the actions of their component individuals tend to preserve the type. Further, that each individual is to be affected more than other individuals by his own actions is a condition of his being an individual. Hence the formula of Justice, from the purely naturalistic standpoint, is nothing more than the statement that if the fittest individuals survive there must be individuals. But Spencer, as usual, confuses the naturalistic and the intuitional standpoints. The *ethical* formula of Justice is not a truism. The authority for it is ethical; it is, as Spencer observes, an *a priori* intuition, not derived from any theory as to what will happen in the limit of evolution, or what is favourable to life.

To sum up these criticisms : Spencer confounds the naturalistic or descriptive method of dealing with ethical questions with the analysis of the intuitional principles of Ethics, and he adopts the following intuitional principles without proving that they are consistent : (1) Ethical Hedonism, (2) Utilitarianism, which we have seen is inconsistent with Ethical Hedonism, (3) the formula of retributive Justice, and its consequence, that unfit races and individuals *ought* to be eliminated.

C. Different Types of Evolution

The idea of evolution has acquired in philosophy, science, and in the history of mankind, a position which it can never lose. So far as psychology, the

history of moral customs, and social science are concerned, this is mainly due to the influence of Spencer.
The so-called "genetic" method, now much used in
studying these subjects, endeavours to understand
things by tracing their past development. It was used
by Hume in reference to ethical beliefs and the theory
of knowledge, but its wider application to the race and
to the whole of nature was made popular by Spencer.
But evolutional philosophy in the proper sense aims
at something more than merely tracing the stages of
growth; it may be described as history ruled by
uniform ideas or principles. Evolution is synonymous
with change, unless it can be shown to "evolve" something definite, to converge towards an end, passing
through a series of stages, each of which foreshadows
the end better than the preceding stages.

Evolutional theories differ, then, according to the
principles they use, and the subjects with which they
deal. The following is a list of the notable types that
have become prominent since the middle of the nineteenth century. (1) The "transcendental" or rational
evolution taught by the Rational Idealists; (2) the
evolution of different forms of life from a common
stock (Lamarck and Darwin), and (3) of special types
of society, and of customs and beliefs (Spencer); (4)
the evolution of solar systems from nebulae—following
the known laws of matter—was suggested by Kant
and worked out by Laplace and modern astronomers
in different forms; (5) the hypothesis that matter,
as we know it, has evolved from one fundamental
substance[1]—following laws of which very little is
known—was revived after the discovery of radium, for

[1] Strangely enough, Greek philosophy began with this theory.

it has been found that some "elements" formerly thought irreducible can be transmuted.

Whatever may be the actual facts, it is certain that the only principle which can make evolution fully intelligible is the idea of good, or of a rational end; no purely mechanical principle can explain anything but change. If there is intelligible evolution it must follow a rational idea, and in the end the good and the rational coincide. The system of T. H. Green lays stress on this truth, which was the guiding thought of Rational Idealism. The moral development of society, which is conceived by Spencer as mechanical, is interpreted by Green as spiritual.

CHAPTER IX

ENGLISH RATIONAL IDEALISM

GREEN

THE Ethics of Thomas Hill Green [1] aimed at giving a practical interpretation—suitable to individual needs —of German Rational Idealism. Unlike Fichte and Hegel, he uses no strict method, but agrees with both in regarding speculative and practical Reason as inseparable. He had much sympathy with the philanthropic spirit of Utilitarianism, but he showed that this spirit is inconsistent with the groundwork of their philosophy. His Ethics is also inspired by opposition to the descriptive and historical method of morality used by Hume and Spencer. The descriptive method is open to the objection that it traces the development, in temporal order, of moral ideas in the individual or in the race, without exhibiting the true ground of moral obligation. Green holds that morality is in no sense a natural development of animal instincts or sympathy

Metaphysics.—Green's Ethics is based on a sublime metaphysical theory of which only an outline is here

---

[1] 1836-1882, Professor at Oxford. The substance of Green's Philosophy is contained in his *Prolegomena to Ethics,* from which the quotations in this chapter are taken.

given. Science presupposes that Nature is a complex
of law-bound relations manifested in the forms of
Time and Space. The existence of such an ordered unity
implies the presence of one conscious Intelligence,
transcending Time and Space, by Whom the spatially
and temporally revealed unity of Nature is created,
and for Whom it exists. Human knowledge, further, is
inexplicable except on the assumption that the spirit
of man is a reproduction of the eternal timeless Spirit ;
for otherwise Nature, the object of Science, would be
different for every person, and would not possess the
unity and objectivity that is presupposed by Science.
Objective morality has its root in the same ground ;
only because man is conscious of himself as a being
transcending the time-series is he able to have a
conception of personal good, which is essentially a good
of the permanent *self* ; only because all persons are
reproductions of the *same* Eternal Spirit is it possible
for each individual to conceive the good of others as
objectively good, while yet remaining a *personal* good.
Thus Morality and Science are explained by the same
principle, that all persons are reproductions of the one
Divine Spirit, for Whom Nature exists.   This reproduction wherever it takes place is Reason.

  Will, Reason, and Freedom of the Will.—Reason
enables man to conceive a future state of the self
that is better than the actual, and Will is the self
realising this conception.   Thus Will and Reason are
intimately connected, but they do not completely
coincide until the ideal is realised.   Will is entirely
distinct from animal want, for the latter is a form
of physical or mechanical causality, whereas the
former is the self-determination of a conscious being.

The freedom of the Will consists in this self-determination. The actions of the self, though free, are *necessary*, not as being the necessary physical results of the past, but because they *really* express the character independently of temporal events. The will, character, self, and person are morally equivalent.[1] It is the power of self-determination that distinguishes man from the lower animals, who are moved by instincts and feelings only.[2] Whatever, therefore, the evolutionists may prove as to the physical origin of life, they can never explain moral responsibility as a development of animal feelings.

The Good Will—Criticism of the Hedonists and Kant.—An act of will is " one in which a self-conscious individual directs himself to the realisation of some idea, as to an object in which for the time he seeks self-satisfaction." The fundamental problem of Ethics is to find the distinction between the good and bad will. From the definition just given it follows that this distinction must depend on the nature of the objects willed. The Kantian theory,[3] which derives the goodness of an action from the *motive* and ignores the effect, cannot be accepted in its entirety, because a will is not completely good unless it realises its objects. The Hedonists, on the other hand, lay stress on the pleasurable *effects*, and regard the motive as of secondary importance;[4] but they are wrong, because the self-satisfaction which constitutes the good cannot be identified with pleasure. It is true that all satisfaction is attended by pleasure, but this pleasure is not always the object of desire, nor is it identical

---

[1] Cf. pp. 21, 22.
[2] Cf. Kant on Autonomy and Free-Will (pp. 198, 199).
[3] See pp. 193, 205.   [4] See p. 236.

with the satisfaction of desire. Even the voluptuary
seeks, not pleasure, but the supposed satisfaction of
self by means of the attainment of ends that yield
pleasure. The motive determining the will is always
an idealised future state of the self, whether as feeling
pleasure or as finding satisfaction otherwise. The
generic conception of the good is that it satisfies desire,
or, what is equivalent, that it gives satisfaction to
some person.

Moral Good.—The good, however, as just described,
may be more apparent than real. The true or moral
good alone is permanent and fully satisfying. The
philosophy of Ethics has here to face the difficulty
that we cannot completely know what the moral ideal
is until it has been realised. We have to be satisfied
with a partial knowledge of the good, of the direction
in which the ideal is to be sought. This partial
knowledge—which is practically sufficient—is to be
derived from the past moral experience of the individual
and the race. " Of a life of completed development,
of activity with the end attained, we can only speak
or think in negatives. . . . Yet the conviction that
there must be such a state of being . . . may have
supreme influence over conduct, in moving us to that
effort to the Better, which, at least as a conscious
effort, implies the conviction of there being a Best."
This ideal is for ever actualised in the Divine Consciousness, which transcends the limits of Time, and
it is just because the soul of man is a reproduction
of the Divine Spirit that he is able to conceive,
however dimly, the truth of the ideal and to work
towards its realisation.

Character of the Moral Ideal.—Though we cannot

fully apprehend the ideal, we know something about it. The moral good must realise itself in persons, in beings conscious of themselves. It must also realise itself in society, since it is only through society that men become conscious of themselves as persons. The ideal is, then, a society of persons, in which each has reached his own highest satisfaction, and each identifies another's good with his own.[1] The ideal is not a mere progress *ad infinitum* in time, since, as we have said, it is already timelessly realised for the Divine Consciousness.

The formal character of the ideal can also be determined ; for the ideal, being an absolutely desirable end, gives rise to a Categorical Imperative,[2] a law enjoining the unconditional pursuit of that end Particular duties cannot have the same unconditional force ; they are, however, *at least* those which the past experience of man has proved to be good. This experience gives rise to conventional morality, the precepts of which are binding, except in so far as increased experience shows that they are inconsistent with the further development of the moral ideal.

Origin of the Ideal.——According to the naturalists social morality is either the product of a conscious adjustment of rival claims between self-seeking individuals (Hobbes)[3] or, as the naturalistic evolutionists hold, an unconscious adjustment due to the elimination of immoral races and individuals, and the consequent growth of sympathy.[4] Green wholly rejects these explanations. Reason, the consciousness

---

[1] Cf. Kant's "Kingdom of Ends" (pp. 197, 198).
[2] See Kant, p. 194.   [3] p. 132 *sq.*
[4] See Chap. VIII., especially paragraph on *The Limit of Social Evolution* (p. 266).

of ourselves and others as persons, is the only means by which the conception of a moral good is possible ; therefore there can be no gradual evolution of the fundamental essence of morality ; where Reason exists morality is possible, and where Reason does not exist there is no morality. Reason enables us to form the conception of " an absolute and common good " which all can apprehend as such, because each person is the reproduction of the one Eternal Spirit.

Development of the Ideal.—The history of morality then begins with the first appearance of Reason, not with the first appearance of life. But, though the fundamental conception of a personal good has not gradually evolved, it has nevertheless passed through a development in two directions : (1) There has been an *extension of the area of the common good,* which, in the earlier history of humanity, was limited to the family or group to which the person belonged. Later, with the Greeks for example, the area of duty was extended to the nation, but excluded foreigners. Under the influence of the Stoic philosophy, the Roman jurists, and Christian teaching, these limitations of race and nation were abolished, and a duty to humanity is now recognised. (2) A *progressive determination of the content* of the moral ideal has taken place. The " content " consists in the satisfaction of those permanent social interests that present themselves in ordinary life, not in the pursuit and enjoyment of mere pleasure. Even in primitive humanity the idea of a permanent good was the idea of a social good, for man can only think of himself as the subject of permanent satisfaction by " the identification of himself with others, in whose continued life he contemplates himself as living." The element of self-sacrifice is present from the beginning, but is confined by the narrowness of the "content," which at first was identified with the gratification of animal wants; afterwards, with the Greeks, intellectual and aesthetic pleasures took the chief place. Only now has morality reached the point where neither animal gratification nor artistic and intellectual pleasures are seen to be the highest good, but the devotion of self to the interests of humanity. And we have no right to assume, as the Utilitarians do, that the more developed state of the human soul is one in which a larger aggregate of pleasure is enjoyed than in the less perfect state. "The perfection of the human soul may involve the constant presence of a lower nature, consisting in certain tendencies, never indeed dominant, but in conflict with which alone the higher energies of man can emerge." This inspiring and eminently practical thought expresses very finely the attitude which every man must adopt who wishes to get the most out of life.

Concluding Remarks

A complete criticism of Green's philosophy is not here attempted. His metaphysical theory raises religious problems, and this is particularly true of his use of the Hegelian doctrine that there is one self-conscious Mind in society. I have given an account of his metaphysical theory, chiefly because he regarded speculative and practical Reason as inseparable. With the help of the German Rational Idealists he has reached the point where the opposition between social and private good disappears, at least for abstract philosophy. Aristotle really took the correct view in teaching— at least indirectly—that personal well-being *is* the pursuit and attainment of objective good, and, consequently, that it includes the performance of our social duties. We must recognise, however, that all the difficulties of the problem were not considered by Aristotle. Those difficulties were emphasised by Christianity, which taught that each person is of infinite worth. Thus the actual disorders of society, which were, and are, due to the prevalence of Exclusive Egoism, are the source of the practical contradiction which was the stimulus to modern Ethics. If each person is of infinite worth he is entirely justified in pursuing his own good; and, for the same reason, he should sacrifice himself for the good of others, since they likewise are of infinite worth. The conclusion we have reached, by a critical study of the history of Ethics, is this: Either the performance of duty gives the highest satisfaction to a rational being who really thinks about the matter, or the problem is insoluble for *him*. Philosophy cannot go any further than this. As soon as a man has discovered his true position in society, and has become conscious that society is a complex of thinking, willing, and feeling souls, who, like himself, are able to endure pain as well as to enjoy pleasures, the contradiction disappears. But so long as complete good is identified with pleasurable feeling there is a permanent contradiction.[1] The ideal good, so far as it can be conceived as a whole, is a harmony to which each individual contributes his part, not by sacrificing his individuality, but by asserting it,

[1] See pp. 255, 256.

subject to those instinctive moral judgments which, as
Butler taught, form a part of his true nature.   This
harmony is the Platonic Idea of Justice, which
combines the principles of " Temperance " with that
of " Courage " or " Individuality." [1]   And the same
thought is expressed in Mr. F. H. Bradley's doctrine
of " self - realisation," [2] which is an individualistic
interpretation of Hegelian Ethics.

The philanthropic disposition of Green led him to
regard " self-devotion " to the interests of humanity
as the highest of all virtues.   This doctrine expresses
the full truth only if self-devotion is identified with
" self-realisation," not with " self-abnegation."   The
self to be " realised " is fundamentally a social self,
but that it is likewise a subject of private interests
is an important truth kept alive by Hedonism in spite
of its defects.   Self-abnegation derives its value mainly
from the spontaneous interests which it helps others
to gratify, interests always containing *some* emotional
or intellectual elements not having a reference to the
interests of other persons. [3]   If the content of the good
were *merely* the consciousness that it is shared by others,
it would really have no content.   This is quite consistent
with the truth that sympathy and other social relations
increase the number and value of private interests.
Hence arises naturally the problem of *Applied Ethics*,
How are the special interests of individuals to be
regulated with a view to securing the good of the
whole ?

Applied Ethics.——In the preceding pages we have
dealt chiefly with pure Ethics, which differs from

---

[1] See pp. 45, 46.   [2] *Ethical Studies* (1876).
[3] See Spencer on Egoism and Altruism, pp. 266, 267.

applied in being more general and seeking for fundamental principles. But it is not always possible to draw a sharp line between them. Pure Ethics inevitably leads to applied, since taken alone it is too abstract to fulfil any practical end. Applied Ethics deals with more concrete subjects, the Family, the State, and special economic social and legal questions; these again require special knowledge, and thus it happens that applied Ethics cannot altogether be regarded as a distinct science; it is rather the intelligent application of Science, Art, and the other results of human experience in accordance with the spirit of the ethical ideal that is adopted. Very few general ethical principles can be used with precision in actual life, because they cannot take into account all the particular circumstances which may arise; consequently there is often uncertainty about the answers to moral problems until we come to particular cases. Hence the individual has to use his own judgment, to construct his own system of applied Ethics; and here *conscientiousness*, the permanent will to act in the spirit of the objective ideal in which he believes, is indispensable, though it may mislead, unless guided by reflecting intelligence. And some "moral sense," or an intuitive practical insight, is essential, though, as we have seen, it cannot be regarded as infallible. The practical use of pure ethical theory, and of the study of its history, is to correct moral insight by arousing reflection, which is one of the stepping-stones by which man can rise to higher things.

INDEX

The numbers refer to the pages. Principal references are marked *.

Abbott, 196 *note*

Absolute (*see also* Good, absolute):
  Schelling on, 214, 216
  Idea, Heg l on, 216
  Mind, Hegel on, 227

Absolutism, political, 136, 142

Affections:
  Shaftesbury's division, 155
  Butler on, 168, 170

Altruism (*see also* Social Ethics, etc. ; Good, individual and social ; Benevolence):
  and Egoism, Sidgwick on, 248-9
  Spencer on, 266 *sqq.*

Apathy, Stoic, 100

Aristotle, 64 *sqq.**
  relation to predecessors, 41, 42
  influence of, etc., 115, 118, 120, 126, 145, 167, 175, 258, 289
  on Well-Being and Virtue, 68, 175, 206

Art (*see also* Beauty):
  Schelling on, 214
  Hegel on, 227
  Spencer on, 268

Associationists' theory of Virtue, 240 (cf. 182)

Atomism:
  Epicurean, 86
  of external Nature, Hegel on, 217

Augustine, 114

Authority:
  of Reason or Conscience
    Aristotle, 67, 68
    Butler, 167, 169
    the Intuitionists, 122, 159

Authority:
  of motives, Spencer on, 264
  of Formula of Justice, Spencer on, 273

Autonomy (*see also* Self-Determination, Free-will, Freedom):
  defined, 167 *note*
  in Butler's ethics, 167
  Kant on, 197 *sqq.**
  Fichte on, 212
  in Hegel's ethics, 225

Axioms, ethical:
  Clarke, 150, 151
  Sidgwick, 244-246

Bacon, Francis, 125, 126, 127, 178, 180, 234

Bad (*see* Good)

Beatitudo, 143, 145

Beauty, 53, 55, 62, 83 and *note*
  sense of, compared with moral sense, 153, 154, 157, 181

Benevolence (*see also* Altruism):
  Hobbes on, 132
  Clarke on, 150
  Shaftesbury on, 155
  Hutcheson on, 158
  Butler on, 169
  Kant on, 195, 197
  Rational, Sidgwick's axiom of, 246

Bentham, Jeremy, 235 *sqq.**
  criticised, 237, 240 *sqq.*

Biological view of evolution of conduct:
  Spencer on, 263

Biological view of good criticised, 274

Bradley, F. H., 233, 290
Butler, 159, 162, 163 sqq.*, 243, 257
  criticism of, 172 sqq.
  relation to Kant, 192, 193

Cambridge Platonists, 148
Cardinal Virtues, Plato on, 44 sqq.
Character, 21, 22
Charity, 19 and note, 20, 21
Christianity, 108, 110, 113-115,
  117, 174, 221, 287, 289
Chrysippus, 93
Clarke, 149 sqq.*, 191
  influence on Sidgwick, 243, 246,
Classification of modern systems,
  119 sqq., 123, 124, 229-233
Cleanthes, 93
Common-sense morality, Sidgwick
  on, 243, 244, 247
Communism, Spencer on, 272
Compassion (see also Pity), Butler
  on, 170
Comte, 115, 230 sq.*, 257
  on development, 231, 258
Conduct, 1, 12
  as deliberate action, implies
    knowledge, 15
  Spencer on, 261 sqq.
  on evolution of, 263
Conscience (see also Obligation,
  Ought), 159, 161
  Butler on, 165-170*, 172, 173
Conscientiousness, 14 note, 291
Consciousness, Hegel on, 218
Contradiction, apparent, in idea of
  objective good, 289
Cosmopolitanism, 38 and note, 102,
  104, 108
Courage (see Fortitude)
Cudworth, 121, 124, 148 sqq.*, 191
Custom, a source of moral judg-
  ments, 181 sqq.
Cynics, 36, 37 sqq.*, 41, 62, 66,
  78, 106, 120
Cyrenaics, 36, 39*, 41, 62, 78, 106,
  121

Darwin, Charles, 259 sqq.
Deductive science, 126
Descartes, 125

Descriptive method, 122, 276
Desire :
  relation to Good, 6, 203
  Aristotle on, 65-68
  Plato on, 46
  Epicurus on, 87, 90, 91
  Stoics on, 96
  Hobbes on, 129, 131
  Kant on, 193 note, 202, 203
  Hegel on, 219, 220
Development (see also Evolution,
  Social Evolution), 231, 258
  ethical, Hegel on, 222
  ethical, Green on, 287
Dialectic, Plato on, 52, 56, 82
  method, Hegel's, 215 sqq.
Divine Spirit, Green's doctrine con-
  cerning, 283, 285, 287
Dogmatic Intuitionism, Sidgwick
  on, 243, 244
Duties, particular :
  Kant on, 202
  Green on, 286
  perceptional theory of, 243
  remarks on, 291
Duty (see also Conscience, Obliga-
  tion), 11, 118, 121, 122
  Hobbes on, 134
  a motive distinct from pleasure,
    188, 189, 193 sqq.
  Kant on, 193 sqq.
  and Well-Being, 204, 206, 228,
    229

Education, a source of moral
  judgments, 182
  of Rulers, Plato on, 50-52
Effect (see Motive)
Ego (see also Self) :
  Hobbes on, 128, 131 note, 140,
    142
  Hume on, 178, criticised, 187
  Fichte on, 212
Egoism (see also Self-Love), 34
  exclusive, 26, 34, 41, 132, 156,
    289 (see also Hobbes) ; criti-
    cism of, 137 sqq., 213
  Hobbes on, 130 sqq.
  Kant on, 198
  Fichte on, 213
  Hegel on, 219, 224

Egoism :
 Utilitarian difficulty concerning, 248, 249, 255, 256
 inverted, 255
 and Altruism (*see also* Benevolence), Spencer on, 266 *sqq.*
Emotion, 46, 67, 68, 98 *sqq.*
Empiricism, 148, 180
End of absolute worth, Kant on, 196
Ends, 3
 kingdom of, 197
Epictetus, 93
Epicurus, 85 *sqq.**, 109, 115, 116, 121
 criticism of, 90
Equality :
 Sidgwick's axiom of, 245
 and Justice, Spencer on, 272, 273
Equity :
 Clarke's rule of, 150, 151
 Spencer's principle of natural, 273
Erigena, 114
Ethics :
 general description of, 1, 6
 Sidgwick's description of 242
 individual and social, 6
 pure and applied, 6, 117, 291
 Spencer on, 261 *sqq.*
Evil (*see also* Good), Plato on, 58, 59, 63
 Spinoza on, 144
 Hegel on, 224, 227, 228
Evolution (*see also* Naturalism, evolutional) :
 general meaning, 258, 259
 Spencer's use of, 261
 different types of, 279 *sqq.*
 naturalistic, 257 *sqq.**
Existence of God :
 Cudworth on, 149 *note*
 Kant on, 200, 201

Feeling (*see also* Emotion, Moral sense, Pleasure) :
 Hume on, 178, 180
 Kant on, 198, 199 (*see* Inclination)
 relation to good, reason, and moral law, 203 and *note*. 209

Feeling :
 Comte on social, 231
 Sidgwick on, 246
 difficulty of separating from other mental elements, 251
 relation to function, Spencer on, 263 *sqq.*
Felicity, Hobbes on, 130
Fichte, 211 *sqq.**, 257
 connection with Kant, 207 *note*, 211, 212
 connection with Hegel, 215, 216
Formalism, 38, 110, 203 *sqq.*
Fortitude (or Courage) :
 Plato on, 44 *sqq.*, 199 *note*, 290
 Aristotle on, 74
 Epicurus on, 88
 Stoics on, 98
Free-Will (*see also* Nature, external ; Necessity and Freedom) :
 elementary, 11
 Aristotle on, 72, 73
 Epicurus on, 87, 89
 opposite views on, 121, 122
 Kant on, 192 *note*, 199 *sqq.*, 201
Freedom (*see also* Free-Will) :
 Socrates on, 36
 Stoics on, 100
 Spinoza on, 145
 two meanings of, 145, 146
 Fichte on, 212
 of knowing mind, 212
 Hegel on Freedom of Mind, 217 *sqq.*, 221
 Hegel on Freedom of Will, 220
 Hegel on unity of Freedom and Necessity, 225
 Spencer on Freedom of Individual, 271
Friendship, 39, 76, 89, 102, 132
Future life, Butler on, 171, 172

Genetic Method, 189 *sq.*, 280
Golden Rule, 239, 246, 273
Good :
 general sense of term, 6-9 ; a form of conscious life, 25, 32, 159, 246, 250, 276 ; Aristotle's definition, 65 ; Hobbes', 129, 136 ; Hegel, 223, 224 ; Kant

on relation to moral law, 202 ;
    Kant criticised, 203, 208 ;
    Utilitarians, 237, 246, 250 ;
    Spencer, 262 ; Green, 285.
absolute (*see also* Ideal), 14
    Plato, 55; Aristotle, 66 ;
        Hobbes, 130 ; Green, 287
immediate, remote and moral,
    6-9 ;
    Spencer, 264
moral, 9, 209
    Green, 285
and Knowledge, 15 *sqq*.
    various theories concerning,
        37, 39, 42, 70, 78-79, 82-
        83, 85, 93, 118, 127, 144,
        149, 212, 214
objective and subjective, 24, 25,
    32, 33
and Useful, 22
individual and social (*see* also,
    Altruism, Egoism), 25, 26,
    41, 42, 116, 118, 119
    Plato, 47, 82, 83, 108 ; Aris-
        totle, 65, 77, 82, 83, 108 ;
        Shaftesbury, 155 ; Hutche-
        son, 158 ; Butler, 164 *sqq*. ;
        Fichte, 213 ; Hegel, 225 ;
        Comte, 231 ; Spencer, 266 ;
        Green, 286 *sqq*.; concluding
        remarks on, 289, 290
individual, Plato on, 59 *sqq*.
Gorgias, 33, 35, 105
Government, Civil, Hobbes on, 135,
    138
Greek Ethics : Pt. I.
    survey of, 105 *sqq*.
    influence on modern, 115 *sqq*.,
        174
    Green on, 287, 288
Green, T. H., 14, 282 *sqq*.*
    relation to predecessors, 210, 233,
        256, 281

Habit, 69, 71
Happiness :
    distinct from Pleasure and Well-
        Being, 23
    and Virtue (*see also* Self-Love),
        Shaftesbury, 153-156 ; But-
        ler, 164 ; Kant, 200 *sqq*.

Happiness :
    Kant on, 193 and *note*
    Hegel on, 220
    Utilitarians on, 234 *sqq*.
Harmonious Life, 61, 70, 72 *note*,
    107, 109, 168, 289 *sqq*.
Hedonism (*see also* Pleasure) :
    defined, 24 *note*, 38
    psychological, 87, 168 *note*, 188
        used as basis of Utilitarianism,
            185, 236, 237
        same use criticised, 241 *sq*.
    ethical, 87, 92, 246
        Plato's criticism of, 60
        criticised, 250 *sqq*.
    egoistic, 90 *sqq*., 242
    universalistic, 234, 242
    opposed to moral purism, 193
        sqq., 206 *note*
    evolutional naturalists on, 262 ;
        criticised, 278
    criticised by Green, 284
    source of contradiction in Ethics,
        289
    merit of, 290
Hegel (*see also* Idealism, Rational),
    215 *sqq*.*, 257
    method, 215
    relation to Fichte and Schelling,
        215, 216
    compared and contrasted with
        Comte, 231, 258
Heredity, 260
Heteronomy, Kant on, 198
Hobbes, 115, 116, 125, 126 *sqq*.*
    criticism of his ethics, 137 *sqq*.
    inconsistencies in his philosophy,
        140
    influence of, and criticisms of,
        144, 147, 148, 152, 156,
        164, 165, 168, 173, 177,
        178, 179, 198, 202, 213,
        236, 257
    compared and contrasted with
        Hume, 184
    contrasted with Kant, 207 and
        note
    his starting-point different from
        that of evolutional natural-
        ists, 258
Hume, 119, 157, 161, 177 *sqq*.*

Hume :
  criticised, 185 *sqq.*
  relation to Kant, 192
Hutcheson, 156 *sqq.**, 234, 243

Idea of Justice :
  Plato's (*see* Justice)
  Spencer's, 271, 272
Ideal and Actual, 57
Ideal Life, 47, 61, 79 *sqq.*
  Green on, 285 *sqq.*
Ideal State, 47 *sqq.*
Idealism, 14
  rational, 123, 211 *sqq.**, 227,
    282 *sqq.**
    distinct from Naturalism and
    Intuitionism, 229
Ideals and scientific conceptions, 53
Ideas, Plato's theory of, 52 *sqq.*
Immortality, 63, 81
  Kant on, 192 *note*, 201
Immutable morality :
  Hobbes, 134, 135
  Cudworth and Clarke, 148 *sqq.*
Impartiality, principle of, 151, 208,
  236, 245, 246
  a difficulty for Utilitarians, 253
Imperative :
  Kant's categorical, 194 *sqq.*
  interpreted, 195 *note*
  Sidgwick on, 246
  Spencer on, 273
  Green on, 286
Impressionism, 178
  criticised, 185 *sqq.*
Inclination, contrasted with duty
  by Kant, 193 *sqq.*
Individual Good (*see* Good)
Individualism, 34 and *note*, 139,
  176
Individuality, Fichte on, 212
Inductive method, 66, 163
Industry, 20
Intellectualism, 42, 82, 109
Intelligence and Will, Hegel on,
  219-221, 221 *note*
Intention, 13
  Hegel on, 223
  Bentham on, 236
Interests, 3 and *note*, 6, 290
  Green on, 287, 288

Intuition, 72, 202
  the clearest moral, Sidgwick on,
    249
Intuitionism :
  and Naturalism, defined, 119 *sqq.*
  and Rational Idealism, 229
  rational, 148 *sqq.**
    relation to Kant, 191
  aesthetic, 152 *sqq.**
    opposed by Kant, 192, 198
  sympathetic, 160 *sqq.**
    opposed by Kant, 192, 198
  autonomic, 163 *sqq.**
  Kant combines two forms, 192
  Sidgwick's use of term, 242 *sqq.*
Intuitive element in judgments
  about good, 159, 291
Intuitively known ethical principles
  (*see also* Axioms) :
  Spencer, 273

Judgments :
  ethical, 9, 158, 159, 166
    are free, not mechanical, 274,
      275
Justice, 8, 121
  mercy, and charity, 19 *note*
  Plato on, 43 *sqq.**, 121
  Plato's justice the true social
    ideal, 290
  Aristotle on, 75
  Epicurus on, 89, 121
  Stoics on, 98, 101-102
  Hobbes on, 134
  Hume on, 183, 184
  Sidgwick on popular theories of,
    244
  Sidgwick's axiom of, 245
  contract theory of, 89, 134, 184
  Spencer on, 269 *sqq.*
    criticised, 279
  formula of, Spencer's, 271, 273

Kant, 191 *sqq.**, 12, 243
  relation to English predecessors,
    191, 192
  criticised, 202 *sqq.*
  influence of, etc., 207 *sqq.*, 211,
    246, 250, 257
  criticised by Hegel, 224 and *note*
  criticised by Green, 284

Knowledge (*see also* Science) :
 and Good (*see* Good)
 and Virtue (*see* Virtue)
 theory of, Epicurus', 86
 theory of, Stoic, 94

Law (*see* Nature ; Moral law ;
 Right, legal)
Laws, Plato's, 62
Life :
 Spencer on, 261 *sqq.*
 criticised, 274
Locke, 150 *note*, 157 *note*, 178,
 180, 181, 185 *note*, 186
Logic (*see also* Knowledge, theory
 of ; Dialectic) :
 Hobbes', 126
 Hegel's, 216
Love and Self-Love, 76, 77

Marcus Aurelius, 93
Materialism, 86, 94, 127, 128
 criticism of, 140, 141
Mean :
 Aristotle's doctrine of, 70 *sqq.*
 compared with Plato's theory,
 72 *note*
Mercy, 19 *note*
Merit, Hobbes on, 134
Metaphysics (*see also* Philosophy), 3 ;
 Green's, 282
Method, ethical :
 Aristotle's, 66
 Plato's (in the *Republic*), 43
 naturalistic or descriptive, 122,
 282
 Clarke's deductive, 150
 Butler's inductive, 163
 Hume's inductive, 178
 genetic, 189, 190, 280
 Kant's, 193
 Hegel's dialectic, 215
 Mill's, 237
 Sidgwick on, 242 *sqq.*
 Sidgwick's axiomatic, 244,
 245
 Sidgwick's, in proving Utilitari-
 anism, 246
 evolutional, 259
 Spencer's, 261, 263, 274, 276,
 279

Method, ethical :
 Spencer's, in analysing Justice,
 269, 274, 279
Mill, J. S., 180, 237 *sqq.**
 criticised, 240 *sqq.*
Mind, Hegel's Philosophy of, 217
 sqq.
Modern Ethics, Pt. II.
Moral approval and disapproval
 (*see also* Conscience) :
 Hume's theory of, 181 *sqq.*
Moral Law, Kant on, 194 *sqq.*,
 202
Moral nature of man, Butler on,
 166
Moral sense, 153, 154, 156 *sqq.*
 criticism of, 158-160, 291
 Hume on, 180, 181
 Kant on, 198
 Bentham on, 235
Morality :
 positive, 2-3, 37
 Hegel on, 228
 Mill on, 239
 Sidgwick on, 248
 ideal, 2
 Hegel on, 223, 224
Motive, 12, 71 and *note* 3
 prominent in modern Ethics,
 118
 and effects, Kant on, 193 *sqq.* ;
 criticised, 204 *sqq.*
 Bentham on, 236
 Green on, 284

Natural equality, Hobbes on, 132,
 134
Naturalism :
 and intuitionism, 119 *sqq.*, 177,
 229, 275 *sqq.*
 evolutional, 116, 117, 123, 257
 *sqq.**
 relation to Kant, 210
 and rational idealism, 229, 232 (3)
 egoistic, 126 *sqq.*
 rationalistic, 143 *sqq.*
 sympathetic, 177 *sqq.*
 defect in naturalistic methods,
 188 *sqq.*
Nature (*see also* Nature, external) :
 Stoics on, 95, 96, 120

Nature :
  Butler on human, 120, 166 *sqq.**
  various meanings of, 120, 166
  Hobbes' Laws of, 133 *sqq.*
  Hume's Laws of, 184
  Spencer on, 261, 264, 265
Nature, external :
  and freedom :
    Kant on, 199 *sqq.* ; criticised,
      207
    Fichte on, 212, 213
  Schelling on, 214
  Hegel on, 217
  Green on, 283
  relation to Mind, 217, 230, 231
    283
Necessity and freedom :
  Kant on, 200
  Schelling, 214
  Hegel, 225
  Green, 284
Neo-Platonists, 113

Objective (*see also* Good, Right) :
  Mind, Hegel on, 221 *sqq.*, 227
Obligation, moral (*see also* Duty,
    Conscience), 11, 118, 121,
    241
  Hobbes on, 134
  Intuitionists on, 146
  Butler on, 164, 167
  Hume on, 183 ; criticised, 189
    natural obligation to Justice,
      184
  Kant on, 193 *sqq.*
  Bentham on, 235
  Spencer on, 264, 265
Optimism, 209
  hedonistic, 232, 262, 263
  Spencer on, 262
Origin of moral beliefs or truths, 3
  different theories of, in Modern
    Ethics, 119-124, 286
  Green on, 286, 287
Ought (*see also* Obligation)
  implies free-will (Kant), 199
  implies contingency (Hegel), 224

Pain, 37, 232 (*see also* Pleasure)
Paley, 234

Panaetius, 93
Pantheism, 95
Passion (*see also* Affections, Feeling),
    Hume on, 178, *sqq.*
Patristic, 114
Peace, Hobbes' Articles of, 133
Person, 21, 22
Personal meaning of good (*see
    also* Good, individual ; Indi-
    vidualism), 32, 34, 283, 286,
    289 *sqq.*
Pessimism :
  Schopenhauer, 209, 231, 232
  Spencer on, 262
Phaedo, 63
Philebus, 42, 59 *sqq.**
Philo, 113
Philosophic Intuitionism, Sidgwick
    on, 243, 245 *sqq.*
Philosophy :
  Plato on, 49
  Hobbes on, 126, 127
  Kant on ethical, 193
  Schelling on, 214
  Hegel's division of, 216, 217
Physical view of evolution of Con-
    duct, Spencer's, 263
Physics :
  Epicurean, 86
  Stoic, 94 and *note*
Pity (*see also* Compassion), Hobbes'
    definition of, 132
Plato, 41 *sqq.**, 14, 15, 66,
    120
  compared with Aristotle, 82-84,
    107
  contrasted with other Greek
    systems, 103, 104, 109, 110
  influence of, etc., 113, 114, 121,
    145, 148, 153, 156, 167, 174,
    227, 290
  on Ethical Hedonism, 60, 253,
Pleasure (*see also* Hedonism), 24
    and *notes*
  Cynics on, 37
  Cyrenaics on, 39, 40
  Plato on, 59 *sqq.*
  Aristotle on, 77, 78, 81, 108
  Epicurus on, 87 *sqq.*
  Stoics on, 99
  Hobbes on, 129 and *note*

Pleasure :
  Hume on, 178, 181, 185
  Kant on, 193 and *note*, 198
  Bentham on, 235
  Mill on, 237 *sqq.*
  ambiguity in meaning of, 239, 251
  difficulty of separating from other mental elements, 251
  Spencer on, 262, 263, 264, 266
  criticised, 277, 278
Plotinus, 113
Porphyry, 113
Posidonius, 93
Positive Morality (*see* Morality)
Positivism, 230, 231
Postulates of Morality, Kant's, 192, 200 *sqq.*
Power, desire for (Hobbes), 130 *sqq.*
Problems, general, 27
Proclus, 113
Protagoras, 31 *sqq.**, 35, 41, 105
  dictum of, 31, 62
Providence, 62, 95, 226
Prudence (practical insight, sometimes called practical wisdom), 35, 37, 39, 49, 78, 79, 88, 98
Psychological divisions :
  Plato's, 46
  Aristotle's, 67
  Hobbes', 128
  Hume's, 178
  Sidgwick's, 246
    criticism of, 251
  Stout's, 246 *note* 2
  Spencer's, 264
Psychological view of evolution of conduct, Spencer's, 264
Public affections, 165
Punishment, 223, 236, 237, 270, 271
Purism, moral (*see also* Kant), 174 *note*, 191 *sqq.** ; defeats itself, 205

Quality and quantity of pleasures, 238, 239
Quantification of happiness, 253, 254

Realism and Idealism, 14, 84
  in another sense, 218
Reason (*see also* Idealism, Rational) :
  Plato on, 54, 62, 63
  Aristotle on, 67, 70, 77, 80-81
  Stoics on, 96 *sqq.*, 103, 109
  Cudworth and Clarke on, 148 *sqq.*
  Practical and speculative, 149, 152, 187 ; Kant on, 192 and *note* ; united by Fichte, 212 ; united by Schelling, 214 ; Hegel on (*see* Intelligence)
  Hutcheson on, 157
  Butler on, 169
  Hume on, 178 *sqq.*; criticised, 185 *sqq.*
  opposite views on, 180
  concrete and abstract, 185, *sqq.*
  Kant on, 192 and *note*
  as regulative principle, 46, 67, 169, 209
  Hegel on, 216, 219
  Green on, 283, 287
Relativity, principle of, 32, 33
Religion, 114, 158, 171, 227
Republic, 42, 43, *sqq.**, 167
Resentment, Butler on, 171
Resignation, 98
Responsibility :
  Aristotle on, 73
  Spinoza on, 144, 145
  Butler on, 176
Right, 9
  objectively and subjectively, 10
Right, legal, Hegel on, 222, 223
Rulers, Plato's ideal, 48-52
Rules of Righteousness, Clarke's 150, 151

Sacrifice of individuals, Spencer on, 265, 271
Sanctions of Utilitarianism, 237, 238
Scale, ethical, 14
Schelling, 211, 213 *sqq.**, 215, 216
Scholastic philosophy, 114
Schopenhauer, 231
  relation to Kant, etc., 209
  relation to Fichte, 231

Science (*see also* Knowledge):
  ethical value of, 17, 231
  the highest, 65
  of morals, 1 *note*, 178
Selection, natural, 260
Self, 21, 22
  double meaning of, 39, 77
  Hobbes on, 128, 140, 142
  Smith's two selves, 160, 161
  the true self, 77, 162, 167, 187, 198, 203
  Hume on, 178
    criticised, 187
  Green on, 283, 285, 287
Self-consciousness, 211, 212, 215
  Hegel on, 218, 219
Self-control, 38, 39, 98
  involves Reason, 186, 187
Self-devotion:
  Green on, 288
  correct view of, 290
Self-determination (*see also* Autonomy):
  Aristotle on, 73
  Green on, 283, 284
Self-Love (*see also* Egoism):
  Aristotle on, 76, 77
  Aesthetic intuitionists on, 153, 158
  Butler on, 165, **169**, 172
  Kant on, 195 *sqq.*
  Rational, Sidgwick's axiom of, 245
  and Virtue, if disjoined cannot be reunited, 256
Self - preservation (*see also* Self-Love):
  Stoics on, 95
  Hobbes on, 129, 131
Self-realisation, 290
Self-sacrifice, 290
  Mill on, 239
Seneca, 89, 93
Sense, Sensation (for Moral Sense *see* Moral):
  Epicurus on, 86
  Plato on, 54, 55
  Hobbes on, 128
  Cudworth on, 148
  Hume on, 178
  Spencer on, 264

Sentiment of Justice, Spencer on, 271, 272
Shaftesbury, 153 *sqq.**, 164, 173, 234, 257
Sidgwick, 242 *sqq.**
Smith, Adam, 160 *sqq.*
Social Ethics, Hegel on, 224, 225
Social Evolution, limit of, Spencer on, 266
Social good (*see* Good)
Social nature of man:
  Butler on, 164 *sqq.*
  Evolutional naturalists on, 258
Society and Individual (*see also* Good, individual and social; Altruism):
  Spencer on, 265, 271
Sociological view of evolution of conduct, Spencer on, 265
Socrates, 15, 34 *sqq.**, 79, 105, 118, 120
Sophists, 32-34
Soul:
  Aristotle on, 67 and *note*
  Hegel on, 218
Speculative (*see also* Reason, Practical and Speculative):
  wisdom, 42
  knowledge, explained by morality for Fichte, 212, 213
  knowledge, the explanation of morality for Schelling, 214
Spencer, Herbert, 115, 232, 261 *sqq.**
  criticised, 274 *sqq.*
Spinoza, 121, 125, 143 *sqq.**, 229
  compared with Greeks, 144-147
Standard, ethical, 18
State:
  Plato on, 43 *sqq.*
  Aristotle on, 65
  Hobbes on, 135, 136
  Hegel on, 226
  Spencer on, 273
Stoics, 93 *sqq.**, 89, 109, 115, 120, 144, 166, 174, 287
  criticism of, 103, 109, 110
  relation to Spinoza, 144
    to Kant, 202
Stout, 246 *note*
Struggle for existence, 260

Subjective (*see also* Good, Right):
  Mind, Hegel on, 218, 227
Subjectivity:
  principle of, 32
  Hegel on, 224
Substance, the ethical (Hegel), 225
Suicide, Kant on, 195, 197
Summum Bonum, Kant on, 201, 203
Supremum Bonum, Kant on, 200
Survival of the fittest, 259, 260 and *notes*, 270, 272
  ethical use of the principle, criticised, 274, 279
Sympathy:
  as source of moral judgments:
    Smith, 160
    Hume, 181, 183
    Bentham's criticism, 235
    Green's criticism, 286
  in evolution of Justice, Spencer, 272
Synthetic philosophies, 65

Tautology in ethical maxims, Sidgwick on, 245
Temperance:
  Plato on, 44 *sqq.*
  Aristotle on, 72, 73 *sqq.*
  Epicurus on, 88
  Stoics on, 98, 99
Theism, 94
Theological principles, used by Hutcheson and Butler, 158, 163 *note*, 173, 175
Theoria, 80, 81 and *note*, 82, 107, 108, 115
Theory, ethical, practical use of, 291
Thomas Aquinas, 114, 115
Thrasymachus, 34, 43
Truth, 49, 55, 80, 81 *note*, 151

Universality of moral law:
  recognised by rational intuitionists, 151
  Kant on, 194 *sqq.*
  correct meaning of, 208
Utilitarianism, 124, 127, 234 *sqq.**
  Shaftesbury, 154 and *note*, 234

Utilitarianism:
  Hutcheson, 158, 234
  Hume, 185, 189, 234
  relation to Kant, 209
  egoistic (Bentham, J.), 235
  sympathetic (Mill, J. S.), 237
  intuitional (Sidgwick), 242
  general criticism of, 249 *sqq. esp.* 255
  Spencer on, 269 and *note*, 271
  Green on, 282, 284, 288
Utility (*see also* Utilitarianism):
  and Goodness, 22, 23
  public, as standard, 185, 235

Veracity:
  Kant on, 193, 205
  Utilitarians on, 239, 248
Virtue, Virtues, 9 *sqq.*
  moral and special, 17 *sqq.*
  cardinal, 44 *sqq.*, 96
  and knowledge, 15, 35, 37, 39, 49, 78-79, 98, 106
  Aristotle on, 68 *sqq.*
  Epicurus on, 88, 89
  Stoics on, 96 *sqq.*
  unity of, 35, 106
  Hobbes' definition, 131
  Hume on 180, 181 ; his division of virtues, 182
  Kant on, 200, 201
  Utilitarians on, 236, 240, 247 etc.
  popular conceptions of, inconsistent, 244
  and Happiness (*see* Happiness)
Voluntarism, pessimistic, 209, 231
Voluntary action (*see also* Free-Will):
  Aristotle on, 72, 73
  Hobbes on, 129

Well-being, 23, 24, 36, 37, 39, 47, 61, 66-68, 87, 95, 106, 143, 145
  distinct from Happiness, 23 *sqq.*
  wrongly separated from Duty, 204, 206
Westermarck, 190 *note*

Will (*see also* Free-Will), 21, 22
  prominent in Stoic theory, 103, 109
  Hobbes on, 130
  not the source of moral distinctions, 148
  the good, Kant on, 193 *sqq.*
  Green on, 284
  Fichte on, 212
  Hegel on, 220
  Schopenhauer on, 231

Will and Reason, Green on, 283
Will, Universal and Individual :
  Hegel on, 222, 224, 225
  Green on, cf. 283
Wisdom, 37, 39
  Plato on, 44 *sqq.*, 49
  practical (*see* Prudence)
Wise man, Stoic, 101
Wrong, 9

Zeno, 93

THE END

PRINTED BY R. & R. CLARK, LTD., EDINBURGH